Haugh — Courteney

GIDEON'S BAND; A TALE OF THE MISSISSIPPI

→ Begins with launch of new
   boat —— and scenes of
   wealth on levee.

p. 6 — black crew sing.

⊗ — p. 12 — Roosevelt,
      first steamboat
      down Mississippi

p. 13 — paean to the
        steamboat.
        "majestic" etc.

p. 19 — Ramsey - "deep in love with river
                  life".
                  "Shall flows like water?"

20 - River

24 — "left this world"

25 — most wonderful thing in the world.

28 blended consciousness

(on one,
with the
death of
that boat)

119 — meteor in heaven

120 — "only civilization they knew"

137 — River vs Plantation.

Abolition

Democratization vision of river
love compared to Twain — river
love permeates conversation of men
and women.

166 — "truth, justice" etc.,
210 - 211 — Eden

GIDEON'S BAND; A TALE OF THE MISSISSIPPI

36 — boats humanly alive

Cholera — inequalities of immigrants experience

George Washington Cable

Hope twins anti-immigrants

47 — "re little whole world"
boat

86 — Green Notion deaths

59 — Abolitionism — Mr Hayle?

61 — actor — opposed to scheme to
remove deck passenger
travels river by flatboat.
Gilmore

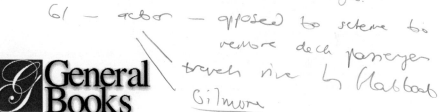

www.General-Books.net

67 — "exalted and exalting life"

75 — dead deck hand.

99 — hurricane deck: "What space! What freedom!"

Publication Data:

Title: Gideon's Band
Subtitle: A Tale of the Mississippi
Author: George Washington Cable
General Books publication date: 2009
Original publication date: 1914
Original Publisher: Charles Scribner's Sons
Subjects: Mississippi River
Fiction / General
Fiction / General
Fiction / Classics
Fiction / Historical
Fiction / Literary
Literary Criticism / American / General

How We Made This Book
We automated the typing, proof reading and design of this book using Optical Character Recognition (OCR) software on a scanned copy of the original rare book. That allowed us to keep your cost as low as possible.

If the book is very old, worn and the type is faded, this can result in a lot of typos or missing text. This is also why our books don't have illustrations; the OCR software can't distinguish between an illustration and a smudge.

We understand how annoying typos, missing text or illustrations can be. That's why we provide a free digital copy of most books exactly as they were originally published. Simply go to our website (www.general-books.net) to check availability. And we provide a free trial membership in our book club so you can get free copies of other editions or related books.

OCR is not a perfect solution but we feel it's more important to make the book available for a low price than not at all. So we warn readers on our website and in the descriptions we provide to book sellers that our books don't have illustrations and may have typos or missing text. We also provide excerpts from each book to book sellers and on our website so you can preview the quality of the book before buying it.

If you would prefer that we manually type, proof read and design your book so that it's perfect, we are happy to do that. Simply contact us via our website for the cost.

CONTENTS

1

SECTION 1

BOOKS BY GEORGE W. CABLE
  Publishpsy"D4 Bt CHARLES SCRIBNER'S SONS
  Qideon' Band. Illustrated. 12mo *net* $1.35
  Posson Jone' and Pere Raphael.
  Illustrated. 12mo *net* S1.3S
  Kincaid's 12mo
  Battery. Illustrated.
  net
  net
  nel
  ml
  Bylow Hill. Illustrated. 12mo .
  The Cavalier. Illustrated . . .
  John March, Southerner. 12mo
  Bonaventure. 12mo *net*
  Dr. Sevier. 12mo *net*
  The Qrand issimes. 12mo . . *net*
  Illustrated. Crown

The Same.
8vo
Sl.35
Si.25
SI. 35
SI.: 15
Sl.35
Sl.35
Sl.35
Old Creole Days. IL'ino . . . .
Illustrated. Crown
net
net
S2.50
Sl.35
The Same.
8vo
net S2.50
Strange True Stories of Louisiana.
Illustrated. Urno *net* Sl.35
Strong Hearts. 12mo . : . . . *net* S1.25
Illus-
... net S2.50
The Silent South. 12mo . . . *net* Sl. OO
The Negro Question. 12mo . . *net t* .75
Madame Delphine *net* S .75
The Cable Story Book. *[ScrUmer*
" ' ". - "ifl. 1 Illus-
$ .50
The Creoles of Louisiana.
trated. Square 12mo
Series of School Reading.]
trated. 12mo
Illus-
. . *net* GIDEON'S BAND
THE STEAMBOAT LEVEE
Saturday, April, 1852. There was a fervor in the sky as of an August noon, although the clocks of the city would presently strike five.

Dazzling white clouds, about to show the earliest flush of the sun's decline, beamed down upon a turbid river harbor, where the water was deep so close inshore that the port's unbroken mile of steamboat wharf nowhere stretched out into the boiling flood. Instead it merely lined the shore, the steamers packing in bow on with their noses to it, their sterns out in the stream, their fenders chafing each other's lower guards.

New Orleans was very proud of this scene. Very prompt were her citizens, such as had travelled, to remind you that in many seaports vast warehouses and roofed docks of enormous cost thronged out so greedily to meet incoming craft that the one boat which you might be seeking you would find quite hidden among walls and roofs, and of all the rest of the harbor's general fleet you could see little or nothing. Not so on

this great sun-swept, wind-swept, rain-swept, unswept steamboat levee. You might come up out of any street along that mile-wide front, and if there were a hundred river steamers in port a hundred you would behold with one sweep of the eye. Overhead was only the blue dome, in full view almost from rim to rim; - anjd all about,, amid a din of shouting, whip-cracking, scolding, knd laughing, and a multitudinous flutter of 'ffiaflyrooloreH foot-square flags, each marking its special lot of 'goods,'Were swarms of men – white, yellow, and black – trucking, tumbling, rolling, hand-barrowing, and "toting" on heads and shoulders a countless worth of freight in bags, barrels, casks, bales, boxes, and baskets. Hundreds of mules and drays came and went with this same wealth, and out beyond all, between wharf and open river, profiled on the eastern sky, letting themselves be unloaded and reloaded, stood the compacted, motionless, elephantine phalanx of the boats.

The flood beneath them was up to the wharf's flooring, yet their low, light-draught hulls, with the freight decks that covered them doubled in carrying room by their widely overhanging freight guards, were hid by the wilderness of goods on shore. Hid also were their furnaces, boilers, and engines on the same deck, sharing it with the cargo. But all their gay upper works, so toplofty and frail, showed a gleaming white front to the western sun. You marked each one's jack-staff, that rose mast high from the unseen prow, and behind it the boiler deck, high over the boilers. Over theboiler deck was the hurricane roof, above that the officers' rooms, called the "texas." Above the texas was the pilot-house, and on either side, well forward of the pilot-house and towering abreast of each other and above all else – higher than the two soaring derrick posts at the two forward corners of the passenger and hurricane decks, higher even than the jack-staff's peak – stood the two great black chimneys.

And what a populace teemed round and through all! Here was the Creole, there the New Englander. Here were men of oddest sorts from the Missouri, Ohio, and nearer and farther rivers. Here were the Irishman, the German, the Congo, Cuban, Choctaw, Texan, Sicilian; the Louisiana sugar-planter, the Mississippi cotton-planter, goat-bearded raftsmen from the swamps of Arkansas, flatboatmen from the mountains of Tennessee and Kentucky; the horse trader, the slave- driver, the filibuster, the Indian fighter, the circus rider, the circuit-rider, and men bound for the gold- fields of California.

More than half the boats, this April afternoon, flew from the jack-staff of each, to signify that it was her day to leave, a streaming burgee bearing her name. A big-lettered strip of canvas drawn along the front guards of her hurricane-deck told for what port she was " up," and the growing smoke that swelled from her chimneys showed that five was her time to back out.

In the midst of the scene, opposite the head of Canal Street – the streets that run to the New Orleans levee run up-hill and get there head first – lay a boat whichspecially belongs to this narrative. A pictorial poster, down in every cafe and hotel rotunda of the town, called her "large, new, and elegant," and such she was in fair comparison with all the craft on all the sixteen thousand navigable miles of the vast river and its tributaries. Her goal was Louisville, more than thirteen hundred miles away. Her steam was up, a velvet- black pitch-pine smoke billowed from her chimneys, and her red-and-white burgee, gleaming upon it, named her the *Votaress.* II

THE "VOTARESS"

Her first up-river trip! The crowd waiting on the wharf's apron to see her go was larger and included better types of the people than usual, for the *Votaress* was the latest of the Courteney fleet, hence a rival of the Hayle boats, the most interesting fact that could be stated of anything afloat on Western waters.

So young was she, this *Votaress,* so bridally fresh from her Indiana and Kentucky shipyards, that the big new bell in the mid-front of her hurricane roof shone in the low sunlight like a wedding jewel. Its parting strokes had sounded once but would sound twice again before she could cast off. Both pilots were in the lofty pilot-house, down from the breast-board of which a light line ran forward to the bell's tongue, but neither pilot touched the line or the helm. For the captain's use another cord from the bell hung over the hurricane deck's front and down to the boiler deck rail, but neither up there on the boiler deck nor anywhere near the bell on the roof above it was any captain to be seen.

At the front angle of the roof's larboard rail a youth, quite alone, leaned against one of the tall derrick poststo get its shade. He was too short, square, and unani- mated to draw much attention, although with a faint unconscious frown between widely parted brows his quiet eyes fell intently upon every detail of the lively scene below.

The whole great landing lay beneath his glance, a vivid exposition of the vast, half-tamed valley's bounty, spoils, and promise; of its motley human life, scarcely yet to be called society, so lately and rudely transplanted from overseas; so bareboned, so valiantly preserved, so young yet already so titanic; so self-reliant, opinionated, and uncouth; so strenuous and materialistic in mind; so inflammable in emotions; so grotesque in its virtues; so violent in its excesses; so complacently oblivious of all the higher values of wealth; so giddied with the new wine of liberty and crude abundance; so open of speech, of heart, of home, and so blithely disdainful of a hundred risks of life, health, and property. And all this the young observer's glance took in with maybe more realization of it than might be looked for in one not yet twenty-one. Yet his fuller attention was for matters nearer and of much narrower compass.

He saw the last bit of small freight come aboard and the last belated bill-lading clerk and ejected peddler go ashore. He noted by each mooring-post the black longshoreman waiting to cast off a hawser. He remarked each newcomer who idly joined the onlooking throng. Especially he observed each cab or carriage that hurried up to the wharf's front. He studied eachof the alighting occupants as they yielded their effects to the antic, white-jacketed mulatto cabin-boys, behind whom they crossed the ponderous unrailed stage and vanished on their up-stairs way to the boiler deck, the cabin, and their staterooms. Had his mild scru- tinizings been a paid service, they could hardly have been more thorough.

By and by two or three things occurred in the same moment. A number of boats above Canal Street and several of lesser fame below sounded their third bell, cast off, and backed out into the stream. The many pillars of smoke widened across the heavens into one unrifted cloud with the sunbeams illumining its earthward side. Now it overhung the busy landing and now, at the river's first bend, it filled the tops of the dark mass of spars and cordage that densely lined the long curve of the harbor's up-town shipping.

At the same time, while the foremost boats were still in sight, the two pilots in the pilot-house of the lingering *Votaress* quietly took stand at right and left of the wheel with their eyes on a distant vehicle, a private carriage. It came swiftly out of Common Street and across the broad shell-paved levee. As quietly as they, the youth at the derrick post regarded it, and presently, looking back and up, he gave them a slight, gratified nod. Through the lines of onlookers the carriage swept close up to the stage and let down two aristocratic-looking men. The taller was full fifty years of age, the other as much as seventy-five, but both were hale and commanding.

As they started aboard the younger glanced up brightly to the unsmiling youth at the roof's rail and then threw a gesture, above and beyond him, to the pilot-house. One of the pilots promptly sounded the bell. Down on the forecastle a dozen deck-hands, ordered by a burly mate, leaped to the stage and began, with half as many others who ran ashore on it, to heave it aboard. But a sharp "avast" stopped them, and four or five cabin-boys gambolled out on it ashore. A smart hack came whirling up in its own white shell dust, and a fledgling dandy of seventeen sprang down from the seat of his choice by the driver before the vehicle could stop or the white jackets strip it of its Ill

CERTAIN PASSENGERS

From his dizzy outlook the older youth dropped his calm scrutiny upon the inner occupants as they alighted and followed the boy on board. First came a red- ringleted, fifteen-year-old sister, fairly good-looking, almost too free of glance, and – to her high-perched critic – urgently eligible to longer skirts. Behind her appeared an old, very black nurse in very blue calico and very white turban and bosom kerchief; and lastly a mother – of many children, one would have said – still perfect in complexion, gracefully rounded, and beautiful.

This was the first time he on the hurricane deck had ever seen them, but he knew at once who they were and looked the closer on that account. The self-oblivious elation with which the slim lass gave her eyes and mind to everything except her own footing caused him to keep his chief watch on her. He even beckoned a black deck hand to do the same. Wherever her glance went her gay interest went with it, either in a soft soliloquizing laugh or in some demonstration less definite though more radiant; some sign of delight from her lips, her eyes, her brow, her springing step, dancing curls, or supple arms. The youth on the roof's edge deepened his frown. At a point on the stage where its sheer, naked sides spanned the narrow chasm through which the waters swept between boat and wharf, her feet strayed too near one perilous edge, and just then her eyes went up to him. The two glances had barely met when she tripped and staggered. With a dozen others aboard and ashore, he gave a start. She sent him a look of terror, then turned from deadly pale to rosy red and gasped her thanks to the smiling deckhand, whose clutch had saved her life. The next instant she was laughing elatedly to her horrified nurse, and so disappeared with her kindred on the lower deck and front stairs.

The mellow boom of the third and last parting signal diverted the general mind, and a glance behind him showed the youth the close and welcome presence of that superior-looking man in answer to whose gesture the pilot had tolled the earlier bell. But this person was closely preoccupied. Now his capable glance ran aft along every marginal line of the boat, now it dropped below to where the big stage lay drawn in athwart the forward deck from guard to guard. Now he gave short, quiet orders to wharf and forecastle, now a single word or two to the pilot-house. Far below, the engine bells jingled. The bowline was in. A yeast of waters ran forward from the backing wheels, the breast line slacked away in fierce jerks, and the *Votaress* began to depart.

Meantime there was an odd stir on shore. A cab whirled up furiously and two more youths, shapely, handsome, and fashionable, twins beyond cavil and noticeably older than their twenty years, visibly rich in fine qualities but as visibly reckless as to what they did with them, sprang out, flushed and imperious, to wave the *Votaress*. One of her guards was still rubbing along the steamer beside her, but before the pair could dash aboard this other boat and half across her deck, a gap had opened, impossible to leap. They halted in rage as the more compact youth on the moving steamer's roof, catching their attention, pointed a good two miles up the river front. Yet what he said they would not have known had not her mate repeated from the forecastle:

" Post forty-six! Drive up thah! We stop thah fo' a load of emigrants!"

They fled back to the cab. Aboard the receding boat the ruthless engine bells jingled on; the broad waterside and the city behind it seemed, from her decks, to draw away into the western clouds, and the yellow river spread wide its shores in welcome to her swinging form. Now its mighty current seemed to quicken and quicken as she gradually overcame her down-stream drift, the ship-lined shores ceased to creep up-stream – began to creep down – and her black crew, standing close about the capstan, broke majestically into song:

"Oh, rock me, Julie, rock me."

From the forecastle her swivel pealed, her burgee ran down the jack-staff, a soft, continuous tremor setin among all her parts, her scape-pipes ceased their alternating roars, her engines breathed quietly through her vast funnels, the flood spurted at her cutwater, white torrents leaped and chased each other from her fluttering wheels, her own breeze fanned every brow, and the *Votaress* was under way.

2

SECTION 2

IV

THE FIRST TWO MILES

The youth whom we have called short, square, and so on crossed to the starboard derrick post. Several passengers had come up to the roof, and one who, he noticed, seemed, by the many kind glances cast upon her, to be already winning favor, was the tallish lass with the red curls.

The nurse was still at her back. She drew close up beside him and stood in the wind that ruffled her hat and pressed her draperies against her form. Her servant betrayed a faint restiveness to be so near him, but the girl, watching the steamer's watery path as it seemed of its own volition to glide under the boat's swift tread, ignored him as completely as if he were a part of the woodwork. The very good-looking man who was "taking out" the boat returned from a short tour of the deck and halted by the great bell over the foremost skylights; but soon he moved away again in mild preoccupation. The maiden's frank scrutiny followed him a step or two and then turned squarely to the youth. Her attendant stirred uncomfortably and breathed some inarticulate protest, but in a tone of faultless composure the girl spoke out:

"Is that the captain yonder?"

"No," he said, equally composed, though busy thinking that but for his eye she would at this moment be lying, in all these dainty draperies, as deep beneath the boiling flood as she now stood above it. " That's not the captain."

"Then why is he running the boat?"

"He owns her."

"Oh!" The girl's soft laugh was at herself. Presently – "Where's her captain?"

"Ashore, in the hospital.7

"What's he got?"

"Missy!" murmured the dark woman beseechingly.

But missy gave her no heed. "Got cholera?" she ventured, "the Asiatic cholera?"

"No, a broken leg."

"Oh! Is that all he's got?"

" No, he has another, not broken." The speaker was so solemn that, with mirth in every drop of her blood, the inquirer contrived to be grave, herself.

" How'd he get it – I mean get it broken? "

" He was superintending "

"And fell? When'dhefall?"

"This afternoon, about "

"Where'd it happen?"

" Down on the lower deck as he "

"Which is the lower deck?"

"The deck you came aboard on."

"They told me that was the freight deck!"

"It is."

"Then, why – ?" She ceased, pondered, and spoke again: "Is there any deck lower than the lower deck?"

"None."

She mused once more: "Why – that's strange."

"Yes," he said, "strange, but true."

"Then how could the captain fall " Again she

ceased and yet again pondered: "Are the boilers – on the boiler deck?"

"No, the boiler deck is just over the boilers."

"Then why do they – " Once more she pondered.

"The boilers," said the youth, "are down on the freight deck."

The questioner brightened. "Do they ever put any freight on the boiler deck?" she asked.

Before he could say yes, and without the slightest warning, a laugh burst from her tightened lips. He could not have called it unmusical and did not resent it, although he did regard it as without the slenderest excuse. Her eyes and brow, still confronting his in a distress of mirth, confessed the whim's forlorn senselessness, while his face returned not the smallest sign of an emotion. As the moment lengthened, the transport, so far from passing, spread through all her lithe form. Suddenly she turned aside, drew herself up, faced him again, and began to inquire, "Do they ever – " but broke down once more, fell upon the old woman's shoulder with a silvery tinkle, shook, hung limp, threw one foot behind her, and tapped the deck with her toe. A married couple drifting by, obviously players and of the best of their sort, enjoyed the picture.

"Why, missy !" the nurse softly pleaded, "yo' plumb disgracin'yo'seff! Stop! Stop!"

"I can't!" whined the girl, between her paroxysms, "till he stops looking like *that.*" But as the youth was merely looking like himself he saw no reason why he should stop.

To avoid the current the steamer suddenly began to run so close beside the moored ships that the continuous echo of all her sounds – the flutter of her great wheels, the seething of waters, the varied activities of her lower deck – came back and up to the three voyagers with a nearness and minuteness that startled the girl and drew her glance; but just as her dancing eyes returned reproachfully to the youth the big bell at her back pealed its signal for landing and she sprang almost off her feet, cast herself into the nurse's bosom, and laughed more inexcusably than ever.

The woman put an arm about her shoulder and drew her a few steps back along the rail to where four or five others were gathered. The young man gave all his attention downward across the starboard bow. The engine bells jingled far below, the wheels stopped, the giant chimneys ceased their majestic breathing, and the boat came slowly abreast of a ship standing high out of the water.

3

SECTION 3

V

RAMSEY HAYLE

The flag of Holland floated aft of a deck crowded with a sun-tanned and oddly clad multitude. The Dutch sailors lowered their fenders between the ship's side and the boat's guards, lines were made fast, a light stage was run down from the ship's upper deck to the boat's forecastle, and in single file, laden with their household goods, the silent aliens were hurried aboard the *Votaress* and to their steerage quarters, out of sight between and behind her engines.

Up on the boiler and hurricane decks her earlier passengers found, according to their various moods and capacities, much entertainment in the scene. The girl with the nurse laughed often, of course. Yet her laugh bore a certain note of sympathy and appreciation which harmonized out of it all quality that might have hurt or abashed the most diffident exile. Childlike as she was, it was plain she did not wholly fail to see into the matter's pathetic depths.

The youth at the derrick post, scrutinizing each immigrant that passed under his eye, could hear at his back a refined voice making kind replies to her many questions. He knew it as belonging to the older of thetwo men for whose coming aboard the *Votaress* had delayed her start. Between the girl's whimsical queries he heard him indulgently explain that the Dutch ensign's red, white, and blue were no theft from us Americans and that at various periods he had lived in four or five great cities under those three colors as flown and loved by four great nations.

Amazing! She could not query fast enough. "First city?"

First in London, where he had been born and reared.

"And then?"

Then in Amsterdam, where he had been married.

"And then?"

Then for ten years in Philadelphia.

"And then?"

Why, then, for forty years more, down to that present 1852, in New Orleans, while nevertheless, save for the last ten, he had sojourned much abroad in many ports and capitals, but mainly in Paris.

The girl's note of mirth softly persisted, irrepressible but self-oblivious, a mere accent of her volatile emotions, most frequent among which was a delighted wonder in looking on the first man of foreign travel, first world-citizen, with whom she had ever awarely come face to face. So guessed the youth, well pleased.

Presently, as if she too had guessed something, she asked if the boat's master was not this man's son.

He now running it? Yes, he was.

"And was he, too, born in England? – or in Holland?"

In Philadelphia, 1803.

"And did he, too, marry a – Dutch – wife?"

"No, a young lady of Philadelphia, in 1832; an American."

" Did you ever see Andrew Jackson? "

"Yes, I knew him."

"Were you in the battle of New Orleans?"

"Yes, I commanded a battery."

"Did you know anybody else besides Jackson? Who else?"

"Oh, I knew them all; Claiborne, Livingston, Duncan, Touro, Sheppard, Grimes, the two Lafittes, Dominique You, Coffee, Villere, Roosevelt "

" I know about Roosevelt; he brought the first steamboat down the Mississippi. My grandfather knew him. Did you ever have any grandchildren?"

Yes, he had had several, but before she could inquire what had become of them the attention of every one was arrested by the second approach of the cab bearing the two hotspurs who had missed the boat at Canal Street. All the way up from there their labored gallop, by turns hid, seen, and hid again, had amused many of her passengers, and now, as the pair shouldered their angry way across the ship's crowded deck and down the steep gang-plank, a general laugh from the boat's upper rails galled them none the less for being congratulatory. So handsome and dangerous-looking that the laugh died, they halted midway of the narrow incline, impeding the stream of immigrants at their heels, and sent up a fierce stare in response tothe propitiatory smiles of the boat's commander and the youth standing near him. Only one of the twins spoke, but the eyes of his brother vindictively widened till they gleamed a flaming concurrence in his fellow's high-keyed, oath-bound threat:

"We'll get even with you for this, Captain John Courteney. We warn you and all your tribe."

The old nurse on the roof, to whose arm her slim charge was clinging with both hands, moaned audibly: " Oh, Lawd, Mahs' Julian! Mahs' Lucian!"

The girl laughed, laughed so merrily and convincingly – as if to laugh was the one reasonable thing to do – that most of the passengers did likewise. Even the grave youth whose back was to her inwardly granted that the lamentable habit could make itself useful in an awkward juncture. While he so thought, he observed the unruffled owner of the *Votaress* motion to the chagrined young men to clear the way by coming aboard, and as they haughtily did so he heard the commander's father say to the girl still at his side:

"Ibelieve those are your brothers?"

"Yes," she responded, for once without mirth, "my brothers," and the peace-loving but conscientious nurse added with a modest pretence of pure soliloquy:

"One dess as hahmless as de yeteh."

The bell boomed. The last transatlantic stranger shuffled aboard, wan and feeble. Now to one wheel, now to the other, the pilot jingled to back away, then to stop, then to go ahead, then to both for full speed, and once more the beautiful craft moved majesticallyup the river. Her course shifted from south to west, the shores for a time widened apart, the low-roofed city swung and sank away backward, groves of orange and magnolia grew plainer to the eye than suburban streets, and the course changed again, from west to north. Soon on the right, behind a high levee and backed by a sombre swamp forest, appeared the live- oaks and gardens of Carrollton, and presently on the left came Nine-mile Point and another bend of the river westward. As the boat's prow turned, the waters, from shore to shore, reflected the low sun so daz- zlingly that nearly all the passengers on the roof moved aft, whence, ravished by the ascending odors of supper, they went below.

But the handsome old man, the sedate youth, the girl, the nurse, remained. Captain Courteney came along the deck and crossed toward the four, eyed from head to foot by the girl even after he had stopped near her. But her gaze drew no glance from him.

"Well, Hugh," he said.

The youth turned with a smile that bettered every meaning in his too passive countenance: "Well, father?"

"Oh!" breathed the startled girl. She looked eagerly into the three male faces, beamed round upon her dark attendant, and then looked again at grandfather, father, and son. "Why, of course!" she softly laughed.

"John," said the older man, "this young lady is a daughter of Gideon Hayle."

"I thought as much." The benign captain lifted his hat and accepted and dropped again the dainty hand proffered him with childish readiness. "Then you're the youngest of seven children."

Her reply was a gay nod. Presently, with a merry glint between her long lashes, she said: "I'm Ramsey."

The captain's smile grew: "That must be great fun."

The girl looked from one to another, puzzled.

" Why, just to be Ramsey," he explained. " Isn't it? "

She gave him a wary, sidewise glance and looked out over the water. " My three married sisters all live near this river," she musingly said; "one in Louisiana, two in Mississippi." Her sidelong glance repeated itself: "I know who it would be fun to be – for me – or for anybody!" Her eyes widened as her brother's had done, though in an amiable, elated way.

"Your father?" asked the captain.

She all but danced: "How'd you know?"

"I saw him – in your eyes," was the placid reply. "Your father and I, and your grandfather Hayle, and this gentleman here "

"Ya-ass, ya-ass!" drawled the nurse in worshipping reminiscence, and Ramsey laughed to Hugh, and all the while the captain persisted: "We've built and owned rival boats "

"Fawty yeah'!" murmured the nurse. "Fawty yeah'!"

"Yes, yes!" chirruped the girl. "Pop-a's up the river now, building the *Paragon!* We're on our way to join him !"

"Law', missy," gently chid the nurse, made anxious by a new approach which Ramsey was trying to ignore, "dese gen'lemens knows all dat."

Ramsey twitched her shoulders and waist. Her lips parted for a bright question, but it was interrupted. The interrupters were the restless twins, whose tread sounded peremptory even on the painted canvas of the deck, and the fineness of whose presence was dimmed only by the hardy lawlessness which, in their own eyes, was their crowning virtue.

"Ramsey," drawled one of them, who somehow seemed the more forceful of the two. He spoke as if amazed at his own self-restraint. She whisked round to him. He made his eyes heavy: " Have you had any proper introduction to these – gentlemen?"

A. white-jacket, holding a large hand-bell by its tongue, bowed low before the captain, received a nod, and minced away. With suspended breath the girl stared an instant on her brother, then on the captain, and then on his father; but as her eyes came round to Hugh his solemnity caught her unprepared, and, with every curl shaking, she broke out in a tinkling laugh so straight from the heart, so innocent, and so helpless that even the frightened old woman chuckled. Ramsey wheeled, snatched the nurse round, and hurried her off to a stair, hanging to her arm, tiptoeing, dancing, and carolling in the rhythm of the supper-bell below:

"Ringading tingalingaty, ringadang ding,
Ringading tingalingaty, ringadang ding."

Red and dumb, the questioner glared after them until, near one of the great paddle-boxes, they vanished below. But his brother, the one who had the trick of widening his eyes, found words. "Captain Courte- ney," he said, " by what right does your son – or even do you, sir – take the liberty, on the hurricane-deck of a steamboat, to scrape acquaintance with an un- protec ?"

The captain had turned his back. "Hugh," he affably said, " will you see what these young gentlemen want?" And then to the older man: "Come, father, let's go to supper." They went.

4

SECTION 4

VI

HAYLE'S TWINS

Hugh was grateful for this task in diplomacy, yet wondered what mess he should make of it.

He was here for just such matters, let loose from tutor and books for the summer, to study the handling of a steamboat, one large part of which, of course, was handling the people aboard. Both pilots, up yonder, knew this was his role. Already he had tried his un- skill – or let "Ramsey" try it – and had learned a point or two. She had shown him, at least twice, what value there might be in a well-tuned, unmanageable laugh. But a well-tuned, unmanageable laugh is purely a natural gift. If it was to come to his aid, it would have to come of itself. Lucian, the twin who had asked the last question, turned upon him.

Hugh smilingly lifted a pacifying hand. "You're entirely mistaken," he said. "Nobody's tried to scrape acquaintance." In the midst of the last two words, sure enough, there broke from him a laugh which to him seemed so honest, friendly, well justified, and unmanageable that he stood astounded when hia accuser blazed with wrath.

"You lie, damn you !" was the answering cry. "And then you laugh in my face! We saw you – all three of you – just now!" The note was so high that one of the pilots began to loiter down from the pilothouse.

Hugh crimsoned. "I see," he said, advancing step by step as the frenzied boy drew back. "You really don't want a peaceable explanation, at all, do you?"

The other twin, Julian, arrested his brother's back step by a touch and spoke for him: "No, sir, we don't. You can't 'peaceably explain' foul treatment, you damned fool, and that's all we Hayles have had of you Courteneys this day. We want satisfaction! We don't ask it, we'll take it! And we'll get it" – here a ripping oath – "if we have to wait for it ten years!"

This time Hugh paled. "It needn't take ten minutes," he said. "Come down to the freight deck, into the engine room, and I'll give both of you so much of it that you won't know yourselves apart."

"One more insult!" cried Lucian, the boy who so often widened his eyes, while Julian, narrowing his lids, said in a tone suddenly icy:

"That classes you, sir, on the freight deck."

"We don't fight deck hands," said Lucian.

"Nor emigrants!" sneered his brother. "And when we fight gentlemen we fight with weapons, sir, as gentlemen should."

Hugh's awkward laugh came again, and the pilot who had come down from beside his fellow at the wheel inquired:

"What's the fraction here?"

"Oh, nothing," said Hugh.

"Everything!" cried Julian. "And you'll find it so the first time we get a fair chance at you – any of you!"

The pilot was amiable. "Hold on," he suggested. "See here, my young friend, what do you reckon your father'd do to this young man" – touching Hugh – "if he should rip around on a Hayle boat as you're doing here?"

"That's a totally different matter, sir!"

The pilot smiled. " Don't you know Gideon Hayle would put him ashore at the first wood-yard? "

" He'd be wrong if he didn't," gravely said Hugh.

"Do you mean that for a threat? – either of you?" snapped Lucian.

"No," said the pilot, "I was merely trying to reason with you. Come, now, go down to supper. It's a roaring good one: crawfish gumbo, riz biscuits, fresh butter, fried oysters, and coffee to make your hair curl. Go on, both of you. You've had – naturally enough – last day in the city – a few juleps too many, but that's all right. A square meal, a night's rest, and you'll wake up in the morning with Baton Rouge and all the sugar lands astern, the big cotton plantations on both sides of us, you feeling at home with everybody, everybody at home with you."

"Many thanks," sneered Julian. "We'll go to our meals self-invited. Good evening."

Hugh granted the pair a slight nod. As they went, Lucian, looking back over Julian's shoulder with eyes bigger than ever, said: "We'll wake up in the morning without the least change of feeling for this boat's owners, their relatives, or their hirelings."

The relative and the hireling glanced sharply at each other. But then Hugh said quietly: "A man can't quarrel with boys, Mr. Watson."

" No," mused the pilot aloud as he watched the pair go below, "but he can wait. They'll soon be men."

"And this be all forgotten," said Hugh.

"Not by them!" rejoined Mr. Watson. "They'll remember it ef they have to tattoo it – on their stomachs."

"I should have managed them better," said Hugh.

" Lord, boy, nobody's ever managed *them* sence they was born." The speaker sauntered back toward the pilot-house, coining rhetoric hi his mind to relieve his rage. "It's only the long-looked-for come at last," he thought, "and come *toe* last." As he resumed the bench behind his partner his wrath at length burst out:

"Well, of all the hell-fry I ever come across !"

"And they 'How to keep things fryin'," said his mate.

Which made Watson even more rhetorical. "Yes, it's their only salvation from their rotten insignificance." He meditated. "And yet – hnn!" He was about to say something much kindlier when suddenly he laughed down from a side window upon the twins returned. "Well, I'll swear!"

"We heard, sir," said Julian with a lordly bow.

"And you," chimed Lucian, "shall hear later." Rather aimlessly they turned and again disappeared, and after a moment or two the man at the wheel asked, with playful softness, with his eyes on the roof below:

"D'you reckon yon other two will ever manage to offset the tricks o' Hayle's twins?"

His partner rose and looked down. The old nurse and the third Hayle brother stood side by side watching the beautiful low-lying plantations unbrokenly swing by behind the embankments of the eastern shore. The level fields of young sugar-cane reposed in a twilight haze, while the rows of whitewashed slave cabins, the tall red chimneys of the great sugar-houses, and the white-pillared verandas of the masters' dwellings embowered in their evergreen gardens, still showed clear in the last lights of day. But the query was not as to the nurse and the boy. Near them stood Ramsey, with arms akimbo, once more conversing with Hugh.

"Oh!" said the glowing Watson. "If that's to be the game, Ned, I'm in it, sir! I'm in it!"

"Just's well, Watsy. You're in the twins' game anyhow."

Meantime Ramsey's talk flowed on like brook water, Hugh's meeting it like the brook's bowlders:

"Guess who's at the head of the table!"

"Who? my grandfather?"

" No, he's 'way down at the men's end."

"Well, then, father?"

"Yes! And who's sitting next him – on his right?"

"Your mother?"

"Yes! And guess who's going to sit at the head of the children's table. You!"

"How do you know that?"

The reply was chanted: "I asked the steward to put you there." She laughed and glanced furtively at her unheeding brother. Then her eyes came back: "And I'm to be the first on your right!" She spread her arms like wings.

"Why, Miss Ramsey!" protested the nurse.

Hugh blushed into his limp, turn-down collar. "I don't believe you'd better," he said.

"I will !" said Ramsey, lifting her chin.

5

SECTION 5

VII
"
SUPPER

Deep in love with the river life was Ramsey.

She had tried it now, thoroughly, for an hour, and was sure! The twenty-four hours' trip down from her plantation home, on the first boat that happened along, a rather poor thing, had been her first experience and a keen pleasure; but this, on the *Votaress,* was rapture.

One effect was that her mind teemed with family history. Her grizzly, giant father, whom she so rarely saw, so vehemently worshipped, son of a wild but masterful Kentucky mountaineer who had spent his life floating "broadhorns" and barges down the Ohio and Mississippi, counted it one of the drawbacks of his career that so few of his kindred cared for the river. One of his brothers was an obscure pilot somewhere on the Cumberland or Tennessee. Another, once a pilot, then a planter, and again a pilot, had been lost on a burning boat, she knew not how nor when. The third was a planter in the Red River lowlands. Her three sisters, as we have heard her tell, were planters' wives, and the father's home, when ashore, was on a plantation of his Creole wife's inheritance, four or five miles in behind the old river town of Natchez.

There Ramsey had been born and had grown up, knowing the great Mississippi only as a remote realm of poetry and adventure out of which at intervals her mighty father came to clasp to his broad breast her sweet, glad mother, tarry a few days or hours, and be gone again. She, herself, had seldom seen it even from the Natchez bluffs, yet she could name all its chief boats apart, not by sight but by the long, soft bellow of their steam-whistles, wafted inland. But now, at last, she was a passenger on its waters. As Hugh, so well grown up as to breadth and gravity, took his seat at the head of the dazzling board that filled the whole middle third of the cabin, and as she sat down next him with all the other adolescents and juveniles in places of inferior dignity, the affair seemed the most significant as well as most brilliant in which she had ever taken part.

Most significant, because to love the river for itself would be to find herself easily and lastingly first in her father's love and favor – her only wish in this world. And most brilliant: without an angle or partition the cabin extended between the two parallel lines of staterooms running aft through the boat's entire length from boiler deck to stern guards. Its richly carpeted floor gently dipped amidships and as gently rose again to the far end, where you might see the sofas and piano of that undivided part sanctified to the ladies. Its whole course was dazzlingly lighted with chandeliers of gold bronze and crystal that forever quivered, glittered, and tinkled to the tremor of the boat's swiftadvance. It was multitudinously pilastered, gleam- ingly white-painted and shellacked, profusely gilded and pictorially panelled, and it bewilderingly reflected itself and Ramsey from mirrors wide or narrow wherever mirrors wide or narrow could be set in.

A new decorum came into her bearing. She ceased to ask questions. She waited for them to be put to her – from the head of the table – and smiled where an hour earlier she would have laughed. Above all, she felt in her spirit the same dreamy strangeness she had so lately felt in her bodily frame when the boat first began to move: a feeling as if the young company about her were but stayers behind on a shore from which she was beginning to be inexorably borne away. The wide river of a world's life, to which the rillet of her own small existence had been carelessly winding, was all at once clearly in sight. She could almost have written verse! She yearned to tell her whole history, but not one personal question could she lure from Hugh. Silently she recalled the story of her Creole grandmother, married at fifteen – her own present age. That young lady had met her future husband just this way on Roosevelt's famous *New Orleans,* earliest steamboat on the Mississippi. But there sat Hugh, as square, as solid, and as incurious as an upended bale of cotton. And still she kept her manners.

It was but the custom of the time and region that the most honored guest of the *Votaress,* wife of her owner's most formidable competitor, with her family, not only should enjoy her journey wholly without cost, but thatshe should receive every attention courtesy could offer. The heat of the contest counted for nothing. And so, while Ramsey ate and talked with Hugh, his grandfather, near by in the ladies' cabin, at her left and at Hugh's back, conversed with her mother on a sofa. It was a heavenly hour. The resplendent boat kept her speed with no inward sign of her ceaseless ongoing except the tremor of her perfect frame, the flutter of her hundred-footed tread, and the tinkle and prismatic twinkle of her pendent glass, all responsively alternating with the deep breathings of her stacks, and with no sign of her frequent turnings but the softly audible creepings of her steering-gear.

While never failing duly to receive and return Hugh's rather stiff attentions, and while doing superb justice to the repast, Ramsey, with side glances from her large, unconscious eyes emotionally enriched by long auburn lashes, easily and with great zest contemplated her mother's charming complexion, so lily-white and shell pink for a Creole matron, as well as the lovely con- fidingness of her manner, so childlike yet so wise. It was not for her to know that her mother, while hanging on every word of the courtly old man, was closely observing both her and Hugh.

The grandfather, too, her blue-and-auburn glances took in sidewise, as their closer scrutiny had earlier done pointblank on the hurricane-deck. He was small, unmuscular, clean-shaven, erect, placid. She noted again his snowy, waving hair, thin only on his pink crown. It shone like silk. He still kept a softflush of unimpaired health and an air of inner cleanness equal to that which showed outwardly from gai- tered shoes to the bell-crowned beaver in his hand. She observed the wide cambric ruffle that ran down his much-displayed, much-pleated shirt-front. His stiff, high stock was tied with a limp white bow-knot. His standing collar covered half of either cheek. He wore a jewelled breastpin and a heavy gold fob-chain and seal. In his too delicate hand, along with the beaver and his gloves, was a stout, gold-headed cane, and from his coat skirt his handkerchief painstakingly peeped out behind. All of which seemed quite natural on him and well related to the highly attractive attire of the lady beside him.

Yet suddenly Ramsey had a painful misgiving. Hugh was remarking upon some matter on the other side of the world, when she asked him as abruptly as a boat might strike a snag: "Is your grandfather a Whig?"

"He is," said Hugh. They laid up their napkins.

"Oh!" sighed Ramsey, but then laughed. "Is your father a Whig, too?"

"Yes, my father, too."

"Not a Henry Clay Whig? " she hopefully prompted.

"Yes, a Henry Clay Whig yet."

Self-consciously she dropped her head over the back of her chair to be rid of her curls. "My father," she musingly observed, "is a Democrat."

"Yet we can be friends," said Hugh, "can't we?" wondering, when he had asked, why they need be.

Ramsey did not say. With her chin in her collar she looked herself over carefully while she brokenly remarked, "All our men folks – four men – three boys – are – red-hot Democrats."

But on the last word she checked and hearkened, and they smiled together at the far-away whistle of another steamer, deep-toned, mellowed by distance, and long sustained.

"That's a Courteney boat," quietly began Hugh, but Ramsey was up and off.

" *The Empress !"* she called to her mother as she flew.

6

SECTION 6

VIII

QUESTIONS

Our forward of the texas and close beside the great bell, Ramsey halted, alone in the boundless starlight and rippling breeze on the cabin roof. The stately *Votaress,* with her towering funnels lost in the upper night, was running well inshore under a point, wrapped in a world-wide silence broken only by the placid outgo of her own vast breath, the soft rush of her torrential footsteps far below, and the answering rustle of the nearer shore. Even on that side the dark land confessed no outline save the low tree tops of two or three plantation-house groves, from each of which shone a lighted window or two, tinier and lonelier than a glowworm.

Across the point, between its groves, the flood revealed itself at intervals in pale shimmerings, and just beyond one of these gleams, in mid-river, shone the nearing boat, her countless lights merged into a single sheen brokenly repeated in the water beneath her. Hugh came to the girl's side at a moment when a wood on the point's extreme end concealed the steamer's approach; but in the next the fleet comer swept out of hiding, an empress in truth to Ramsey, jewelled, from furnace doors to texas roof, with many-colored lights as if in coronation robes.

"That is how we look to her," said Hugh.

But his words were lost. With a startled laugh the girl shrank low over the bell, clutching it as if a whirlwind had struck them, while its single, majestic peal thundering, "I pass to starboard, hail! farewell!" drowned speech and mind in its stupendous roar. Mirth, too, was drowned in awe. And now the vast din ceased, and now the *Empress,* every moment more resplendent, responded, first with her bell, then with the long, solemn halloo of her whistle, and presently with huzzas from all her glittering decks as she passed within a cable's length.

Ramsey gazed entranced. Not until the fading vision had dwindled down and around the great bend did her tread realize again the quivering deck, or her sight reawaken to the wonder of the ever coming, parting, passing flood, its prostrate, phantom shores, and the starry hosts and illimitable deeps of the sky. Even then she was but half-way back to earth, unconscious that she had stepped down forward to the captain's chair and into a group including Hugh and his grandfather, her mother and youngest brother.

"Oh!" she cried, turning, "it's as if – " and found herself face to face not with Hugh but his father.

"As if – what?" smilingly asked the boat's master.

"As if," she said more softly, "we'd left one world and were hunting another."

His smile grew. Her own resented it. "I know what you're thinking," she said, and glanced away. Her curls twitched, her chin tilted, and she sent down from it one of those visible waves that ended at her feet, as if they were the cracker of the whip. When he spoke, her eyes came back at him sidelong.

"I was thinking only," he rejoined, "that at your age it's always as if we'd just left one world and were seeking another."

Her eyes – and lashes – were sceptical. "Weren't you going to say it would seem more so if we should blowup?"

"No," he laughed, "nothing like it."

She began absently to scrutinize his entire dress. It was like the old man's though without the jewelry and ruffles. "Were you ever in an explosion?" she asked. The words came of themselves. She was backsliding from her table decorum.

"No," he replied, "I was never in an explosion."

"Ah, my child!" broke in the mother, "questions again? And even to Captain Courteney? "

Ramsey laughed, gave the deck a wilful scuff, and demanded of the captain: "Were you ever on a burning boat?"

Madame Hayle flinched, gasped, and drew her from him as he replied: "Yes – once – I was."

The mother started again. "There!" she cried; "so! you 'ave it! Now, go" – she laughingly pushed the querist – "go, talk with Hugh – allong with yo' brotheh."

The girl, as she backed away, turned to the grandfather: "Was Hugh on the boat – when it burned?"

Her mother smiled with new pain, but while the captain bowed himself away the old man replied: "Come, Miss Ramsey, sit down with me and I'll tell you the story – if we may, madam? – Hugh – some chairs, will you?"

Ramsey sprang to Hugh's aid, but her brother had a mind for mutiny. "You told me," he accused his mother, "that I could go watch them play cards!"

"Yes?" she asked in a pretty irony; "well, then, of co'se, sisteh or no sisteh, you muz' instan'ly go!" The steady tinkle of the sister's laughter as she passed with a chair provoked her own: "Yes, go! Me, I'll rimmain with her till Joy" – the nurse – "ritturn from suppeh."

The boy went, flinging back for a last word: "You want to hear the story as bad as Ramsey does!"

"'Tis true!" she brightly said to the old gentleman. "Since all those nine year', me, I've want' to hear the Courteney side of that!" – little supposing that this was what neither she nor Ramsey would then or ever quite lay hold upon.

"No," laughed the irrelevant girl to the old man, "you sit here." She faced him up-stream, her mother on his "stabboard," as she said, herself on his "lab- board," and Hugh on her left, "labboardest of all." But – to Hugh – "now, wait – wait! If I'm on your stabboard – how can you be – on my lab' – ? Oh, yes, I see!" She dropped into her chair and, to Hugh'sgreat weariness, laughed till her curls fell on her cheeks, larboard and starboard by turns.

Yet she ceased sooner than any one had hoped and the four sat silent while several ladies sauntered past on the arms of escorts, all highly entertained to see such cordiality between any Hayles and the Courteneys. One trio that paused near by to catch some Hayle or Courteney utterance praised aloud the enchantment of the night and of the boat's speed, and as they strolled on again, having caught nothing, Ramsey breathed softly to the old man:

" They can't describe it ! Nobody can! I've tried!"

Through four or five breathings of the giant chim- , neys she waited for the story she was not to hear, and at length herself broke silence. "I think," she said, "this boat is the most wonderful thing in the world."

No one rejoined that it was or was not. "Don't you?" she airily challenged the "labboardest of all," defensively letting herself realize how nearly a woman she was, how merely a boy was he.

" It's very wonderful," replied Hugh indulgently, as one so nearly a man should to one so merely a child. "I've never seen anything in this world that wasn't."

"Neither have I!" cried the girl and clapped her hands.

In that moment, for the first time, each thought how admirable the other, as yet so absurd, was – some day – probably – going – to be, and right there arose between them a fellowship more potent than either would recognize for a length of hours or days which ishere best left unstated. Their two seniors saw; saw, but kept still – *mais pourquoi rum?* – and why not? – while the great steamer breathed on, quivered on, breathed and quivered, on and on.

Ramsey transiently forgot them. "Do you, too," she asked her " labboardest," " feel yourself widen out of yourself and down and round into all this wonderful boat till you are it and it's all – you?"

"Yes," Hugh confessed, and they in turn were still, even though the seniors resumed converse, one mildly telling which sugar estates along the shore had been whose and the other recounting how their heirs had intermarried.

7

SECTION 7

IX

SITTING SILENT

Thus they sat, Hugh and Ramsey, not recognizing that sitting silent is a symptom.

They sat and together felt their consciousness, his and hers, wing and wing, widen beyond their own frames to a mightier embodiment in this great cloud- white structure breasting the air that cooled their brows and cleaving unseen the flood so far beneath them. Together in this greater self they felt the headway of the long, low hull, the prodigious heart glow of the hungry fires, the Cyclopean push of steam in eight vast boilers, the pulsing click and travail of the engines – whisper of valve and cylinder, noiseless in-plunge and out-glide of shining rods – the ten-foot stroke of either shaft and equal sweep of crank, the nimble beat of paddle-wheels and tumble of their cataracts, the tranquil creep of tiller-ropes, and the compelling swing and sage guidance of the helm.

In this vaster consciousness, by a partnership which had to be tacit or instantly perish, they easily lifted and carried the abounding freight, of every form and substance, destined for the feeding, apparelling, or equipment of thousands awaiting it in homes and families whose strivings and fortunes helped to makethat universal wonder of things which kept Hugh grave and Ramsey laughing. Especially the teeming human life of the great craft did these two jointly draw into this magnified *sett*. They drew in deck-hands, mates, watchmen, firemen, engineers, and strikers, each with some aspiration and some appetite. They drew in stewards, cooks, chambermaids, and cabin-boys, every one' with yearnings and sacrifices; pilots, clerks, and mud clerks, full of histories and dreams. Down in dim spaces behind the engines and between the two wheels they drew in the immigrant deck passengers, so mutely sad for the distant homes behind them, so mutely hopeful and fearful for the distant homes before. And on the deck above these exiles they took in the cabin passengers – ladies who told their lives over their knitting or embroidery in floods of lamplight and the cushioned ease of feminine seclusion; children here and there battling against sleep or yielding to it in stateroom berths; the ruder sex at card-tables in the forward cabin – from which, oddly, the twins were refraining; three or four tipplers at the fragrant bar, and one or two readers under the chandeliers. Outside, scores of non-readers sat in tilted chairs, their heels breast-high on the guard-rails and their minds tobacco-lulled to a silent content with the breezy lantern- light of the boiler deck, the occasional passing of a downward-bound flatboat or steamer, the gradual overhauling of some craft that had backed out earlier at New Orleans, and the wide, slow oscillations of the unbounded starlight overhanging land and flood. These too the young pair included. All these were parts of their blended consciousness as the alert Ramsey noticed that the grandfather's talk had turned upon Hugh and boats.

"He and the *Quakeress* were the same age," he was remarking, when Ramsey's laugh jingled.

"Both," she broke in, "built the same year!" Her curls switched backward at the old man. She faced Hugh. " Where were you born? "

But he only signed for her not to interrupt. In the dim light she made a wry face at him and jingled again while her mother said: "On the *Quakerezz!* – end of trial trip! – whiles landing at New Orleans! Me, I was there, ad the landingg! Yes! on the boat of my 'usband, the *Conqueror* – also trial trip) – arrive' since only one hour biffo'l"

Ramsey, with her eyes roaming over Hugh, faintly kept up her laugh, yet parallel with it her mother managed to continue: "Yes, that was in eighteen-thirty- three, Janawary. Because that was the winter when Jackson he conquer' Clay in the election and conquer' Calhoun in the nullification, and tha'z the cause why my 'usband he name' his boat the *Conqueror*. Ah, veree well I rimember that; how the *Quakerezz* she came cre-eepingg in, out of that fog, an' like the fog so still an' white, cloze aggains' the *Conqueror*. And the firz' news they pazz "

The old nurse reappeared, laid thin shawls on the mother and daughter, and sat down on the deck close below Ramsey.

"Firz' news they pazz," resumed the speaker, "'tis that Captain Courteney he's got with him his wife, from Philadelphia, and "

Ramsey broke in merrily: "Was *she* the Quakeress? Was the *Quakeress* named for her?"

"Yes, and she's juz' have, they say, a liT son! An' my 'usband he di'n' like that! Because "

" But you had three little girls!" said Ramsey.

"Girl', they di'n' count! Because those girl', you know, they can' never run those *steamboat'.*"

"I don't see why," said Ramsey. Hugh might sit silent if he chose; her silent sitting was over.

"They di'n' count," repeated the lady. "And so my 'usband he di'n' want those Courteney' to be ahead of those Hayle' in having boys!"

"He little knew what was coming," said Ramsey, and wondered why the remark was ignored, especially when

"Me," said the pretty matron, "I was nearly ready to 'ave those twin', but Gideon Hayle he di'n' know they was goin' be twin', an' he di'n' know those twin' goin' be boys!" She gently laughed. The daughter stared as if in no light – or shade – could those twins be a laughing matter, but the mother spoke on gayly: "Never I 'ear my 'usband swear so hard – an' so manny way' – like that day – at everything – everybody. Not because that liT babee – if that be all; but because he see that *boat,* that she's the mo' fine boat, that *Quak- erezz,* an' when they ripport her run from Loui'ville, he's already affraid – to hisseff – that she's goin' to be the mo' fas'."

" And was she? " asked the girl.

"Barely," said the grandfather. "It took years to prove it and by that time your father had built another boat."

"The *Chevalier!"* she exclaimed.

"Yes, which beat the *Quakeress* once or twice nearly every season until the *Quakeress* burned."

" Burned!" cried Ramsey, while Hugh, stirred to rise, yet remained. "Was it the *Quakeress* that – ?" But the old man was telling earlier history and she sank repiningly in her seat. "You're going backward," she softly whined.

"In 'sixteen," he said, "I built the *Huntress,* and "

"We already know about that," sighed Ramsey, bracing her feet in old Joy's hands. " I know it from old nursie."

"Ramsey!" murmured her mother.

"In 'seventeen," said the chronicler, "Miss Ramsey's grandfather built the *Hunter.* In 'twenty he built the *Charioteer* "

"Ain't we ever going to hear about the burning?" laughingly whimpered the girl, but the narrator kept on:

"In 'twenty-one I built the *Shepherdess* "

Ramsey all at once revived. "And did the *Shepherdess* outrun the *Charioteer?"*

"A trifle, yes."

"Humph!" she said to herself, and twice again, on a higher key and with a grimace at Hugh, "humph!"

" But in 'twenty-five the *Charioteer* was run into and sunk, and the Hayle boat that came next," continued the historian, "was the best ever seen till then on these waters, of the hundred and sixty-five steamers launched."

"Yes," said Madame Hayle, "and the firz' boat what my 'usband was captain."

Ramsey started wildly. "The *Admiral!"* she cried at Hugh. She whisked round on his grandfather. "And then – to beat the *Admiral* – you built ?"

"My son built – the *Abbess."*

"And did the *Abbess* beat the *Admiral?*"

" Not for a long time. But in 'thirty-three the *Conqueror's* very first run broke the *Abbess's* record."

But madame was not to be outdone in generosity. "Ah, yes," she cried, "but that same day the *Quakerezz* she beat the *Conqueror !*" At which the teased Ramsey, suddenly seeing that all this was but a roundabout peacemaking where she could discern no strife, laughed herself so limp that she all but tumbled into old Joy's lap.

"That's where we began!" she commented.

"True," said the old man to her mother, "but in 'thirty-eight came your husband's *Chevalier* "

"Came – yes! only to get beat racing yo'" – the name eluded her

"Ambassadress," prompted Ramsey. "Everybody knows about that – 'way back in the country – even the dates. The *Ambassadress* beat the *Chevalier,* the *Autocrat* beat the *Ambassadress,* the *Empress* beatthe *Autocrat,* the *Regent* beat the *Empress,* te turn, te turn, te turn! Didn't the *Quakeress* ever burn up, after all?"

"Ramsey "

"Oh, well! this forever sitting silent! I- " Ramsey! " PERIL

Ramsey clutched the old man's arm, pressed curls and brow against it, and laughed in a rillet of pure silver.

Hugh bore it, sitting silent, while the great boat, so humanly alive and aglow in every part, ceaselessly breathed above and quivered below, and the ruffling breeze as ceaselessly confirmed her unflagging speed. The mere "catalogue of the ships" had lighted in him a secret glow that persisted. In his roused imagination the long pageant of the rival steamers still moved on through the rudely thronging, ever-multiplying fleet of the boundless valley's yearly swelling commerce, ocean-distant from all disparaging contrasts of riper empires; moved, yeasting, ruffling, through forty years of a civilization's genesis, each new boat, Hayle or Courteney, more beautifully capable than her newest senior, and each, in her time and degree, as cloud-white by day, as luminous by night, and as rife with human purpose and human hazards as this incomparable *Votaress.*

The girl's mirth faded. From behind the four a quiet tread drew near. From another quarter came two other steps, lighter yet more assertive. The onewas John Courteney's; the two, that halted farther away, meant again the twins.

"Well, captain?" mildly said the grandfather.

"Well, commodore?" said the captain, declining his son's chair.

"Oh, good!" cried Ramsey, and rose with her nurse. "I didn't know anybody but my father was called commodore!"

"Yes," replied the captain, "my father too."

" Where've you been?" asked the fearless girl.

His answer was mainly to her mother: "I've been making myself acquainted in the ladies' cabin. This is no Hudson River boat, you know – whole trip in a day's jaunt."

"Ah, 'tis a voyage!" said madame.

"So it's well to know one's people," added he. He looked up into the night. "What a sky! Miss Ramsey, did you ever see, through a glass, the Golden Locks of Berenice?"

"'The gold – " she began eagerly – "no-o! What are the golden – ?" But there she checked, fell upon old Joy, and laughed whimperingly, "That's a dig at my red hair!"

One of the twins gravely accosted his mother, but she and the captain were laughing at Ramsey while the grandfather said: "My dear child, your hair is beautiful."

With face still hid on Joy's bosom, the girl shuffled her feet, then turned upon the old man and playfully intoned:

"I'm not a child!"

"Ramsey!" said the mother, and "Missie!" said the nurse.

"Hugh," said the captain, "suppose you take Miss Ramsey up to the pilot-house and show her the "

The girl laid a hand on his arm. "Do you want to tell mom-a something you don't want me to hear?"

"Why – " began the captain, and laughed. "On second thought, no. I want to tell your mother and the commodore something before any one else can, and before I tell any one else; but you may hear it if "

" If I won't get frightened. Has anything happened to the boat?"

. "Ramsey!" "Missie!" lamented matron and servant again.

"Mother," with much dignity pleaded the twins.

"Oh, no," said the captain, "not to the boat."

"I want to stay and hear it," whined Ramsey, jerking up and down. "I won't get scared."

" Tu'd be de fust time sence she wuz bawn ef she did," audibly mused the nurse, and Hugh said: "I believe that."

The girl stared round at him and then back at his father, her eyes wide with merriment. " No Ramsey to the pilot-house with him if he can help it!" she managed to say, and fell over her mother and nurse, down into her chair and across its arm, her laughter jingling like a basket of glass rolling down-stairs. Suddenly she hearkened. The captain was speaking to her mother:

"Must you reach Loui'ville as quickly as you can?"

"Ah! – well? yes? we muz' do our possible. My 'usband he – Ramsey!"

The girl had turned face down in a play of collapse. "Nobody," she piped, "finishes what he starts to tell!"

"Ho!" playfully retorted the mother, "an' you muz' go? – cannot wait? Well, good night." But no one went.

Her mother turned again to the captain. "There is something veree bad – on the boat?" Ramsey sat up alert.

The captain's reply was heard by none but her mother and the grandfather, but evidently the twins knew whatever there was to tell. " It was no time to take deck passengers at all!" said one of them to the other, in full voice, while the grandfather was asserting:

"We are as wholly at your command, madam, as if this were Gideon Hayle's boat. Our one thought is your safety."

"And comfort of mind," added the captain, about to go.

Ramsey guessed the trouble. "We are veree oblige'," said her mother; "we'll continue on the *Votarezz.*"

" Goody 1" murmured the daughter to old Joy, to Hugh, and to the captain as he left the group. "Goody!"

"Mother!" protested the twins, "you must not!"

"Oh-h! you?" she radiantly inquired, "you rather go ashore, you, eh? Veree well. Doubdlezz the captain be please' to put you." Her smile grew stately as Ramsey laughed. She turned to the grandfather. "Never in my life I di'n' ran away from sicknezz. I billieve anybody can't die till his time come'. When his time come' he'll die. My 'usband he billieve that, too."

"Don't the Germans come from Germany?" asked Ramsey, but no one seemed able to tell her.

"And also," pursued the lady, "I billieve tha'z a cowardly – to run away from those sick." She looked around for the twins but they were conferring aside. "And also I billieve, me – like they say – to get scare' – tha'z the *sure* way to catch that kind of sicknezz.. 'Tis by that it pazz into the syztem! My 'usband he tell me that. He's veree acquaint' with medicine, my 'usband, yes! And "

"Is Germany in Asia?" Ramsey drawled, but nobody seemed to know anything.

" And I billieve," persisted madame, " to continue on the boat, tha'z also the mo' safe. Because if we leave the boat, where we'll find one doctor for *that* mala- dee-e? An' if we *find* one doctor, who's goin' nurse us in that maladee?"

"Is Asia – ?" tried Ramsey again, but hushed with a strange thrill as her ear caught, remotely beneath her, a faint sawing and hammering.

" Mo' better, I billieve," continued her mother, " we continue on the boat and ourselve' nurse those sick. When the Mother of God see' that she'll maybe privent from coming our time to die."

"If Germany – " whined Ramsey, but huddled down in her seat as the sawing and hammering came again

"What, my chile?"

Light at last! She instantly sat up: "Why do they call it the Asiatic cholera if – ?" She stopped short. From the open deck far below rose an angry cry:

" Stop that fool! Stop her!"

Ramsey darted so recklessly to the low front guard that Hugh darted also and held her arm as she bent over, while close upon the cry came a woman's long, unmistakable wail for her dead. Twice it filled the air, then melted out over the gliding waters and into the night, above the regardless undertones of the boat's majestic progress. Grandfather, nurse, mother, brothers pressed after the girl and Hugh. Clutched by the nurse, released by him, she still looked wildly down, seeing little yet much. At their back the great bell boomed. The boat's stem began to turn to the forested shore. A glare of torches at the lower guards crimsoned the flood under the bows. She flashed round accusingly upon Hugh:

"What are we landing in the woods for?"

He met her gaze and it fell. Her mother tried to draw her away but she dropped to her knees at the rail and bent her eyes upon a dark group compacting below. Hugh muttered to his grandfather:

"She'd better leave the boat. She'd rather." Catching the words, she leaped and stood, her head thrown high. "I wouldn't! I won't!"

She glared on him through brimming tears, but something about him, repeated and exaggerated in the twins as she whipped round to them, reversed her mood. She smote her brow into her mother's bosom and, under the stress of a silvery laugh that would not be stifled, hung to the maternal neck and rocked from side to side.

8

SECTION 8

XI

FIRST NIGHT-WATCH

Often through the first half of that night, while many other matters pressed on them, the minds of the three Courteneys turned to one theme. Ramsey's inquiries had called it up and the presence and plight of the immigrants, down below, kept it before them: the story of Hugh's grandmother, born and bred in Holland.

With Hugh standing by, the girl had drawn its recital from his grandfather; as whose bride that grandmother had been an immigrant, like these, though hardly in their forlorn way and with Philadelphia, not New Orleans, for a first goal. Thence, years later, with husband and child, she had reached and traversed this wild river, when it was so much wilder, and had dwelt in New Orleans throughout her son's, John Courteney's, boyhood. Thence again, in his twenty-first year, she had recrossed the water to inherit an estate and for seven years had lived in great ports and capitals of Europe, often at her husband's side, yet often, too, far from him, as he – leaving his steamboats to good captains and the mother to her son – came and went on commercial adventures ocean-wide. It was thesefirst seven years of John Courteney's manhood, spent in transatlantic study, society, public affairs, and a father's partnership, that had made him – what Ramsey saw.

The tale was fondly told and had made Hugh feel very homespun compared with such progenitors. But Ramsey had looked him up and down as if he must have all his forebears' beautiful values deep hid somewhere in his inside pockets, and had wondered, as she tossed away to the pilot-house, if he was destined ever to show the father's special gift of winning and holding the strongest and best men's allegiance. A very mature thought for her, but she sometimes had such, and had once heard her father frankly confess that therein lay the Courteneys' largest advantage over him, he being signally able to rule the rudest men by a more formidable rudeness, but not to command the devotion of men superior to that sort of rule.

At length the stars of midnight hung overhead. The amber haze of Queen Berenice's hair glimmered to westward. Where the river had so writhed round on itself as to be sweeping northeastward, the *Votaress,* midway of a short "crossing" from left shore to right, was pointing southwest. An old moon, fairly up, was on the larboard quarter, and in the nearest bend down-stream the faint lights of a boat recently outstripped were just being quenched by the low black willows of an island. In the bend above shone the dim but brightening stern lights of the foremost and speediest of the five-o'clock fleet. A lonely wooded point beneath the brown sand of whose crumbling water's edge the poor German home-seeker had found the home he least sought lay miles behind; miles by the long bends of the river, miles even straight overland, and lost in the night among the famed sugar estates that occupied in unbroken succession College Point and Grandview Reach, Willow Bend, Bell's Point, and Bonnet Carre. Past was Donaldsonville, at the mouth of Bayou Lafourche, and yonder ahead, that boat just entering Bayagoula Bend, and which the *Votaress* was so prettily overhauling, was the *Antelope.*

"Fast time," ventured the watchman to the first mate.

"Yes, fast enough for a start."

No word from either as to any trouble aboard.

A cub pilot risked a remark to his chief: "' – Chase the antelope over the plain,' says the song, but I reckon we won't quite do that, sir."

No, they wouldn't quite do that. Not a breath as to any unfortunate conditions anywhere. But on every deck, wherever equals met, the fearful plight of the queer folk down nearest the water was softly debated. Distressing to feminine sympathy was the necessity of instant burials, first revealed up-stairs by that woman's cry of agony down on the lower gangway. But masculine nerve explained that such promptness would save lives and might confine the disease to the lower deck. Was no physician on the boat? No, one would be taken aboard in the morning. Of course you could ask to be set ashore, but, all things considered, to stay seemed wiser. Where was Madame Hayle? Few passengers knew, none of the boat's "family" chose to tell, and at bedtime the majority "retired." So much for t] e surface of things.

But beneath the surface – "Good God, sir! if any one is to go ashore, why shouldn't it be *they* – the foreigners?"

For the full bearing of this speech let us recount certain doings in this first half of the night. The Hayle twins, coming aboard at "Post Forty-Six," had begun, by the time the boat backed away, to offer exchanges of courtesy with such men on the boiler deck as seemed best worth while, and this they kept up with an address which, despite their obvious juleps, unfailingly won them attention. Even a Methodist bishop, who "knew their father and had known his father, both stanch Methodists," was unstintedly cordial. No less so was a senator.

"Know Gideon Hayle?" He had "known him before they had! Hoped to know him yet when his sons should be commodores." Was on the *Chevalier* when the *Chevalier* outran the *Quakeress*. One twin heard the tale while the other brought the bishop.

"Senator, you already know Bishop So-and-So?"

"Senator, we'd like you to know Judge So-and-So,
sir."

Judge, senator, and bishop were pleased. The senator reminded the judge that they had met years before for a touch-and-go moment as one was leaving and the other boarding the *Autocrat* – or was it the *Admiral ?*

Hayle boat at any rate – how time does fly! The brothers took but a light part in the chat and were much too wise to betray any degree of social zeal. Each new introduction was as casual as the one before it. Sometimes they were themselves introduced but only those here named stayed in the set. Chairs were found for four, and Julian, stepping aside for a fifth chair, came upon another worthy, as well juleped as himself and carrying his deck load quite as evenly.

"Bishop So-and-So, this is our father's boyhood friend, General So-and-So. Judge So-and-So – Senator So-and-So – you both know the general?" The general accepted Lucian's chair, and presently Lucian, with two more chairs, brought one more personage, tall and solemn.

"Senator, have you never met Squire So-and-So?" The senator had long wished to do so, the judge was well acquainted, the general shook hands grandly, and the bishop blithely said the squire had the largest plantation on the Yazoo River. The squire was too thirsty to smile but said he hoped the bishop would not feel above joining the others as his guest at the bar. The bishop declined, but kept the seats of all till their return. They came back talking politics, having found themselves of one democratic mind, southwestern variety, and able to discuss with quiet dignity their minor differences of view on a number of then burning questions now long burned out with the men who kindled them: Webster, Fillmore, Scott, Seward, Clay, Cass, Douglas, Garrison, Davis, and others.

By and by, without a break in the discussion, the seven walked back into the cabin and stood where, on the first tap of the supper bell, each could snatch a seat near the upper end of the table and so collectively assume among the hundreds on the boat that separate and superior station to which the laws of nature and nature's God entitled them. The squire had his motherless children aboard but could leave them to a sister and brother-in-law. Which reminded the twins to look after their sister, on the roof, as hereinbefore set forth. But both the bishop and the senator were thoughtful for them and when they came tardily to the board they found the group close about the old commodore, their own places saved and the judge and the general sustaining the squire's rather peppery assertion to the courteous but vilely unconvincible commodore, that certain new laws of Congress must be upheld with all the national power, Yankee mobs be squarely shot into and their leaders hanged, or the Federal Union would not long be worth a rap.

The senator had almost thought of something tactful to say and the bishop had just the right word on the end of his tongue, when Julian, with very good manners in a very bad manner, asked leave to speak, and the squire, ignoring the commodore, said: "Certainly, Mr. Hayle, sir, do!"

"One thing to be stopped at all cost," said Mr. Hayle, "is this deluge of immigration. Every alien who comes to New Orleans, and especially every alien who passes on up this river into the West, strengthensthe North and weakens the South commercially, industrially, and politically, and corrupts the national type, the national speech "

"The national religion," prompted the bishop.

"The national love of law and order," said the judge.

"And of justice and liberty," put in the general.

"And the national health," said the youth. "New Orleans should refuse every immigrant entrance to the country, and every steamboat on the Mississippi ought to decline to carry him to his destination!"

The commodore smiled to reply, but the senator broke in with an anecdote, long but good, of a newly landed German. The judge followed close with the story of a very green Irishman; and the general, with mellow inconsequence, brought in a tale to the credit of the departed Jackson and debit of the still surviving Clay. A new sultriness prevailed. The judge's palliative word, that many a story hard on Clay was older than Clay himself, relieved the tension scarcely more than did Lucian's inquiry whether it was not, at any rate, true beyond cavil that Clay had treated Jackson perfidiously in that old matter

That old matter's extreme deadness reminded the group that the repast was over and Whiggism amply squelched. Besides themselves only the ladies'-cabin people and the captain, away aft, lingered. The long, intervening double line of mere feeders was gone and the cabin-boys were setting the second table. The commodore rose and the seven drifted out again, withtheir seven toothpicks, to the boiler deck. There men who had passed the salt to each other at table were giving each other cigars, some standing in knots, others taking chairs about the guards. Almost every one had related himself to some other one or more as somehow his or their guest and host combined, and had taken his turn or was watching his chance to recognize the captain as social and civil autocrat and guardian angel over all. The conspicuousness of the twins led to stories, in undertone, of the long Hayle-Courteney rivalry.

" Remarkable, how it's run on and on without their ever locking horns, eh?"

"Mighty nigh did it when the *Quakeress* burned."

"Oh! do you really think so?"

"I know it, sir!" He who knew spat over the rail, and the one who had dared to doubt moved on. Between stories there were debates on the comparative merits of the two types of hull favored respectively by the rival builders: the slim Hayle model and the not so slim of the Courteneys.

"After all, sir," asserted a man of eagle eye, "a duck flies faster than a crane."

" I doubt that, sir," said one with the eye of a stallion. "Not that I question your word, but "

Their friends had to separate them.

At that point along came the *Empress,* as we know, a sight only less inspiring on this deck than to Ramsey on the roof; shining, saluting, huzzaing, then fading round the bend. When the card-tables were set out our group of seven fell into three parts. The squire and the general sat down to a game with a Vicksburg merchant and a Milliken's Bend planter, who " couldn't play late," their wives being on the boat. The twins, ceasing to tell the senator and the bishop what damnable things *some* boats were known to have done for the sake of speed, went down-stairs to take a glance at the safety-valve, following a few steps behind the captain. For him they had just seen, as he came down from the roof to their deck and met an unexpected messenger from the engine-room, promptly turn with him and go below. But their needless glance at the safety-valve they never took. They saw only two or three poor women sobbing like babes, the dead body of a young man being prepared for burial, and the carpenter finishing his coffin. When the captain, as will be remembered, went back to the hurricane-deck to tell their mother, they went too.

The boat's torches enabled all on the various decks to view the burial. It ended the game of cards. During the swift ceremony and long after it the twins consulted the squire, the general, the Vicksburger, the senator, the bishop, the judge, and the planter from Milliken's Bend as to what ought to be done. They took care to advance their questions and suggestions singly and according to the nature of each hearer's inflammability, and as each one kindled they brought him close to another, Julian always supplying the hardihood, Lucian the guile. Here were men, they said, and soon had others saying – the squire to the merchant, the general to the Milliken's Bend planter – here were men, gentlemen, scores on scores, not to say hundreds, who at all times and everywhere could take the chances of life like men, like gentlemen, native American gentlemen. But here also were women and children, the families of many of these gentlemen. Such risks were not for such women and children. Was no step to be generally agreed upon? Was it to be supinely assumed that the owners of the *Votaress,* now mainly preoccupied in overhauling the *Antelope,* knew all that was best to do and would punctually do it all? The twins did not originate half the inquiries or replies, they merely started the ferment and kept it working. "You saw at table, did you not, the positive contempt the commodore – who is a foreigner himself – showed for the direst needs of our country?" To be sure that had little to do with the management of the boat, but it made it easier to think that the Courteneys, the captain himself being half Dutch in his origin, might incline to do more for those people down-stairs than was just to those above them – every way above them. The general called it a criminal error to plant the victims of a deadly contagion along a great national highway, like fertile seed in a fertile furrow. The bishop counted it no mercy to the aliens themselves to keep them aboard when they could be set ashore in a rough sort of roofless quarantine on some such isolated spot as Prophet's Island, which should be reached by sunrise, was heavily wooded, and lay but six miles below the small town of Port Hudson. Nor could he call it a mercy to consult the immigrants' wishes. How could they be expected to view the matter unselfishly?

A deputation of seven elected itself to wait on the captain. The masterful twins, finding themselves not of its number, sought him in advance, alone. But their interview was brief. We pass it. The first *watch* turned in. The men who had served through the first two hours' run came again on duty as " middle watch," and in their care, after their four hours' rest, the shining *Votaress,* teeming with slumberers, breasted the strenuous flood as regally as ever.

9

SECTION 9

XII

HUGH AND THE TWINS

In the captain's chair, between the derricks and the bell, far above and behind which the chimneys' vast double plume of smoke and sparks trailed down the steamer's wake, sat Hugh Courteney, quite uncom- panioned.

So his father had just left him, leaving with him the thought, though without hint of it in word or tone, that some night, on some boat as deeply freighted with cares as this one, he must sit thus, her master. The wonder of it, with the wonder of the boat herself and all she carried, sounded a continuous stern alarum through his spirit like a long roll sounding through a camp: " Be a man ! Make haste! See even those Hayle twins, with all their faults, and up! Make haste! Rise up and be a man!" Had the wonder-loving Ramsey been there she must have laughed again; looking into his round, heavy visage was so much like looking into the back of a watch – one saw such ceaseless movement of mind yet learned so little from it. Amid his won- derings he wondered of her; not only where at that moment she might be, but what a child she still was, and yet in how few years – as few as two or three – she would be a woman, might be a bride.

But soon a bride or never, the boat was full of matters only less remarkable and he gently let the girl out of his thought by looking behind him. The windows of the captain's room – between the chimneys – front room of the texas – gave shining evidence that somewhere the captain was yet astir. From the rayless pilot-house above it faint notes of speech showed that some one was up there with the pilot, but at the same time a near-by tread drew Hugh to his feet with quick pleasure and again his father stood before him, looking at the lights of the *Antelope,* a few hundred yards ahead.

"She'll soon be astern," said Hugh.

"We can't keep her so," replied the captain, accepting his chair. "We must land too often. Where's your crony?"

"The commodore? He's turned in." After a pause – "Father, you've shipped a lot of trouble."

"Yes," was the light response, "counting Hayle's twins."

" I wish you'd give me full charge of them."

"Do you?" laughed the father. "Take it. You hear them, don't you?"

They were easy to hear, down on the forward freight deck, dancing round a bottle of liquor, and

"Singing 'Gideon's Band,'" said Hugh listening.

"Yes," said the amused captain, "after pledging me on their honor to go straight to bed." Hugh started away so abruptly that his father asked: "Where are you bound? "

"I'm going to send them to bed."

"Both of them?" smilingly asked the captain.

"Yes, both."

"Not both at once?"

" Yes, both at once. Do you know where their sister is?"

"Why, abed and asleep long ago, is she not?" "I don't know," said Hugh, going; "I doubt it." On his way he glanced about for her. Taking charge of the twins seemed logically to involve a care of her. Where the mother was he knew. Down in the after parts of the lower deck, between the ceaseless torrents of the wheels, most of the people from overseas had spread their beds wherever they might, while in one small place apart some five or six lay smitten with the deadly contagion, two or three in agony, one or two in painless collapse, under the unskilled, heartbroken care of a few terrified kindred. There, by stealth at first and by the captain's helpless leave when he found her there, attended by a colored man and maid from the cabin service, was Madame Hayle, ministering, now with medicine, now with the crucifix, amid the hammer's unflagging din. To this Hugh was reconciled; but it would never, never do, he felt, to let the daughter share such an experience. Better to find her, even at that hour, on the boiler deck.

But on the boiler deck he found only its wide semicircle of chairs quite empty and no one moving among the high piles of trunks and light freight under the hanging bunches of pineapples and bananas. He lookedinto the saloon. It was bright though with half its lamps cold, but the barber's shop and the clerk's office were shut, and double curtains of silk and wool cloistered off the ladies' cabin. The fragrant bar stood open, and at two or three card-tables sat heavy-betting, hard-chewing quartets, but no one else was to be seen; even the third Hayle brother had gone to bed. Halfway down the double front stairs to the lower deck, on a landing where the two flights merged into one, Hugh paused. All about beneath him forward of the wheels, clear out to the capstan and jack-staff, slept the deckhands, except a few on watch, a few more who with eager crouchings, snapping fingers, and soft cries gambled at dice in the red glare of the furnaces, and one who had become an amused onlooker of the Hayle twins – the negro who, six hours before, by merely putting out a hand had saved their sister's life.

And there, close before Hugh, at the stairs' foot, under the open sky, were the twins. In their hunger for notice, their equal disdain of the captain and the deputation of seven, and their belief that the gayest defiance of the plague was its best preventive, they had set their bottle on the deck and in opposite directions were daintily pacing round it in a long ellipse and chanting to a camp-meeting tune their song of Gideon:

"O, Noah, he did build de ahk,
O, Noah, he did build de ahk,
O, Noah, he did build de ahk,
An' shingle it v. id cinnamon bahk.
Do you belong to Gideon's band?
Here's my heart an' here's my hand!
Do you belong to Gideon's band?
Fight'n' fo' yo' home!"

A glance at Hugh gave them new life. Singing on, they halted at opposite ends of the beat, patted thighs, called figures, leaped high, crossed shins, cracked heels, cut double-shuffles, balanced, swung round the bottle, lifted it, drank, replaced it, and resumed their elliptical march to another stanza:

"He couldn't tote de whole worl' breed,
He couldn't tote de whole worl' breed,
He couldn't tote de whole worl' breed,
He los' de crap, but he save' de seed!
Do you belong to Gideon's band?
Fight'n'fo'yo' home!"

Hugh moved on down. " Both at once," he had said, but on every account – their mother's, her daughter's, his father's – it must be both at once without a high
Do you be-long –
word from him. On the bottom step he was about to speak, when a tall, flaxen-haired German in big boots and green cap and coat, meek of brow and barely a year or two his senior, came out from behind the stair and stepped between the dancers, silent but with a hand lifted to one and then to the other.

"No," said Hugh to him. The alien's meekness vanished. He motioned toward the sick. His blue eyes flashed. But in the same instant he was jolted hah off his feet by the lunging shoulder of one of the Hayles marching to the refrain:

"Do *you* belong to Gideon's band?"

His answer was a blow so swift that Hugh barely saw it. The singer fell as if he had slipped on ice. Yet promptly he was up again, and from right and left the brothers leaped at their foe. But while men rushed in and hustled the immigrant aft the negro who had saved Ramsey caught one twin as lightly as be had caught her, and Hugh, jerking the other to his knees, snatched up the bottle and whirled it overboard. A moment later he found himself backing up-stairs, followed closely by the pair. These were being pushed up from below by others, and, in lofty phrases hot with oaths, were accusing all Courteneys of a studied plan to insult, misguide, imperil, assault, and humiliate every Hayle within reach and of a cowardly use of deckhands and Dutchmen for the purpose.

His replies were in undertone: " Come up! Hush your noise, your mother'll hear you! Come on! Come up!"

On the boiler deck they halted. The crowd filled the stair beneath and he marvelled once more as he gazed on the two young Hectors, who, true to their ideals and loathing the obliquities of a moral world that left them off deputations, blazed with self-approval in a plight whose shame burned through him, Hugh Cour- teney, by sheer radiation.

" And as sure," said Julian, " as sure as *hell,* sir, your life's blood or that of your kin shall one day pay for this! To-night we are helpless. What is your wish?"

"My father's wish is that you go to your stateroom and berths and keep your word of honor given to him."

"That, sir, is what we were doing when a hired ruffian "

"Never mind the hired ruffian. Charge that to me."

"Oh, sir, it is charged!" said the two. "And the charge will be collected!" They went their way.

10

SECTION 10

XIII

THE SUPERABOUNDING RAMSEY

In his hurricane-deck chair, with eyes out ahead on the water, John Courteney gently took his son's hand as the latter, returning to his side, stood without a word.

"Tucked in, are they, both of them?"

No reply.

"Hugh, I hear certain gentlemen are coming to ask me to put our deck passengers ashore."

"You can't do it, sir."

"Would you like to tell them so?"

"I'd like nothing better."

"Now that you've tasted blood, eh?"

No reply.

" It wouldn't be a mere putting of bad boys to bed, my son. It would be David and Goliath, with Goliath in the plural."

" Can't I pass them on to you if I find I must? "

"Of course you can. Hugh, I'm tempted to try you."

"I wish you would, sir."

" With no coaching ? No ' Polonius to the players' ?"

"I wish you would."

The father looked into the sky. "Superb night," he said.

Again no reply.

" Were you not deep in the spell of it when I found you here awhile ago?"

"Yes, I was."

"My son, I covet your better acquaintance."

"You mean I – say so little?"

"You reveal yourself so little. Even your mother felt that, Hugh."

"I know it, father. And yet, as for you "

"Yes – as for me ?"

"I've never seen you without wanting to tell out all that's in me." The pair smiled to each other.

"And you say that at last, now, you can do it?"

"Did I say that, sir?"

" Not in words. But you seem all at once to be seeing things – taking hold of things – in a new way."

"The things themselves are new, sir. They're small, but – somehow – they've helped me on."

"Couldn't I guess one of them?"

"I hardly think so, sir; they're really such trifles."

"Well, for a first attempt, Ramsey."

"Yes. How did you guess that?"

"She's such a persuasive example of perfect openness."

"Her mother's a much lovelier one."

"No, Hugh; allowing for years, Miss Ramsey's even a better. But – another small thing – shall I mention it?"

"Yes, please."

"All these Hayles, to-night, bring up the past – ours."

"Yes!" said Hugh, and said no more, as if the remark had partly unlocked something and then stuck fast.

The questioner tried a smaller key. "What were you thinking," he asked, "when I joined you here to-night?"

" When you – ? Oh, nothing we're thinking of now."

"At the same time, what was it?"

"Why – something rather too fanciful to put into words."

"All the same, let's have it."

"Well, for one thing, seeing and feeling this boat, with all its light and life, speeding, twinkling on and on through the night like a swarm of stars, the thought came – and I was wishing I could share it with you "

The elder hand pressed the younger.

"The thought that since infinite space – " The thought seemed to stall, take breath, and start again – "since infinite space is lighted only by the stars, the rush and roll of this universe through space is forever and ever – in the large – a night scene – an eternal starlight. Is that absurd – to you? "

The father smiled: "Why, no. I merely – doubt it. All starlight is sunlight – near enough by."

"Yes. But between stars there is no near-by, is there?"

"That depends on who's looking, I think. We mustn't impute human eyes to God – or angels – or saints. You remember the word: ' Darkness and light are both alike to thee'?"

"Yes," pensively said Hugh, rejoicing in this converse yet wondering why it made him feel so childish to speak his best while Hayle's twins showed up in so manly a fashion when they spoke their worst. "Yes, I thought of that, too. Yet I was glad to believe there will always be plenty of starlight for those who love it "

"Wow!" yelled Ramsey in his ear.

With a gulp he whirled and faced her where, limp with laughter, she hung and swung on the captain's chair. Its occupant quietly rose. The old nurse wrung her hands, and Ramsey, in an agony of mirth and dismay, cringed back on her. Suddenly the maiden stood at her best height and with elaborate graciousness said:

"I *hope* I haven't interrupted!"

The father's hand appeasingly touched the son's while playfully he said: "You have a hopeful nature, Miss Ramsey." And then, as her disconcerted eyes widened, he asked: "Where did you come from just now?"

He saw that if she spoke she must weep. Instead she jauntily waved a whole arm backward and upward to the pilot-house. Then, her self-command returning, she remarked, for Hugh in particular: "It's nice up there. They don't snub you." She twitched ashoulder at him, made eyes to his father, and once more tinkled her laugh, interiorly, as though it were a door-bell.

The captain was amused, yet he gravely began to ask: " Does your mother ? "

" Know I'm out? She doth. First time I've been out o' bed this late in all my long and checkered career."

"If she does, Miss Ramsey, will you go up to the pilot once more and tell him to land the boat at the wood-yard just this side of Bonnabel plantation?"

Her mouth fell open: " Who, me? Tell the – ? " She swept the strategist with a quick, hurt glance, but beamed again beneath his kind eyes. "*I get your idea,*" she said, snatched the nurse's arm, and hurried off with her, humming and tripping the song she had quoted.

The captain looked again into " infinite space." The wide scene was shifting. High beyond the *Votaress's* bow the stars of the west swung as if they shifted southward. The moon crossed her silvering wake from larboard quarter to starboard. The *Antelope* shone close ahead. "To me, Hugh," he lightly resumed, "this boat, full of all sorts of people, isn't so much like your swarm of stars as it is like just one little whole world."

"Yes," said the son, facing him sidewise so that no Ramsey might again surprise them: "I see it that way too. Father" – the father had stirred as if to leave him – " I want to tell you some things about our past. But I can't tell them piecemeal. I must find some time when you're off watch."

"And when Miss Ramsey's asleep?"

"Yes."

" Why have you never told me before? "

"I've tried for years. The power wasn't in me. I've had to grow up to it. But, as you say, 'now, at last,' I can do it."

The captain turned away and looked up to the dim pilot-house. Out of it came the tranquil voice of the pilot who earlier had talked with the twins: "Caving bank above has planted snags at that wood-yard, sir. Whippoorwill Ferry's a better landing, on t'other side, head o' the crossing."

"Well, Mr. Watson, land there."

The boat was sweeping close by the west-shore village of Bayagoula, that lay asleep where the stream for a brief space widened to a mile. Her veering jack-staff hid the north star a moment, then crept to right of it and pointed up a five-mile reach of dim waters and dimmer shores, hard on the heels of the panting *Antelope*. But the captain's eye lingered behind and above him. Between him and the pilot-house, softly veiled by its moonlight shadow, stood in unconscious statuesqueness on the front overhang of the texas roof, between the towering chimneys, Ramsey.

Her rippling curls and slim shoulders stood above the shade that enveloped the rest of her form and showed dark against the feeble light of the moon at her back. As he looked she uttered a droll sound – fair counterfeit of the harsh note a mocking-bird speaks to himself before his nightly outburst – and then broke forth in avoice as untrained, but as fresh and joyous and as reckless of reproof or praise, as the bird's:

"O, the lone, starry hours give me, love,
When still is the beautiful night '"

At sight of a second and third figure he moved that way, while below the singer's feet sounded a mother's moan: "Ramsey! mon Dieu! my chile! come down from yondeh!"

The girl's eyes stayed in the sky, but one mutinous foot so keenly smote the roof that her nurse, approaching behind, stopped short, and from Hugh came a laugh, a thin, involuntary treble, which caused Ramsey visibly to flinch.

"Ramsey!" entreated her mother again, but

"Just this one moment, beloved mom-a! Listen, oh, listen, everybody! to my midnight thought!" The rhapsodist struck a stiffer pose and began with all her voice, " Since infinite space is lighted only by the stars! their rush and roll – te rum te riddle, te ruin te ree "

"Ramsey!"

" – Is an eternal starlight!" The girl hugged and kissed her black nurse: "Oh, mammy Joy! is that absurd to you?"

"Ram-zee!" cried the mother. But a toll of the great bell silenced her. Another solemnly followed, and when a third completed the signal to land, the staggering footsteps of the vanished girl dragging old Joy with her in full retreat were a relief to every ear. As madame turned to say good night a last bleat came out of the darkness:

"Please don't, anybody, tell about the *Quakeress* to-night!" XIV

THE COMMITTEE OF SEVEN

"hitherto," said the senator, in his stateroom, to the bishop and the judge, "there really has been no need to take any assertive step."

He was explaining his slowness as head of the deputation and was glad, he said, to have a word apart with these two. The room could not seat seven and for the moment the other four were at the bar, where standing was so much easier than elsewhere.

Their business, the seven's, he added, was with the captain, and officially the captain had gone off duty at eight o'clock and was on again only now, at midnight, in the "middle watch." Even yet there need be no hurry; what they wanted done could not be done before early morning, at Prophet's Island.

The bishop approved. "Don't cross the bridge till you get to it," he quoted.

The judge – whose elderly maiden sister was aboard and abed but awake and alarmed and amazed and astounded that he should be so helpless – assented, too, but thought there was now no call for further delay; Prophet's Island was nearer every moment and the sooner "those people" were well ashore the safer – and easier – for everybody.

"I was giving our numbers time to grow," remarked the senator.

"And the cholera time to spread?" queried the judge.

"We're but a small minority yet," persisted the senator.

"A minority always rules," smilingly said the bishop.

The senator smiled back. " There are two or three hundred of those deck passengers alone," he responded.

"Senator," said the judge, "what of that? We've taken upon ourselves to speak for all the cabin passengers on this boat, whether as yet they agree with us or not. They are as numerous as those foreigners, sir, and, my God! sir, *they* are our own people. Self-preservation is the first law!"

"Oh, surely you know," protested the senator, "I'm with you, heart and soul! We must extricate these people of our own from a situation whose desperate- ness most of them do not recognize. We'll go to the captain now, as soon as – as we must. But let us agree right here that whatever we require him to do we also require him to do of his own free will. He must shift no responsibility upon us. You have, of your sort, bishop, a constituency quite as sensitive as the judge's or mine, and we don't want-to give any one a chance to start a false story which we might find it difficult to run down. And so we can hardly be too careful "

The absent four had returned while he spoke. " Sir," interrupted the general, whose th's were getting thick, "ththat is what we have been – too careful!"

The hearts of the four were on fire. A chance wordof the barkeeper, they said, had sent them to the stateroom of Hayle's twins, who, with tears of wrath, had confessed themselves prisoners; prisoners of their own word of honor – " after being knocked down "

"What?" cried senator, judge, and bishop.

"Yes, sirs, one of them literally knocked down by the acknowledged minion of one Courteney, for having ventured to differ politically with another and for daring to mention the pestilence to a third."

The seven poured out to the guards and started for the roof. The bell up there tolled for the landing at Whippoorwill Ferry. About to ascend a stair, they uncovered and stood aside while Madame Hayle and a cabin maid passed down on their way back to the immigrants' deck. By the time the roof was reached the boat was close inshore.

The captain had begun to direct her landing. The engine bells were jingling. Tall torch baskets were blazing on the lower-deck guards, and another burial awaited only the running out of the big stage. Now it hurried ashore, a weirdly solemn pageant. The seven, looking down upon it, regained a more becoming composure. When the swift task was done, the torches quenched, and the boat again under way and her movements in control of the pilot, they once more looked for the captain. His chair was empty, but his room was bright and its door ajar. Within, however, was only the wholly uninspiring figure of Hugh, at a table, where he was just beginning to write. He rose and seemed sedately to count his visitors.

"We are looking for the captain," said the senator.

"He's down on the after lower deck, sir."

"Oh!" The bushy brows of the inquirer lifted. "Will you send for him? We can't very well go down there."

"That's true, sir," said Hugh, feeling the irony, "unless you wish to help." He looked from one to another, but none of the seven wished to help.

"Do you mean to say," broke in the general, "ththat we can't sssee ththe captain of ththis boat unless we nurse the cholera?"

" No, sir, I don't mean that, though he's very much occupied. If you will state your business to me I will send for him unless I can attend to it myself."

"Why, my young friend," said the senator, "does that strike you as due courtesy to a delegation like this?"

"No, sir, ordinarily it would not be, sir. But my father – I am the captain's son – knowing you were coming and what you were coming for, waited for you as long as he could. Just now he is extremely busy, sir, doing what he can – short-handed – for the sick and dying." The captain's son, in spite of himself, began to warm up. "Those hundreds of people down yonder, sir, are homeless, friendless, dumb – you may say – and in his personal care. He has left me here to see that your every proper wish has every attention. Gentlemen, will you please be seated?" He resumed his own chair and at top speed began again to write.

It was a performance not pleasant for any one. Hefelt himself culpably too full of the resentful conviction that this ferment, whose ultimate extent nobody could predict, was purely of those Hayle twins' brewing, and he knew he was speaking too much as though to them and them alone. He was the only Courteney who could do this thing so badly, yet it must be done. Still writing, he glanced up. Not a visitor had stooped to sit. He dipped his pen but rose up again. "What can I do for you, sirs?"

"We have told you," said the senator. "Send for the captain!"

"Will you please say what you want him for?"

"No, sir! We will tell him that when he comes!"

"He'll not come, sir. I shan't send."

The senator glared steadily into the youth's face, and the youth, forgetting their disparity of years, glared as steadily back. The bishop blandly spoke:

"Senator, will you allow me, for an instant – ? Mr. Courteney, you will admit that this steamboat is not your property?"

"She's as much mine as anybody's, sir. I am one third owner of her."

The bishop's pause was lengthy. Then – "Oh, you are! Well, however that may be, sir, your father . ought to realize – and so ought you, sir – that we cannot consent to conduct an aifair like this in a second- handed way."

"It really isn't second-handed, sir; but if you think it is and if you're willing to put your request in writing and will dictate it to me, here and now "

The senator exploded: "Damn the writing!" He whirled upon the bishop: "Your pardon, sir!"

"Some one had to say it," jovially answered the bishop. Everybody laughed. Hugh dipped his pen once more.

"Shall I put that down, also?" he asked, looking to the bishop and the senator by turns.

"Put what? – down where?" they asked. "What are you writing there, anyhow?"

" Our conversation."

The senator stiffened high: "For what, sir?"

And the bishop asked, "A verbatim report to the captain?"

"Yes, sir, and the newspapers."

"Insolence!" exclaimed the general, but was hushed by the squire, though the squire's own brow lowered.

"Who will vouch for your accuracy?" loftily asked the senator.

"I'll send now for witnesses." The youth reached toward a bell-cord. But the senator lifted a hand between:

"Stop, sir. There will be nothing to witness. Nevertheless you know, of course, that this is not the end."

"I see that, sir."

"When your passengers awake in the morning, your real, your cabin passengers, they will, they *shall* awake to the deadly hazard of their situation. Gentlemen, there will be available landings beyond Prophet's Island. We shall reach Turnbull's Island by noon and Natchez Island before sundown. Meantime, sir, thismortal peril to hundreds of our best people is wholly chargeable to your captain."

"Captain and owners," said Hugh.

" Captain and owners! Good night, sir."

" Good night, gentlemen."

For half an hour the *Votaress* headed west. Then the north star crept forward from starboard beam to bow and then back from bow to larboard beam. Plaquemine town, bayou, and bend swept past, and as she laid her course east for Manchac bayou, bend, and point a tranquil voice came up to the pilot-house from the darkness forward of the bell: "Where is Hugh, Mr. Watson?"

"He's just turned in, sir." XV

MORNING WATCH

Twinkled quite away were the four hours of middle watch.

All the gentler turnings of the journey's first hundred miles were finished and the many hundred miles of its wider contortions were well begun. One winding of thirty-five miles had earned but twelve of northward advance. But at any rate that was now far downstream. Baton Rouge, the small capital of the State, crowning the first high bank you reach, was some six miles astern. In the dark panorama of the shores, decipherable only to a pilot's trained sight, the unbroken procession of sugar estates was broken at last and the shining *Votaress,* having rounded a point from north to west, was crossing close above it with Seven Lakes and the Devil's Swamp on her starboard bow. The *Antelope* glimmered a short mile behind.

It was the first mate's watch. On the hurricane- deck he paced at ease across and across near the front rail, where at any instant his eye could drop to its truer domain, the forecastle. The westerly moon hung high over the larboard bow. Now the boat ran so close along the lowland that in smiting the water each bucket of her shoreward wheel drew a separate echofrom the dense wood, as if a phantom boat ran beside her among the moss-draped cypresses. Ramsey! what thrills you were missing!

She knew it. In her sleep she lay half consciously resenting the loss. Under the next point a close turn led into a long northeastward reach, and as the *Votaress* bore due north across it the morning star, at one flash, blazed out on the dark world and down the flood. Through her stateroom's high window its silvery beam found Ramsey in the upper berth and opened her eyelids with a touch. Staring on the serene splendor, she would soon have slept again, but just then the many lights of a large steamer glided out of the next bend above and Ramsey sprang to an elbow to watch its swift approach and await her own boat's passing call and the other's reply. Now the *Votaress* tolled a single stroke, as if to cry: "Hail, friend, we take the starboard."

With bird-like speed the shining apparition came on, and after a few seconds – that seemed endless – its soft, slow note of assent floated over the waters. Crossing the star's slender path on a long oblique, the wonder came, came on, came close, glittered by, and was gone; now lowland and flood lay again in mystic shadows, and the heavenly beacon of dawn, shedding a yet more unearthly glory than before, swung nearer and nearer to the *Votaress's* course until it vanished forward of the great wheel-house as she headed northeast.

The very pilot at the helm was not more awake than the reclining Ramsey as she pondered the hours, eachone a year, that had passed since she came aboard. AH their happenings, dark and bright; all their speeches; all their faces, male, female, aged, adolescent, juvenile, danced through her fancy with a variety and multiplicity of values which seven such little country-girl minds as hers, thought she, could hardly make room for. It seemed as though a shower of coined gold were overflowing her wee muslin apron of an intelligence and dropping through it. She could scarcely remain in the berth. Listen! Was her mother awake, in the lower one? The boat veered a trifle back northward and suddenly again, hovering over dim water and shore and blazing like a herald angel, was the morning star, a scant point or so to "stabboard." She chuckled, softly, at the word.

Gently her na. me was called, beneath her:" Ramsey? " She let her face into the pillow and shook with the fun of it. If she should squeak half a note of reply she would be ordered to stay abed. Soon the mother rose and began stealthily to dress. No doubt it was to return to those poor Germans below. The thought was very sobering. Ramsey yearned to go with her, but knew she might as well ask leave to ride in the white yawl which, night and day, so incessantly, invitingly skimmed, zigzagged, foamed, and bounded after the *Votaress,* holding on to her fantail by its jerking painter.

The yawl reminded her of the boy Hugh. He seemed to belong to the boat in much the same way as it. He *was* a boy, nothing else – humph! – pooh! – . though he seemed to think himself the elephant of the show. A boy, and yet with what a mind! Not that she should ever want one like it – whoop! what would she ever do with it? No wonder she had laughed in his face. Without laughter she would have been his tossed and trampled victim. Laughter was her ladder; the ladder up which the circus girl runs to sit on the elephant's shoulder.

The lock of the stateroom door whispered. Her mother was going! Now she was gone! The daughter rose enough to look out on the gliding flood. It was day. But, night or day, how it intensified existence, this perpetual, tremulous passing of heaven and earth over and round and by and beneath one! Every least incident, indoors or out, was large and vivid, and a mere look from a window became a picture in the memory, to hang there through life. Nay, a sound was enough, too much. The remote peck-peck of that carpenter's hammer smote into her mind the indelible image of the only thing he could be making at such an hour. Trying to be deaf, she thought of Joy – timely thought! At any moment the old dear might steal in. She dropped from her berth, and when the actual invasion came, when Joy appeared, Ramsey was at the wash-stand, splashing like a canary, while strewn about the cramped place lay a lot of fresh attire, her Sunday best, brightest, longest.

"Now, you needn't say one word!" she cried.

The old woman bridled to say many, but before she could speak there was a fervent challenge to answer:

"Do you realize all I've got to attend to to-day?"

The nurse's mouth opened but another question was shot into it: "Has anybody told about the *Quakeress ?"*

There was a limit to forbearance. " Now, Miss Ramsey Hayle, ef dey is tell it, aw ef dey hain't – to yo' ma – dat's all right an' beseemly. But fo' you, dat ain't no fitt'n' story fo' you to heah!"

Ramsey stared from her towel with lips apart. "Why, you – I'm going to hear it! – all! – this day! – or, anyhow, this trip! – from – from – " She fell upon the nurse's shoulder, convulsed.

"F'om who' is you gwine hear it? Stop, missie, stawp! Dat's madness, dat laughteh. De Bible say' so! F'm who' – ? Lawd! yo' head's a-wett'n' my breas'-han'kercheh!"

Ramsey drew up, her eyes dancing, but went into a new transport as she replied: "From the baby elephant !"

"No, you don't, Miss Ramsey Hayle! No, you don't! An' besides, befo' you heah de story o' de *Quak'ess* you want to heah de story o' Phyllis." XVI

PHYLLIS

From earliest childhood the Hugh whom it gave Ramsey such rapture to nickname had unconsciously worn the dim frown that seemed to her so droll because at once so scrutinous yet so appealing.

To others that faint shade had never meant more than an inborn mental painstaking; a mind as steadily at work as the pulse; seemingly sluggish, really active. But Ramsey, in her stateroom, letting Joy dress her for all the Sabbath could mean afloat or ashore, could not accept such a thought. A feminine eagerness to read the masculine brow had promptly imputed to Hugh's a depth of mystery for which her romantic young soul demanded a romantic interpretation. Hence, mainly, her hunger for the story of the *Quakeress.* She had perceived, she thought, a relation between it and the clouded brow, and was bent on finding for the brow's owner as amazing a part in the tale as could be contrived by any piecing together of its facts which did not absolutely mutilate them. And these facts already she had begun to collect when by the mention of this "Phyllis" she discovered that old Joy had at least a share of the facts and under due pressure would yield them up.

"Phyllis?" asked Ramsey, "who was Phyllis?"

"Humph! Neveh hear o' Phyllis? Well, dey wuz reason fo' dat, too. Phyllis wuz de likeliest yalleh gal I eveh see, not-in-standin' she wuz my full fus' cousin."

Now, one could be as dark as a sloe and yet have a cousin as yellow as a marigold, but Ramsey did not see it so. "How can that be?" she laughed, "when you are so out and out black? " The bare idea seemed too comical for human endurance.

"I ain't no blackeh'n Gawd made me – oh, Lawd! missie, how I gwine button you up ef you shif' an' wriggle like dat? Phyllis wuz nuss to all de Co'teney chil'- en. 'Caze dat same day when de new *Quak'ess* come down de riveh wid dis same Mahs' Hugh, new-bawn, dah wuz yo' pa on his new boat, de *Conjuror* "

"Ow! *the Conqueror!*"

"Yass'm, dat's what I say. And dah wuz yo' ma, an' me, o' co'se, and dah wuz Phyllis, my full fus' cousin – now, ef you cayn't stop a-gigglin' an' wrigglin' long enough fo' me to finish dis "

Ramsey was too unnerved to heed. " How could – " she insisted – "how could a – a mulatto girl be your first cousin?"

"Now, you dess neveh min' how! Phyllis wa'n't no mullatteh, nohow. She wuz a quadroom! Heh mullatteh motheh wuz my own sisteh!"

"Oh, you mean half-sister!"

" I means whole sisteh! Miss Hayle, betteh you dess drap dat subjic' now, an' thaynk Gawd fo' yo' ign'- ance!"

"All right! all right ! whole sister! goon! were you twins?" The querist gave a wild start of surprise at herself and sank to the floor.

"Missie," sighed the old woman, "y'ain't neveh in yo' life stopped to think dat niggehs is got feelin's, is you?"

The speech was hardly begun before the girl was up and about the protester's neck: "Hush! ple-ease hush! You've said it before, you've said it before, you've said it before, before!"

The nurse's eyes filled: "Yass, an' what use it been? De wuss thing I know 'bout good white folks – an' when I says 'good' I means de best! – dat is, dat dey don't *believe* niggehs is got feelin's!" It was hard to speak on, for Ramsey had pushed her into a chair and was in her lap.

"They do! they do, mammy Joy, they do!" She fell to kissing her, first slowly, then wildly as Joy insisted :

"No, dey don't. Ef dey did, Phyllis 'ud neveh 'a' come to de pass she came to. But dey don't! Some o' de bes' *believes* dey believes, dat's all. Oh, I 'llow you, lots o' white folks is got – oh, Lawd! *don't* spile my breas'-han'kercheh! – is got mo' feelin's dan some niggehs; but lots o' niggehs is got *lots* mo' feelin's dan some white folks. Mo' an' betteh! Now, my sisteh, my yalleh sisteh "

"Oh, never mind, there's the rising gong! I know your yellow sister must have had feelings. Tell about Phyllis – and the Courteneys – and the *Quakeress.*"

"Well, I will! Yo' plumb sot on gitt'n' de thing, an' "

"Yes, and it's not a fit story for me to ask *him* about and you know I'll ask him if I have to! And besides, I just know mom-a's told you to keep me off the hurricane roof any way you can and as long as you can – listen! the big bell! we're meeting a boat, maybe half a dozen! And we're passing to labboard. Come! Come on!"

At their own door they espied the passing craft: a single boat, not six; a tiny, cabinless, one-funnelled, unclean, crawling thing, dimly made out in the early dusk of the forested shore which it servilely hugged as if doing all it could to hide its grimy name and identity.

" The *Fly-up-the-Creek!* " gasped Ramsey. " Oh, that *can't* be all!" She sprang up a stair, dragging the old woman after, and on the hurricane-deck, near a paddle-box, stood for a moment in the wide glory of water, land, and early sky, agape again at the squalid object. Then, as the full humor of the thing struck her – but her behavior may as well go undescribed. Yet it could not have been so very bad, for the pilot high above at the wheel, Watson's "partner," glancing down from his side window, enjoyed it much; silently, it is true, unsmilingly; yet so heartily that he took a fresh bite of tobacco, chewed with energy, and thought of home.

When the fit was over, old Joy had been pressed into a chair and the theme was once more Phyllis."Why did they bring her to New Orleans?" was the question.

"Who, Phyllis? She wuz fotch down fo' to be sold."

Ramsey's gaze was roaming every sky-line, but at that word it flashed back: "How, sold? Pop-a's told me, himself, he never in his life sold one of his negroes!"

" Is I said he did? Is I call' heh his niggeh? Ain't I done say she wuz a quadroom?
"

"Why," laughed Ramsey, "a quadroon's a negro!"

"Not in de sight o' Gawd! My Lawd, dat's de shame on it! – dat de likes o' my baby kin say de likes o' dat! Oh, you kin *make* a niggeh out'n a simon-pyo' white gal ef you dess raise heh wid de niggehs and treat heh like a niggeh; but "

Ramsey flushed: "Oh, I don't believe that!"

"Look hyuh, chile! I ain't choosin' to tell about dat, but – I's seen it done! Time an' ag'in! An' Phyllis she see it done! Dat's how come Phyllis to be de kind o' Phyllis she come to be!"

"What kind? Good, or bad? I don't want to hear about her if she was good."

"She was bofe. But I ain't hawngry to tell about heh, naw 'bout de *Quak'ess.*" The narrator shut her lips tight.

The morning air was like a sparkling wine. Ramsey squared her slim shoulders and drank it. The turbid waters next the sunrise showed a marvellous lilac hue, their myriad ripples tipped with pink, silver, and gold. Up-stream the river opened widely to the west, but the*Votaress* bore northward across the foot of the reach, and soon it was plain that she was about to enter a "chute," whose vividly green, low, wooded shore on her larboard bow was a large island: an island of swamp and jungle, ancient fastness of an Indian prophet, hid- denly swarming with all the ravening and venomous brute, reptile, and insect life possible to the region. Prophet's Island, it was, yet no senator, bishop, general, judge, or squire was in sight.

Ramsey had seen it on her down trip, when the boat, as required by law when descending the stream there, went eight miles round it in the main river. She had heard with awe that bit of history – not this history, – the drowning, by collision of a steamboat and a ship, of four hundred Creek Indians who were being deported to make room for the white man, and had felt herself grow older while she listened. But now what unmixed raptures awaited her in the narrow short cut! The recent presence of the *Fly-up-the-Creek* away over here on this morning side of the flood was made clear; she had run the chute, where she had no right to be, coming down-stream.

"My!" cried the girl, "I wish – oh, my, my, *my,* I wish I could be five people at once!"

For here the boat's watchman sauntered by – a boat's watchman must be a world in himself! Yonder at the forward rail the first mate still paced athwart the deck. By the captain's chair stood both the elder Courte- neys, their enthralling conversation all going to waste. Here rushed and quivered all the beautiful boat, her

.- . j - - -,-"'..

great human menagerie still unviewed, her cabin-boys laying her breakfast table, her cook-house smelling of hot rolls, the miracles of machinery pulsing on her lower deck, and down there an awful tragedy going on, with the sweet mother playing angel – oh, my, my! – and here, up yonder, was the pilot, by whose side one might presently look right into the narrow chute's greenwood walls and out over their tops – "Go on, mammy Joy, I can't ever listen to you, once we're in the chute!"

"I ain't bust'n' to tell noth'n'. Phyllis ain't belong to yo' pa, nohow. She belong' fust to yo' grampa Hayle, same like my sisteh do, my yalleh sisteh – aw ruteh to yo' gramma. Yo' gramma she own' a place back o' Vicksbu'g, same like *us* got back o' Natchez, whils' yo' grampa he stick to de riveh, same like yo' pa do now. But yo' grampa he outlive' yo' gramma nigh twen'y-five yeah'. An' 'bout two yeah' ayfteh yo' gramma die' my sisteh, my yalleh sisteh, she house- keep fo' yo' grampa – a shawt spell. Yo' ma she soon bruk dat up."

" Why, that was a funny thing for mom-a to do." "H-it wuz a right thing! Dat's what it wuz." " But, mammy, grandpa died before I was born!" "An' what dat got to do wid de price o' beeswax? Yo' a-mixin' me up a-puppose! Afo' yo' grampa die' – well, I'll stop tell you quits de giggles. . . . Afo' he die', when Phyllis wuz growed up, an' 'bout a yeah ayfteh y'uncle Dan – de bacheldeh – de pilot – quit de riveh a spell fo' to run de Vicksbu'g plantation, yo'ma, down on de Natchez place, she speak up ag'in, an' ax' yo' grampa fo' to loan Phyllis to she. An' yo' grampa, sho' enough, sawnt heh down, bofe Phyllis an" de chile."

"Chi – you skipped! You're skipping! like fury!" "Ef I skips I skips fo' de good o' yo' soul." Ramsey stared. "Why did mom-a borrow her?" "'Caze she couldn' buy heh. Yo' gramma she die' leavin' dat whole Vicksbu'g place an' people, bawn an' unbawn, to yo' grampa, fo' to pass, when he die', to y'uncle Dan, an' y'uncle Dan he wouldn' even 'a' loan' Phyllis ef he could 'a' perwent. Humph-ummm! he tuck on 'bout his 'rights' like a sett'n' hen." "But what did mom-a *want* to borrow her for?"

"Well, I mowt say, fo' heh beauty; but ef I don't skip noth'n' I got to say she 'How to p'otect heh."

Ramsey stared again and suddenly fell into that soft, rippling laugh, keen, merry, self-oblivious, which forty excusing adjectives would not have excused to her nurse.

"Protect her from – from wha-at?" She rippled again.

"F'om herseff! – an' f'om him! – an' him f'om heh! – and de whole Hayle fambly an' de law o' Gawd f'om bofe! An' she done it, yo' ma! – up to de wery day he meet his awful en' in dat bu'nin' pilot-house,

when "

" Ah-h-h! what pilot-house? You never told me "

"Anybody else eveh tol' you? No. Us Hayles-es ain't fon' o' dat story. What I ain't tell you ain't be'nripe to tell. I don't tell noth'n' 'tell it's ripe to tell, me!"

"Oh, it's dead ripe now. Go on, go on! – Burning pilot-house – my uncle Dan – stop! . . . Hmm! . . . That's funny. . . . Why, mammy, how could he be my uncle if he – was burnt up – before I was born?"

"Dat's yo' lookout. He wa'n't bu'nt up tell you wuz goin' on five. Yo' mixin' his las' en' wid yo' grampa's."

"Oh, I see-ee! He was lost on the *Quakeress* /"

"Well, thaynky, ma'am! Yo' perceivin' powehs is a-gitt'n' ahead o' de hounds. I wuz a-comin' to dat "

Ramsey interrupted. Her cry of ecstasy was not for the breakfast bell, which on the deck next below rang joyously up and down both guards and died away in the ladies' cabin. It was for a vision that rose before her and the *Votaress;* an illusion of the boat's whole speed being lost to the boat and given to the shore. Suddenly the fair craft seemed to stop and stand, foaming, panting, quivering like a wild mare, while the green, gray-bearded, dew-drenched forest – island and mainland – amid a singing of innumerable birds, glided down upon her, opening the chute to gulp her in without a twang of her guys or a stain upon her beauty.

"Go on!" cried Ramsey, her eyes enthralled by the scene, her ears by the story: – "Mom-a borrowed Phyllis – goon!"

"When yo' grampa gone," said Joy, "an' de will is read, yo' ma tell y'uncle Dan fo' to neveh mine hisrights aw his lef's; he kin go on ownin' Phyllis and de chile, but, all de same, he cayn't have 'em. An' when he paw de groun' an' th'ow dus' on his back yo' pa dess – go an' see him. Wheneveh yo' pa dess go an' see anybody, you know "

Ramsey knew. She tinkled with delight.

"But den come wuss trouble. 'Caze 'bout dat time "

About that time Ramsey whisked round and stood so as to give Hugh Courteney, as he came on deck, a square view of her young back. He noticed her better length of skirt.

"Go on," she murmured. "Is he coming this way?"

"Co'se he ain't. He gwine up to de pilot-house."

"Humph, how awfuZ busy ! That's just for grandeur. Go on." And while the leafy jaws of the chute drew them in and all the air was suddenly filled with the boat's sounds flung back from every rippling bough, tree top, and mass of draping vines, the nurse went on:

" 'Bout dat time yo' pa he git de hahdess ovehseeh he eveh did git, an' you can't 'spute de fact dat yo' pa he take' natchiully to hahd men, an' hahd men take natchiully to him. You kin say dat to his credits."

"Yes," replied Ramsey, "yes," sighing, gesticulating, whimpering in ecstasies of sight as the walls of the watery lane cramped in to half its first width. They seemed to rush past of their own volition, while out beyond them on either hand the whole dense graygreen interwoven wilderness, with ceremonial stateli- ness, swung round on itself in slow time to the windy speed of the *Votaress.* XVII

"IT'S A-HAPPMIN' YIT – TO WE ALL"

Nevertheless, "Go on!" cried Ramsey. "How could the overseer be hard on Phyllis if Phyllis was mom-a's maid?"

"Phyllis fo'ce' him to it! 'Caze all dat time, while she sweet as roses wid yo' ma – so's to keep in cahoots wid heh an' not have noth'n' to do wid niggehs o' no breed, pyo', half, quahteh, aw half-quahteh – she so wild to git back to y'uncle Dan dat she "

"And to leave mom-a! The goosy-goosy! What for?"

"Well, for one thing, by bad luck, f'om fus' sight, de ovehseeh he *fancy* Phyllis. Y'un'stan' "

"I don't! I don't want to – Go on!"

"Humph! Phyllis un'stan'. She un'stan' so well an' so quick dat de fus' drizzly night when de rain Vd spile de trail – de scent – she up wid de chile an' putt out."

"For my uncle Dan! Walnut Hills! Goon!" The moving scene was forgotten though the chute was widening again.

" Well, de ovehseeh, o' co'se, he *got* to run heh down an' fetch heh back. An' same time de creeks an'
bayous "

"Oh, now, that's the same old-

"Yass, oh, yass, de same ole! So ole an' common dat you white folks – what has all de feelin's "

"Now, just hush! You don't know anything about it! Goon! Goon! The bayous were – what?"

"Bank full, dat's all. One place Phyllis an' him nigh got swep' away an' he drap' de chile."

"Oh! ... Oh! ... Oh!"

"He bleeged to do it, he tell yo' ma, fo' to save Phyllis – what ain't want'n' to be save'. Whils' de chile – wuz – de chile wuz drownded." The old woman moved to rise, but the girl, with a. new expression in her face, prevented her.

"Go on! What did mom-a do?"

"Lawd, what could she do – widout yo' pa?"

"Oh, I'd have done something. What did Phyllis do?"

"Phyllis? Dess th'ash' de bed fo' tfi'ee days – eyes a-blazin' murdeh; th'ee days and de Lawd know' how many night'. Yo' ma done one thing but you don't want to know dat, I reckon."

"What did she do? Did she turn Whig?"

"Wuss! – ef wuss kin be. She tu'n' – dat day – Abolitionless. Ain't neveh tell me, but – you ax heh. Mebbe it wa'n't all 'count o' Phyllis. Mebbe it wa'n't plumb hoss-sensible nohow. But dat day – You ax heh!"

Ramsey flashed: "What are you telling me all this for?"

"Lawd! An' how many time' is you say, 'Go on'?" "I meant about the *Quakeress.*"

" Well, ain't dis de story o' de *Quak'ess?* When "

" Stop ! I'll tell it to you. I see it all."

"You! Y'ain't see it de quahteh o' half a quah- teh. Dat story is a-happmin' yit – to we-all – on dis boat!"

The breakfast-bell rang again, and Hugh started down from the pilot-house. But Ramsey would ask the old woman one more question: "Is it happening to him, too?"

"Co'se, him; all o' us; twins an' all. When us brung Phyllis down de riveh yo' ma wuz dead ag'in sellin' heh, an' when us git win' dat de Co'teneys want' a nuss yo' pa he dat glad he snap his fingehs. ' Us'll rent Phyllis to 'em!' he say. 'Dey's Hendry Clay Whigs; dey'd ought to treat heh fine.' (Dat wuz his joke.) An' yo' ma make answeh: 'Ef dey don't, us kin take heh back!. Betteh dat dan sell heh! Nobody o' de Hayle blood shayn't do dat whils' I live.'"

Hugh was near. "Good morning!" sang Ramsey. They met at the head of a stair. She turned away and looked out beyond the jack-staff as radiantly as if she had just alighted on the planet. The chute was astern. A new reach of open water came, sun-gilt, to meet them, and on either hand the low, monotonous green shores crept southward a mile apart.

She faced again to Hugh. "Isn't this God's country?"

" In a way," the youth admitted with a scant smile.

She glanced about. "Most beautiful river in the world!" she urged, and when he faltered she cried: "Oh, you're prejudiced!" She turned half away. "I know one thing; I wouldn't let *my* grandfather prejudice *me.*"

A new thought struck her: "Oh! . . . I've just heard all about it! ... And it helps to explain – you!"

He enjoyed the personality. "Heard all about what?"

"Phyllis!" She jerked up and down. His smile vanished; his lips set; he turned red.

Ramsey was even more taken aback than he or old Joy. She knew the pilot was looking down on her, the mate glancing back at her. Yet she laughed and prattled and all at once frowningly said: "But one thing I just can't make out! What on earth had the *Hayle blood* to do with any right or wrong of selling Phyllis? Do you know? "

Hugh reddened worse, and in that instant, out- blushing him, she saw the truth. "Never mind!" she cried. "Oh, did I stop you? Go on! – I – I mean go on down – to breakfast!"

"Won't you go first?"

"No, thank you; go on! Please, go on!" Glancing up to the pilot and catching his amused eye, she pointed distantly ahead. "What is that high bank on the – the stabboard shore?" she asked him.

"Why" – his tobacco caused but a moment's delay – "nothing much. They call that Port Hudson."

"Thank you!" She darted below, where Hugh was already gone. As she started she caught sight of the twins. They had just come up on the far side of the boat and were approaching the mate. Still flushed, but straight as a dart, at the stair's foot she turned on her attendant and with brimming eyes said softly: "I don't want any breakfast. I'm going to the lower deck – to find mom-a."

" You shayn't! You'll git de cholera!"

"Pooh, the cholera! – after what I've got! – I'm going to tell mom-a on you!"

"On me – me! Good Lawd! Go on, I's wid you!"

"You'd no right to tell me that story!"

"Missie, I on'y tol' you fo' to stop you. You said yo'se'f you gwine ax him all about it."

"Oh, him!" The girl laughed, yet showed new tears. "'I don't mind him; I mind the story! I don't even care who it's about, Hayles or no Hayles!"

"Why, den, what does you care ?"

"I care *what* it's about." She suddenly looked older. "Oh, I'm all over bespattered with the horrid "

"Y'ain't. Y'ain't de sawt fo' dat. Look at yo' ma. She have bofe han's in it. Is she all oveh be- spattud?"

"Oh, you! You know nothing could ever bespatter mom-a! . . . I'm going to her to get clean!"

"Dat's good!" A shrewd elation lit up the black face. "Go on! As you say yo'se'f, go on!"

Ramsey started away but with an overjoyed gasp found herself in her mother's arms. She pressed closerwhile the three laughed, and when the other two ceased she still mirthfully clung in that impregnable sanctuary. Suddenly she hearkened, tossed her curls, and stood very straight. Two male voices were coming down the stairs.

"We cannot," said one, "submit to this alive!"

"Yes," said the other, "we can. It's just *we who* can – till the day we catch them where they've got us to-day!"

"And what, now, is this?" smilingly inquired Madame Hayle as her twin sons halted before her.

The young men uncovered. They were surprisingly presentable after the night they had spent. Julian, in particular, looked capable and proud of their waywardness.

"Good morning," put in Ramsey, on her mother's arm. " See those little houses up on that bank? That's Port Hudson. Up there they can see away down the river, past Prophet's Island, and at the same time away up-stream. If we were on the hurric – ." She made a start, but her mother, while addressing the twins, restrained her.

"Well," she asked, "you cannot submit – to what?"

"We are ordered ashore!" said Julian.

"At the next landing!" quavered Lucian – "Bayou Sara!"

Ramsey slipped from her mother and gazed at the twins with her eyes as large as theirs. "You shan't go!" she broke in. " Where's Hugh? " She darted for the cabin, old Joy following. Julian glared after them.

"See?" he said to his mother. "You don't see – the plot? It's a plot! – to compromise us! – you and her included!"

"Before this boat-load of witnesses!" chimed Lu- cian.

Him the mother waved to a remote chair. "Bring me that," she said, for a pretext, and turned privately to Julian, speaking too swiftly for him to reply: " Was it part of that plot that you was both on that lower deck laz' night? No? But in the city those laz' two-three day' in how many strenge place' you was – lower deck of the whole worl' – God only know', eh? – unless maybe also the devil – an' the scavenger? That was likewise part of that plot aggains' us? No? But anny- 'ow that comity of seven – h-ah!" – she made a wry face – " that was cause' by the wicked plotting of those Courteney'? An' that diztrac' you so bad this morning that you 'ave not notiz' even that change' face on yo' brotheh? – or that change' voice, eh? An' him he's too affraid to tell you how he's feeling bad! As faz' as you can, take him – to his room – his bed – an' say you, both, some prayers. He's godd the cholera." XVIII

RAMSEY WINS A POINT OR TWO

There was half an hour yet before the first mate's watch would end.

He had risen from the captain's seat on the approach of that middle-aged pair who in the first hour of the voyage had enjoyed seeing Hugh and Ramsey together; a couple whose home evidently was far elsewhere – if anywhere – and who as evidently had seen the world to better advantage than most of the *Votaress's* passengers. As he rose Hugh and Ramsey came up near one of the wheels. Seeing them start directly for him, he made a heavy show of attention to the married pair.

While the quick step of the two younger people brought them near, the husband began to reply to the mate: "Why, to the common eye, tiresome, I dare say. To the artist – I wonder! It's the only much-travelled river in the world whose most imposing sight is always the boat."

"It isn't!" whispered Ramsey to Hugh. Then openly, yet decorously, "Ahem!" she said as they lapsed into waiting attitudes. But the mate was not to be ahemmed, and while he hearkened on to the criticshe could do no better than hammer the small of her back and smooth into it a further perfection.

"At the same time," continued the stranger, "it's immensely interesting; politically as to its future, scientifically as to its past." He turned to his wife: "Look, for instance, at this bit of it right here." A trained art in his pose and gesture caused Ramsey and old Joy to look as he prompted. "This is Fausse Riviere Cut-off," he continued, and the mate said it was – 'False River.

"Yes. Now, barely two generations ago" – he animatedly took Ramsey into his glance – "this stream suddenly abandoned twenty-odd miles of its own tremendous length and width and sprang through this two- mile cut-off." There was such fervor in his tone, and in his wife's mien such vivacity of interest, that the amazing event stood before Ramsey as if it had just occurred.

"You've read books about this river!" she said.

"A few, drifting down it by flatboat."

"Oh, by Christopher!" broke out the mate, "I remember you now! Yo're that play-actor! Yo're the man, by gad! who hauled me into yo' skiff half roasted and half drownded when the *Quakeress* was a-burnin'! By George, look here! What do you want on this boat, that you ain't already got? Name it, sir, just name it! Oh, by hokey, sir, I !"

Smilingly the actor shook his head while his wife beamed delightedly. "We haven't a want ungrati- fied," he answered.

"Oh, please!" put in Ramsey, "yes, you have – one!"

"Have we, mademoiselle? Surely we have if you have."

The mate interposed. " That's a daughter of Gideon Hayle, sir – as good a captain, by Joe, as ever took out a boat - "

The wife nodded gayly. "We know him," she said.

"Oh!" laughed Ramsey, scanning the pair up and down.

"What is it we want, worthy daughter of Gideon Hayle?" asked the player – "you and my wife and I – and yjur – this is your brother, is he not?"

Ramsey's mouth and eyes spread wide. She turned to Hugh and at sight of his heavy face whisked round again with her handkerchief to her lips. The mate spoke for her:

"That's Captain Courteney's son, sir."

"What Miss Hayle wants – " began Hugh -

"What *we* want," said Ramsey -

"Yes," said Hugh, "what we want is the recall

"An order," broke in the mate. "I know; my order for them two twins to go ashore. You can't have that, Hugh."

"We can!" said Ramsey, with tears in her laugh.

"No, sir-ee!" said the mate. "Ashore they go!"

"Ashore they don't!" said Ramsey. "You just told this gentleman you'd do anything he - "

"I'd do anything he – yes, but" – the speaker looked beyond her – " Why, Mr. Play-actor, them two youngAmericans come up here a-smellin' o' buckwheat cakes and golden syrup, when they and some others – a general and a senator, wa'n't they? – had had some political tiff with you "

"Oh, not political at all! There's a proposition – I had no idea it was theirs – to land our deck passengers on "

"On TurnbiuTs or Natchez Island!"

Ramsey breathed an audible amazement.

"Exactly," said the player. "Well, I had the ill luck to call their scheme a bad name or two."

"Good! Now, sir, up they come here *a-demanding o'* me to put you ashore, 'where he'll get himself lynched,' says they."

"Oh, bless my soul!" cried the actor. "If that was all and you want to please us, just let them alone."

The mate smiled to Hugh and shook his head. " It wa'n't all. *You* know it wa'n't. Gad, Mr. Hugh, they got to go!"

"Oh, they must not!" begged both players. A few steps away the bishop and the judge were holding an earnest conversation with the grandfather Courteney, and his eye tried to call the mate. But Ramsey, holding to Hugh by his sleeve, gave the old gentleman a toss of her chin, a jerk of her curls, and took the mate by a coat button. Her slim, silken figure intercepting him, and his rude bulk smiling down into her upturned face with a commanding yet amiable restiveness, made a picture to the players and to the distant pilot, but much more than a picture to the captive himself. Hehad thought he had been fending off the banter of a child, but now, suddenly, this was not a child. A being was here not entirely mundane nor quite supernal yet surpassing all his earlier knowledge of feminine quality, something for which a year's hard thinking would not have found him a definition. Holding his button, she spoke low:

" Please change that order." What mysterious compulsion there was in that "please"! Her fingers tapped Hugh. " *He* wants it changed – for me. We'll be responsible!"

" Oh, you will!" The big man did not look at Hugh; his smile broadened on their common captor. Her answering eyes laughed, but even in them, deep down, he saw a pleading ardor at once so childlike, so womanly, and so celestial that suddenly the deck seemed gone.

"Please change it! quick!" she murmured again, "for us!"

He felt an inward start and saw a vision – of the future – with those two in the midst of it. His brightening glance went belatedly to Hugh, and verily there was more of Hugh also than he had ever seen before, but the crass significance of his smile was quite lost on the pair.

"Yes," insisted Ramsey, *"we* want it changed, him and me – I mean he and I!"

The big man's laugh drowned hers. "Oh, it's plain either way. Well, by George! that *is* an argument. You and him! Gad, the case is covered! You and him has got me – by the hind leg!" He began to turnaway, for yonder,-'apart from commodore, judge, and bishop, but with Madame Hayle at his side, stood the captain, giving him a sign which he promptly passed on up to the pilot. "By the hind leg," he repeated, whereat a titter broke from the averted face of old Joy, while Ramsey stood agape at her success.

"They *stay* – the twins – stay *aboard?"* she asked the actors, Hugh, and the mate in turn.

"Lord, yes!" said the latter.

On tiptoes of gratitude she had parted her lips to say more, when the air overflowed with the long bellow of the boat. "Oh," she cried protestingly in the din, "but that's to land!"

His reply was unheard, but a shake of his head reassured her as he moved toward the elder Courteneys, whom bishop and judge had left, and who now stood alone awaiting him. She faced Hugh. He was telling the actor's wife that this landing was to get a physician. Ramsey touched him and spoke low:

"We're going to have an awful time. Don't you think so?"

He did not say. The great bell tolled thrice. She waved him to look at the people ashore, of all sorts and shades, coming down to the wharf-boat to see them, but suddenly, invited by a glance from his father, he stepped away to him. "Humph!" she laughed to old Joy, and started to join her mother, who was leaving the deck. But the mother motioned her back. "Where are you going?" whined Ramsey.

"To Lucian."

The daughter halted, aghast. "Has he got it?" But her mother went on without reply. She turned to the players and, when they smiled invitingly, rejoined them. When she inquired their name they said it was Gilmore.

"Will you tell me about the *Quakeress?"* she asked.

The husband said he would. " But you don't mean now," he qualified, "when so many things are happening?"

"N-no," she replied grudgingly, and presently added: "I'm afraid my brother's got the cholera." But then she brightened triumphantly. "Anyhow," she said, "the mate didn't know that." The engine bells jingled, the wheels paused, and the shore appeared to drift down upon them, pushing the crowded wharf- boat before it. "What d'you reckon this beautiful boat is saying to herself right now?" she asked.

"She ought to say," critically put in the bishop, behind her, to the senator, while she turned and cast her head-to-foot scrutiny up and down the two, " that for the welfare of that wharf-boatful of men and boys, and of the homes they live in, she'd best not land, after all."

"That's what she *is* saying!" defensively cried Ramsey, and, sure enough, while she laughed the scape-pipes roared and the wheels backed till the wharf-boat stood still. At the same time the pilots changed watch. The captain sauntered to the forward rail. The commodore, with the mate and Hugh, went below. So closely did the actor's eyes follow them that Ramsey asked: " What are they going to do? "

"Going ashore in the yawl, I hope, for a doctor."

"And medicines," added some one.

"And for a priest," disparagingly said the smiling bishop as they moved to the shoreward edge of the roof. " Large demands our deck passengers are mak- ing."

"An outrage!" said the senator. "It's an outrage that they, who wouldn't have dared whimper a month ago in their own country, should be allowed to behave this way here!"

"It isn't!" said Ramsey, squarely in his face. There was a general start, old Joy groaned, and Ramsey's eyes, though still in his, looked frightened; yet there was in her tone and bearing something so pertinent and worthy, even so womanly, that she had nearly every one on her side in a moment and the two players audibly murmured approval.

The senator grew benign. "My fair young lady," he said, "if your father, Gideon Hayle, were captain here he'd have those people off this boat in short metre."

" He wouldn't!" said Ramsey. Her eyes flashed and widened. Then as they darted round upon the actor her most tinkling laugh broke out, and she caught his wife's arm and rocked her forehead on it, the laugh recurring in light gusts between her words as they came singingly: "He wouldn't ... he wouldn't ... he wouldn't."

"There they go," said a voice, and down on the waters directly beneath appeared the white yawl like a painted toy, but full of men. The commodore was there and the mate. Beside the mate sat the young German who had fought the twins.

"That's the one they call Otto," said Ramsey, though how she knew is to be wondered; and somebody, to amplify, added:

"Otto Marburg. They're taking him along so the others will be quiet till he comes back."

"Humph!" said Ramsey, arching her brows to old Joy and the Gilmores and by her own glance directing theirs to the aftermost figure in the yawl. It was Hugh. He was steering.

11

SECTION 11

XIX

THIS WAY TO WOMANHOOD

Noon came with a beauty of sky as if it smiled back to the smiles of a land innocent of pain, grief, or strife.

It found the *Votaress* under full headway, with a physician aboard and Bayou Sara one great reach and two great bends behind. In a stateroom of her texas, by madame's grateful acceptance of the captain's offer, lay Lucian, torn with pain but bravely meek, with Julian in close attendance, Ramsey excluded, and the mother looking in often, though very busy yet with the doctor on the lower deck.

In the middle of the forenoon, invited by the captain, the bishop had held divine service in the ladies' cabin and, praying for his country, found himself praying also, resoundingly and with tears, for the " strange people" down under his bended knees, while out on the boiler deck the disputation concerning them steadily warmed and spread, the committee of seven feeling themselves for the moment baffled but by no means beaten – baffled, for their casual brush with Ramsey had most surprisingly, not to say unfairly, discredited their cause. "Gideon Hayle's daughter" had become as universally known by sight as "John Courteney's son," and all about among the male cabin passengersher method of debate – "It won't! They don't! He wouldn't! We shouldn't!" – with a mirth often pro- vokingly unlike hers – was the fashion and had won two or three small victories.

"The side that laughs, nowadays and hereabouts," agreed the two players, " wins." But they said it aside from Ramsey, who, they had begun to fear, would be sadly spoiled, the juveniles were so humbly looking up to her, and so many grown-ups sought her to draw out her brief but prompt utterances upon the situation and repeat them elsewhere to those who liked their seats so much more than anything else. They tried to keep her with them and off the absorbing theme and were not without success.

Just now the word had run all through the boat that the next turn would bring her into the "Raccourci," or, as every one but the players called it, "Raccourci Cut-off." Counting up-stream, it was the second of four great shortenings of the river, which, in the brief century and a half since the country had become a white man's possession, had reduced a hundred and twenty miles of its wandering course to half as many within a straight overland distance of thirty. Wonderful to Ramsey was the story of it. The kindly Gil- more told it with a pictorial and personal interest that made it seem as if he himself had planned and supervised the whole work. One of the shortenings was Shreve's Cut-off, made only twenty-one years before this birth year of the *Votaress.* Yonder it lay, just veering into the remotest view, where Red River, over twelve hundred miles from its source in the StakedPlains beyond the Rocky Mountains, swept, two thousand feet wide, into the Mississippi without broadening the "Father of Waters" a yard.

Yet why look there, so distantly, when here between, right here under the boat's cut-water, was the Rac- courci, barely four years old? The *Votaress* was in it, half through it, before either Ramsey or Mrs. Gil- more could be fully informed, and now their attention was beyond even their own command. For yonder ahead, miles away in Shreve's Cut-off, riding the strong current under Turnbull's Island, came the *Regent,* finest and speediest of Gideon Hayle's steamers.

So late in the season her passengers were few and she was not utterly smothered in a cargo of cotton bales, yet her freight deck showed a goodly brown mass of them, above which her snowy form gleamed against the verdant background of the forested island, as dainty as a swan, while her gliding stem raised on either side a silver ribbon of water that arched itself almost to her gunwales.

"Each to her own starboard," answered the *Regent's* mellow bell to the bell of the *Votaress.* Her whistle whitened and trumpeted in salute, and on jack-staff and verge-staff her rippling flags ran up and dipped, twice, thrice, to the answering flags of the Courteney boat. Well forward on her hurricane-deck her captain, whom many on the *Votaress* pointed out by name, stood alone. Amid-ships her cabin-boys lined her cook-house guards. Her negro crew swarmed round her capstan with their chantey-man on its head and sent over the gliding waters the same stalwart perversion of the wilderness hymn of "Gideon's Band" to which the twins had danced the night before. Now the lone, high voice of the leader sang:

"Fus' come de animals, two by two,
Fus' come de animals, two by two,
Fus' come de animals, two by two,
De elephantine and de kanguiroo,"

and now, while he held the key-note through the refrain's whole first line, the chorus rolled up from an octave below:

"Do you belong to Gideon's Band?

Here's my heart an' here's my handl

Do you belong to Gideon's Band?

Fight'n' fo' yo' home!"

No song is so poor that it may not thrill a partisan devotion. Ramsey stood on her toes. Down in his berth and in torture the shut-in Lucian faintly heard, turned his gaze to his brother, whispered "the *Regent!*" and listened for another verse. The boats were passing widely apart, and when it came only memory made its foolish lines plain to his doting ear:

"Nex1 come de hoss and den de flea,

Nex' come de hoss and den de flea,

Nex' come de hoss and den de flea,

De camomile and de bumblebee.

Do you belong to Gideon's Band?

Fight'n'fo'yo'home!"

On the last line the singers were half a mile downstream, in Raccourci Cut-off, and Ramsey and the *Votaress* were well started up the ten-mile reach from Red River Landing to Fort Adams.

How swiftly and incessantly the scene changed. Down in a stateroom near the boiler deck some beginner on the horn was dejectedly playing " A Life on the Ocean Wave," but even with pestilence aboard and a brother stricken with it what an exalted, exalting life was a life on this mighty stream! Flat lands? Flat waters? It was the highest, widest outlook into the world of nature and of man she had ever had. Monotonous? – when one felt oneself a year older to-day than yesterday and growing half a month's growth every hour? In yesterday's childishness she had begun at Post Forty-six to keep count of all the timber rafts and flatboats met, and here in this long stretch came three more of the one and five of the other, with men hurrahing to her from them – men as wild as the wilderness, yet with homes and families away back up the great tributaries and their tributaries. And here were mile-wide cotton fields, with the black people hoeing in them and looking no bigger than flocks of birds feeding. And here came another steamboat – and yonder anotherl The very drift logs, so countlessly frequent, vast trees from vast forests, some of them not yet dead, told to her sobering mind in tragic dumb show as they came gliding and plunging by, the age-long drama of their rise, decline, and fall. Unbrokenly green, yes, forever the one same green, were the low willow andcottonwood jungles of the creeping shores; but while the "labboard" shore was still Louisiana the "stab- board" was now her own native Mississippi.

Yes, these wild shores were States – States of the great Union, the world's hope; Jackson's, Clay's, Webster's Union, which "must and shall be preserved," "now and forever, one and inseparable." Somewhere between these shores, moreover, and not behind but away on up-stream, probably, Mr. Watson said, in Dead Man's Bend, was, once more, the *Antelope.* In the long wait at Bayou Sara, where Hugh and the outlandish Otto – who could speak French – had found the priest while the commodore and the mate were getting the doctor, the *Antelope* had reappeared, swept up, and foamed by, and now was so far ahead that in hardly less than another hundred and sixty miles could she be again overtaken. But to Ramsey, even without the *Antelope* or any or all of the sights and facts of landscape and history, no moment could go stale while the tale of Phyllis and the *Quakeress* waited like funds in a bank, and while the commodore, the captain, and Hugh, the pilots, the mate, the Gilmores, the judge, general, bishop, squire, senator, Otto Marburg in his green coat, and dozens and scores of others were all over the boat, each more and more a story, a study, as hourly she grew older.

On the bench close behind her in the pilot-house a lady with needlework, a gentleman with *De Bow's Review* (the squire's sister and brother-in-law), had begun to talk with the -Gilmores and presently mentioned the twins, speaking in such a tone of doom as to give Ramsey a sudden panic.

"It's fine!" said the husband, praising Julian's devotion to his stricken brother. "And they are fine. Their faults – which you've had occasion to discover, sir – are spots on the sun; the faults, madam, of all our young Southern gentlemen "

"Would you say of all?" asked the actor's wife.

"No!" said the other lady, "no, not of all!" and her husband was glad to stand corrected.

"No," he admitted, "but still of almost all; faults of which we may almost say, sir, that we may almost be proud!"

"Oh, well," begged his wife, "please almost don't say it! They're the faults of our 'peculiar institution' and I wish our 'peculiar institution' were – " She sewed hard.

" In the deep bosom of the ocean buried," suggested her husband to the players. " Why, honestly, so do I. But it's not, and can't be, and as long as it can't be we "

"Oh, well," said his wife, "don't let's begin on that."

Reckless of institutions Ramsey turned. "Is my brother worse?" she broke in, but a white-jacket entered with the dinner-bell and spoke softly to old Joy. " Yes," said Ramsey to him, " I'm Miss Hayle. What is it? Is my brother worse?"

"Miss Hayle, Mr. Hugh Co'teney make his comp'- ments "

Ramsey laughed in relief.

"Yass'm, an' say' cap'm cayn' come to de table an' yo' ma she cayn't come "

"I know she can't. Is my brother ?"

"And de commodo' he at de gemp'men's table, an' so he, Mr. Hugh, he 'p'inted to de ladies' table, an' will you please fo' to set in de place o' yo' ma? "

"Oh, rid-ic-ulous! Who? me? I?" The laugh grew plaintive.

"Yes, you; why not?" said the pilot at the wheel, with his eyes fixed far up the river.

But Ramsey glanced at her short skirts and laughed to all by turns: "Oh, it's just some ridiculous mistake!"

"No, miss, 'tain't no mistake. All de yetheh ladies incline de place." Every one laughed. "Oh, he on'y off' it to one! But when she say fo' to off' it to you den dey all say de same; yass'm, sawt o' in honoh o' yo' ma."

"They're afraid that seat'll give 'em the cholera," said the pilot in grim jest, still gazing up-stream, but the ladies cried out in denial for all their sex.

"I accept," said Ramsey, with a downward pull at her draperies. "How's my brother?"

"Thank y'ma'am," was the bowing waiter's only reply. He tripped down the pilot-house steps and away.

"Your brother," said the squire's sister as they all followed, "isn't in nearly so much pain, we hear."

Ramsey flashed: " Does that mean better – or worse?"

"Why – we – we can't always be sure."

"Ringading tingalingaty, ringadang ding!" sang the festive bell up and down the deck to which they began to descend by a narrow stair, old Joy at the rear. Madame Hayle, ascending by another with the Bayou Sara priest, espied the nurse and beckoned her. The pilot, high above, observed the three as they met, although his ear was bent to a speaking-tube. Now he answered into it: "Yes, sir. . . . Yes, close above the point – Point Breeze, yes, sir."

As he resumed his up-stream gaze he saw old Joy, still at the stair, stand as if lost and then descend alone while madame and the priest moved toward the sickroom. The helm went gently over and the *Votaress* rounded the point, but the priest waited outside where madame had gone in, and when the door reopened enough to let one out it was Julian who grimly confronted him, holding a pen, half concealed.

"My brother declines to see you, sir."

A flash came from the eyes of the priest, but the youth repeated: "My brother *declines* to *see* you, sir."

The visitor caught breath to speak, but the great bell pealed for another landing and burial, and madame came out. She addressed him a few words in French, and with an austere bow to Julian he humbly turned away at her side.

12

SECTION 12

XX

LADIES' TABLE

Hugh stood at the head of the midday dinner-table, waiting for a full assembly of its guests. The Vicks- burg merchant and his wife, the planter from Milli- ken's Bend and his wife, also stood at their places.

The two ladies glanced about as if listlessly noting the cabin's lavish arabesques and gilding, while each really studied and knew the other was studying the captain's son. For this tale which we tell, they saw. It was "a-happmin'" before their eyes and, in degree, to themselves. Hugh and his father, the commodore and madame, the first mate, the twins, Ramsey, and the committee of seven – who, we shall see, were not taking discomfiture meekly – were scarlet threads in the story's swiftly weaving fabric – cogent reasons, themselves, why these two ladies had helped vote Ramsey to the seat next Hugh.

His face, Hugh's, was not easy reading. Certain shadows cast on it by that part of his mind just then busiest were quite unintelligible. Deciphered they would have meant a solemn joy for his broadening accountability; an awesome anxiety and distressed eagerness to meet and fill that accountability as fast as it broadened. He was just then recalling one of Ramsey'squeries of the evening before, when she had seemed so much younger than now, and when, nevertheless, a germ of fellowship had sprung up between them; that word of hers about " feeling oneself widen out of oneself," etc. He did not at present feel himself nearly so much as he felt things round about him growing and growing.

The *Votaress* had grown, grown wonderfully, and the story happening, the play being acted on her three decks at once, was neither story nor play to him. Which fact was one of the few things the two gentle students of his face made out to read. However, it quite rewarded them; it went, itself, so well into the story.

And certainly, as even the Gilmores would have said, it is not when our spiritual vision sees things at their completest values that *all* the world's a stage and its men and women *merely* players. Nor is it at our best that we discern our own story, as a story, while it happens. It is a poor eye that sees itself. When Ramsey arrived at the table Hugh's gaze was so big with the reality, not the romance, of things on all the three decks that she had to laugh a little to keep her balance.

Yet her question was an earnest and eager one: " Is my brother better, or is he worse?"

The toll of the bell on the deck above – to land, as we have said, near Point Breeze – came like a spectral reply, invoking, as it did, new trouble unknown to her though just beneath her feet.

" He's better not to be worse," said Hugh, and when she frowned whimsically he explained: "His sickness is not quite the same as that on the lower deck."

"How is it different?" she asked, unconsciously keeping the whole company of the ladies' table on their feet. At the gentlemen's table, just forward of them and tapering slenderly away in the long cabin's white- and-gilt perspective, that grosser majority who had come only to feed were mutely and with stooped shoulders feeding like pigeons from a trough, and far down at its end the white-haired commodore had taken his seat, with senator, judge, squire, general, and the seventeen-year-old Hayle boy nearest him on his right and left. The bishop was not there. He was at the ladies' table, paired with the judge's sister – a leaden load even for a bishop.

"Your brother's illness is so much slower," Hugh said.

"So, then – he – he had it when he came aboard?"

"He had it when he came aboard," assented Hugh, moving for the group to be seated. "But "

"Wait," said Ramsey. "Mustn't we all be as gay and happy as we can?" And when every one but the judge's sister playfully said yes she turned to the Vicksburg merchant: "Then will you change places with Mr. Gilmore?"

Faith, he would! It paired him with the actor's wife, and his wife with the actor. Gayety began forthwith. "And will you change – with – with you?" Ramsey asked the planter of Milliken's Bend and the squire's brother-in-law.

Indeed they would. The change not only paired each with the other's wife but brought the brother-in- law next to Ramsey. Underfoot meantime the engine bells jingled, overhead the scape-pipes roared, and in every part the boat quivered as her great wheels churned or was strangely quiet as they paused for another signal. So all sat down, well aware what the landing was for, and began blithely to converse and be waited on, as if the world were being run primarily for their innocent delight.

What a Sabbath feast was there spread for a bishop to say grace upon, and what travellers' hunger to match it. Among Hugh and Ramsey's dozen, if no further, how the conversation rippled, radiated, and out-tinkled and out-twinkled the fine tablewares. One almost forgot his wine or that the boat and her wheels had stopped; might have quite forgotten had not certain sounds, starting in full volume from the lower deck but arriving under the cabin floor faint and wasted – emaciated, as you might say – stolen up and in. A diligent loquacity contrived to ignore the most of them. The soft chanting of the priest as he walked down the landing-stage and out upon the damp brown sands, followed by the bearers of the new pine box and by a short procession of bowed mourners, perished unheard at the table; but many noises more penetrative were also much more discomfiting, and it was fortunate that the talk of the bishop and others could charm most of them away even from the judge's nervous sister, who, nevertheless, amid such remote themes asJenny Lind, Nebraska, coming political conventions, and the new speed record of the big *Eclipse* in the fourteen hundred and forty miles from New Orleans, could not help a light start now and then. It was good, to Hugh and to Ramsey, to see how the actor, Gilmore, despite this upward seepage of ghostly cries – faint notes of horror, anguish, and despair – attenuated groans and wailings of bodily agony – held the eyes of the ladies nearest him with tales of travel and the theatre, and mention of the great cut-off of 1699, which they would soon pass and must notice. But quite as good was it to the wives of Vicksburg and Milliken's Bend to observe with what fluency Hugh, commonly so quiet, discoursed to Mrs. Gilmore and to Ramsey on other river features near at hand: Dead Man's Bend, Ellis Cliffs, Natchez Island, the crossing above it, Saint Catherine's Creek, and Natchez itself.

"Where I was born!" said Ramsey. "Largest town in Mississippi and the most stuck-up."

The other Mississippians laughed delightedly.

"We stop there," said Hugh, "to put off freight."

"Mr. Courteney," asked Ramsey, "what *is* a 'crossing'?"

There were new lower-deck noises to drown and Hugh welcomed the slender theme. "The channel of a great river in flat lands," he said, "is a river within a river. It frets against its walls of slack water "

" I see! – as the whole river does against its banks!"

"Yes. Wherever the shore bends, the current, when strong, keeps straight on across the slack water till it hits the bend. Then it swerves just enough to rush by, and miles below hits the other shore, swerves again, and crosses in another long slant down there."

"Except where it breaks through and makes a cutoff !"

"But a cut-off is an event. This goes on all the time, in almost every reach; so that pilots, whether running down-stream in the current or up-stream in the slack water, cross the river about as often as the current does."

"Hence the term!" laughed Ramsey.

" I think so. You might ask Mr. Watson."

" No, I'll ask him what a reach is – and a towhead – and a pirooter – oh, don't you love this river?"

While the talk thus flowed, what delicacies – pastries, ices, fruits – had come in and served their ends! But also against what sounds from the underworld had each utterance still to make headway: commands and threats and cries of defiance and rage, faint but intense, and which all at once ceased at the crack of a shot! The judge's sister let out a soft note of affright and looked here and there for explanation. In vain. The Vicksburg merchant lightly spoke across the table:

"Shooting alligators, bishop?"

"Oh!" broke in the judge's sister, aggrieved, "that was for no alligator." She appealed to a white-jacket bringing coffee: "Was that for an alligator?"

"I dunno'm. Mowt be a deer. Mowt be a b'ar." His bashful smirk implied it might be none of the three. Ramsey looked at Hugh and Hugh said quietly to a boy at his back: "Go, see what it is." XXI

RAMSEY AND THE BISHOP

"HiGH water like this," casually said the planter, next Ramsey, " drives the big game out o' the swamps, where they use, and makes 'em foolish."

"Yes," said the bishop. "You know, Dick" – for he and the planter were old acquaintances – "not far from here, those long stretches of river a good mile wide, and how between them there are two or three short pieces where the shores are barely a quarter of a mile apart?"

"Yes," replied Dick and others.

"Well, last week, on my down trip, as we rounded a point in one of those narrow places, there, right out in mid-river, was a big buck, swimming across. Two swampers had spied him and were hot after him in a skiff."

"Oh," cried Ramsey, "I hope he got away!"

"Why, / partly hoped he would," laughed the bishop, " and partly I hoped they'd get him."

"Characteristic," she heard the planter say to himself.

"And sure enough," the tale went on, "just as his forefeet hit the bank – " But there Hugh's messenger reappeared, and as Hugh listened to his murmuredreport the deer's historian avoided oblivion only by asking:

"Well, Mr. Courteney, after all, what was it?" "Tell the bishop," said Hugh to the boy. " 'T'uz a man, suh," the servant announced, and when the ladies exclaimed he amended, "leas'wise a deckhan', suh."

"Thank Heaven!" thought several, not because it was a man but because the bells jingled again and the moving boat resumed her own blessed sounds. But the bishop was angry – too angry for table talk. He had his suspicions.

" Did deckhands make all that row? " "Oh, no, suh; not in de beginnin', suh." "Wasn't there trouble with the deck passengers?" "Yassuh, at fus'; at fus', yassuh; wid dem and dey young leadeh. Y'see, dey be'n so long aboa'd ship dey plumb stahve fo' gyahden-sass an' 'count o' de sickness de docto' won't 'low 'em on'y some sawts. But back yondeh on sho' dey's some wile mulbe'y trees hangin' low wid green mulbe'ys, an' comin' away f'om de grave dey make a break fo' 'em. But de mate he head' 'em off. An' whilse de leadeh he a-jawin' at de mate on sho', an' likewise at de clerk on de b'ileh deck an' at

the cap'm on de roof "

"In a foreign tongue," prompted the bishop, to whom that seemed the kernel of the offence.

"Yassuh, I reckon so; in a fond tongue; yassuh." "About his sick not having proper food?" asked Ramsey.

"Yass'm – no'm – yass'm! An' whilse he a-jawin', some o' de crew think dey see a chance fo' to slip into de bresh an' leave de boat. An' when de mate whip' out his 'evolveh on 'em, an' one draw a knife on him, an' he make a dash fo' dat one, he – dat deckhan' – run aboa'd so fas' dat he ain't see whah he gwine tell it's too la-ate."

The bishop tightened his lips at Hugh and peered at the cabin-boy: "How was it too late?"

"De deckhan' he run ove'boa'd, suh."

The ladies flinched, the men frowned. "But," said the querist, "meantime the mate had fired, hmm? Did he – hit?"

"Dey don't know, suh. De deckhan' he neveh riz."

"Awful!" The bishop and Hugh looked steadily at each other. "So that also we owe to our aliens!"

"Yes," said Hugh.

"We don't," said Ramsey softly, yet heard by all.

Across the board Mrs. Gilmore said "Oh!" but in the next breath all but the judge's sister laughed, the bishop, as Hugh and he began to rise, laughing most.

"Wait," said Ramsey, laying a hand out to each and addressing Hugh. "How are those sick downstairs going to get the right food?"

The cabin-boy almost broke in but caught himself.

"Say it," said Hugh.

"Why, dem what already sick dey a-gittV it. Yass'm, dey gitt'n' de boat's best. Madam Hayle and de cap'm dey done see to dat f'om de staht. H-it's de well uns what needs he'p."

"But," said Ramsey, still to Hugh, "for sick or well – the right food – who pays for it? "

"The boat."

"Who pays the boat?" she asked, and suddenly, blushing, saw her situation. Except the bishop and the judge's sister, who were conversing in undertone – except them and Hugh – the whole company, actually with here and there an elbow on the board, had turned to her in such bright expectancy as to give her a shock of encounter. But mirth upheld her, and leaning in over the table she shifted her question to the smiling bishop: "Who pays the boat?"

"The boat? Why – ha, ha! – that's the boat's lookout."

"It isn't," she laughed, but laughed so daintily and in a gayety so modestly self-justified that the group approved and the Vicksburg man asked her:

"Who ought to pay the boat?"

"Wei" she cried. "All of us! It's in the Bible that we ought!" She looked again to the bishop. "Ain't it?"

"Why, I don't recall any mention of this matter there."

"Nor of strangers?" she asked, "nor of sick folks?" and her demure mirth, not flung at him or at any one, but quite to itself and for itself, came again.

"Ah, that's another affair!" he rejoined. He felt her and Hugh, with half the rest, saying to themselves, "It is not!" but was all the more moved to continue: "My fair daughter, you prepare the way of theLord. Brethren and sisters, I want you to gather with me here as soon as those yonder are through" – a backhanded toss indicated the children's table, whose feasters showed no sign that they would ever be through at all. "We must – every believer – and whosoever will – on this passenger-deck – spend an hour – more if the spirit leads – in prayer for this pestilence to be stayed." He fastened his gaze on Hugh; no senator was present to overtop him now, and certainly this colt of John Courteney's should not. Yet the largeness with which the colt's eyes stared through and beyond him was significant to all.

"And we must do more!" he persisted.

"We shall," said Hugh.

"We must!" said the bishop; "we must beseech God for a spiritual outpouring. We have on this boat the stranger of our own land and the sick of our own tongue: the stranger to grace and the sick in soul, who may be eternally lost before this boat has finished her trip; and as much as the soul's worth outweighs the body's is it our first duty to help them get religion!"

With her curls lowered nearly to the table Ramsey – ah, me! – laughed. Her notes were as light as a perfume, but to the bishop all perfumes were heavy. He turned to the actor. "Isn't that so, brother?"

"Oh, bishop, you know a lot better than I do."

"He doesn't," tinkled Ramsey, and, as the bishop swung back to her – "Do you?" she ingratiatingly challenged him. "No, you don't! You know you don't!"

The company would have laughed with her if only to save their face, and when he made a very bright retort they laughed the heartier. They rose with Hugh. Ramsey said she wished she knew again how her brother was, and Hugh sent his servant to inquire. As all loitered aft, the bishop held them together a moment more.

"You don't object to such a meeting?" he asked Hugh.

"Not if you don't alarm or distress any one. The doctor forbids that." While Hugh so replied, the circle was joined by the commodore. The bishop flared:

"Doctors always forbid ! How can we exhort sinners without alarming or distressing them? "

Hugh's answer was overprompt: "I don't know, sir."

But Ramsey, drawing the Gilmores with her, came between. "Just a bit ago," she said to the bishop, "didn't you say yes, we must all be as gay and happy as we can?"

"I did, verily. But surely that shouldn't prevent this."

"Oh, surely not!" exclaimed both the players.

"It needn't," said Ramsey. "But if we five" – Gilmores, Courteneys, and herself – " and some others – help you with your meeting to-day will you help us with ours to-morrow?"

"If I can, assuredly! But how will you help me today, my young sister?"

On three fingers the young sister – so lately his daughter – counted: "First, we'll get the people to come; we'll tell them you're not going to alarm or distress anybody. Second, if you forget and begin to do it we'll remind you! And, third, we'll take up the collection!"

The senator laughed so much above the rest that the bishop colored as he said: "I never exhort and collect at the same time."

"Oh-h!" sighed Ramsey. "We must collect, you know, to pay our share, each of us, for the care of the sick. And we can't collect to-morrow; we'll all be so busy getting up our own meeting." Her eyes wandered to the senator, so fervently was he urging some matter upon the commodore.

"What," asked the bishop, turning to the players, "is to-morrow's meeting to be for?"

"Why," brightly said the wife, "just to keep every one as gay and happy as we can." But Ramsey added: "And to raise money for the not-sick emigrants, to get them the right food."

"Ho, ho! Another collection!"

"No, only admission fees. Six bits for the play, four bits for the dance."

Half offended, hah amused, the bishop swelled. "And you ask me" – he laughed, but she had turned away and he reverted to the players – " on top of our prayers for God's mercy upon our bodies and souls you ask me to help get up a play and a dance!"

Eagerly, amid a general merriment that was not quite merry, the Gilmores answered with amused disclaimersfor themselves and copious excuses for him. Ramsey's eyes, like Hugh's, were on the commodore and the senator, who were starting off together. The commodore's nod called Hugh and he moved to overtake them. The boy whom Hugh had sent to the texas, returning, sought to intercept him, but Hugh passed on and the messenger found Ramsey. She had just been rejoined by her old nurse, and to both servants her questions were prompt and swift. Their low replies plainly disturbed her, and she wheeled to the bishop where he still stood addressing the Gilmores and a dozen others in a manner loftily defensive. He forestalled her speech with good-natured haste. "Now, if our gay and happy young sister will ask me to do something befitting a minister of the gospel," he began

"Amen to dat!" said old Joy, and as Ramsey's eyes showed tears the speaker paused.

"All right," she quietly said. "Come to my sick brother. Won't you, please?"

"Why – why, yes, I – I will. Cer-certainly I will. Yet – really – if I'm forbidden to alarm him" – his smile could not hide his sense of mortal risk.

"Oh, he's already alarmed!"

"He's turrified!" softly said old Joy.

"Why, then, the moment we're through our meeting "

"Don't begin it!" said Ramsey. "It can wait heaps better than he can. He's waiting now and begging for you. Come! You needn't be afraid; I'll go with you!" She laughed.

."No!" cried Joy. "Lawd, Mahs' Bishop, she mus'n't!"

"She need not," said the bishop. "But for me to go now, before I – why, I couldn't come back and min- gle "

" Oh, come!" The girl drew him by the sleeve. But the Gilmores held her back and he went on alone, his face betraying a definite presentiment as he glanced round in response to a clapping of hands.

"Oh, thank you!" cried Ramsey. "Gawd bless you!" droned Joy. "We'll run your meeting while you're gone!" called Ramsey. "And we'll pray for you! Won't we?" she asked the players, and they and others answered: "Yes." XXII

BASILE AND WHAT HE SAW

For these twenty hours of constant activity one young passenger, save only when asleep in his berth, had contemplated the *Votaress* and her swarming managers and voyagers with a regard different from any we have yet taken into account. The Gilmores, softly to each other, termed him "a type." To the face of nature he seemed wholly insensible. As the gliding boat incessantly bore him onward between river and sky, shore and shore, he appeared never to be aware whether the forests were gray or green, the heavens blue or gray, the waters tawny or blue. No loveliness of land or flood could deflect his undivided interest in whatever human converse he happened to be nearest as he drifted about decks in a listless unrest that kept him singled out at every pause and turn. His very fair intelligence was so indolently unaspiring, so intolerant of harness, as we may say, and so contentedly attuned to the general mind, mind of the multitude, that the idlest utterance falling on his ear from any merest unit of the common crowd was more to him than all the depths or heights of truth, order, or beauty that learning, training, or the least bit of consecutive reasoning could reveal. Earlier he had not lacked books or tutelage, but no one ever had been able toteach him what they were for. This was Basile Hayle, the overdressed young brother of the twins. Now that his seventeen years had ripened in him the conviction that he was entitled, as the phrase is, " to all the rights of a man and all the privileges of a boy," he seemed yet to have acquired no sense of value for any fact or thought beyond the pointblank range of the five senses. He could not have read ten pages of a serious book and would have blushed to be found trying to doit.

He was not greatly to blame. That way of life was much the fashion all about him, and he was by every impulse fashionable. Moreover, as he measured success by the crowd's measure, it was the way of life oftenest successful, the way of his father. He did not see the difference between the father's toiling up that way and his idling down it. So, at any rate, agreed the indulgent Gilmores, reading him quite through in a few glances, while all about the boat those who thought they knew best pronounced him more like Gideon Hayle in his regard for "folks just as folks" than were either the twins or the sister, from all three of whom his impulses kept him amiably aloof.

Of the three brothers certainly he had soon become the most widely acceptable among not only the young people of the passenger guards but also the male commonalty of the boiler deck. In a state of society which he, as "a type," reflected they saw themselves; saw their own spiritual image; their unqualified straightforwardness, their transparent simplicity of mind andheart, their fearlessness, their complacent rusticity, their childish notions of the uses of wealth, their personal modesty and communal vanity, their happy oblivion to world standards, their extravagance of speech, their political bigotry, their magisterial down- rightness, their inflammability, and their fine self-reliance. They saw these traits, we say, reflected in him as in a flattering hand-glass, perceived the blemishes rather plainer than the charms, and liked them better.

So it was that our friend the senator had early discovered Basile and later had found a capital use for him. In him he saw a most timely opportunity, one not afforded by anybody besides. He showed the youth marked attentions, affirming in him all the men's rights and boys' privileges he had ever thought of, got him assigned to his sick brother's place at table, presented him to the committee of seven, called him Gideon by mistake, and at the right moment made him an instrument, not to say tool, by diverting his idle course through the crowd into a highly successful soliciting of signatures to the committee's, or let us say his own, the senator's, petition.

Unlucky task! An exceptional feature of the *Votaress* was that her passenger guards ran aft in full width all round her under the stern windows of the ladies' cabin. Beneath, the lower deck ended in a fantail of unusual overhang, around whose edge curved the stout bars of the " bull-ring," to fence it off from the billowing white surge that writhed after the rudder blade and the trailing yawl, so close below. Among the petition'ssubscribers were several pretty girls of an age at which their only important business was beauty and levity and who gave small heed to the document's purport, readily assuming that nothing *they* were asked to sign needed to be taken seriously. There was much laughter over the performance. They turned it into a "Signing of the Declaration," patterned after the old steel engraving. One of them, as the scroll lay open on the rail under her pen hand, unwittingly set foot in a scrubbing bucket kept there with a line attached for bailing water from the river, and was so unnerved by the fun of it that all at once the scroll flirted back into scroll form and fell through the whirling air that eddied behind the boat. Yet it had the luck to drop upon the deck below, and there presently an immigrant stood mutely gazing up with it in his lifted hand. Otto Marburg came and stood looking up beside him.

Dropping the bucket's line through the balusters under the rail, Basile stepped over the guards and proceeded, while the girls acted out their girlish distresses, to let himself down. The foolish exploit was sufficiently unsafe and painful to be its own reward, the rough line cutting his hands and forcing him, as soon as he dared, to drop into the arms of the two men. With them and others he passed from sight between the great wheels but soon was with the pretty signers again, coming up alone by way of the cook-house and pantry. His hands showed ugly red scars as he brushed away a few flies that liked his perfumery and had stubbornly followed him from below.

But the fun was over. It was not his galled palms but his pallid face that struck the young company with a frank dismay. His whole bearing was transformed and betrayed him smitten with emotions for which he found no speech. Had it made him ill, they asked, going down by that dreadful rope? No, he was not ill at all. But when they vacantly proposed to resume the signing he exclaimed almost with vehemence that he had names enough, and left them, to return the petition to the senator.

This was an incident of the forenoon. As he delivered the paper the senator spoke a pleased word and then gazed on him in surprise. " Why, what's the matter? Sick?"

"No, I'm not sick."

"But, look here, where – where's your own signature?"

"You can't have it."

"Oh, you want to sign, don't you?"

"No." A sudden anguish filled the boy's face. "Not for all the gold in California. God A'mighty, sir, I've been down there and seen those people!"

"Oh! my! dear! fellow! If we let mere sights and sounds – of things that can't be helped – upset us – There's the dinner-bell – come, have a cocktail with me – a Rofignac! . . . Ah! general – judge – wet your whistle with us?"

The general and the judge, accepting, looked sharply at Basile. "Why – what's the matter? Sick?"

But he went with them to the bar and to the board.

13

SECTION 13

XXIII

A STATE OF AFFAIRS

Watson was in the pilot-house, though not at the wheel.

So early of a Sabbath afternoon, in the middle of his partner's watch, he might well have been in his texas stateroom asleep, but to a Mississippi River pilot Sunday afternoon, or any afternoon, or forenoon, or midnight, or dusk or dawn, on . watch or off, the one thing in this world was the river. Else what sort of a pilot would he be, when the whole lore of its thousands of miles of navigation was without chart, light, or beacon, a thing kept only in pilots' memories, a lamp in a temple?

Glancing down forward of the bell, he was reminded of a certain young lady the sight of whom on the previous evening just after his brush with Hayle's twins, standing there before Hugh Courteney with her arms akimbo, had led him to say: "If that's to be the game I'm in it." He wished she were there now, or up here again in the pilot-house asking her countless questions about this endlessly interesting world's highway. He would be answering that the mouth of Red River was now twenty miles behind, the mouth of Buffalo Bayouten and of Homochitto River four; that right here they were in the great cut-off of a hundred and fifty-odd years before. He would say they were passing up the west shore because the current was over yonder on the

east side, Palmetto Point, and that behind there, inland, lay the great loop of still
water which had once been part of the river. He would explain that now the slender
Homochitto ran through that still water lengthwise, for miles, until, within forty rods
of the Mississippi, it recoiled again to launch in at last farther down, opposite Black
Hawk Point, still in sight astern. And he would tell how, over here on this west side,
Red River was yet only four miles away and actually sent Grand Cut-off Bayou across
into the Mississippi, but likewise swerved away southward through seven leagues
more of wet forest before it finally surrendered to the mightier stream. All this would
he tell, without weariness, to one who loved his great river.

Yet really he was in the pilot-house at this time not chiefly for the river, nor the girl,
nor the *Votaress,* though the *Votaress* was new, with kinks of character quite her own
and important to be learned. He was there because the stateroom given Hayle's twins
in the texas was next to his, and they, rarely in their life having restricted themselves
to tones of privacy and being now especially in a state of storm and stress, had made
sleep impossible even to a pilot off watch after a midday Sunday dinner. Lounging in
his berth, he had overheard things which ought to be told to one Courteney or another
early, though, of course, casually. Meantime he enjoyed not telling his partner, at
whose back he quietly chatted while the partner stood with hands and foot on the
wheel and with eyes well up the river, holding the jack-staff close to his "mark" far
ahead in the next bend.

" I couldn't stay," drawled Watson. " Noth'n' 'twixt the sick one an' me but a
half-inch bulkhead."

"Cholery can't scratch through a half-inch bulkhead," said the partner.

"Sounds kin. Funny what little bits o' ones kin. An' the sawt o' keen, soft way he
hollas an' cusses through his sot teeth an' whines an' yaps into his piller – why, he's
suffered enough by now to be dead five times over."

"That sufferin', that ain't the peggin'-out stage."

"No, I know that, an' I don't misdoubt but what he's a-goin' to git well."

"Hmm! – sorry fo' that. What's goin' to kyore him?"

"His simon-pyo' cussedness! He's so chuck full of it – looks like it's a-p'isonin'
the p'ison o' the cholery."

"Pity!" said the partner. . . . "Humph! *Now* what's up?"

To see what was up, Watson rose and looked down. On the roof below, evidently
having come there for privacy, were the commodore, the senator, and Hugh. Watson
loitered from the pilot-house and disappeared.

Down on the roof the commodore and the senator conversed across Hugh's front.
The statesman, with heavy "dear sirs" and heavier smiles, was buttonholing the elder
Courteney, who at every least pause affably endeavored to refer him to Hugh. The
grandson's turn to speak seemed not to have arrived. The senator was trying to keep it
from arriving and Hugh was glum. Hence it may be doubted if the senator's cigar was
really cocked as high, or that his silk hat was as dingy, his very good teeth as yellow,
his cheeks as hard, or his forehead as knotty as they appeared to Hugh, or that his
tone of superiority, so overbearing last night, so ingratiating to-day, was any worse for
the change. Hugh was biassed – felt bias and anger as an encumbering and untimely
weight. In self-depreciating contrast he recalled a certain young lady's airy, winning

way – airy way of winning – and coveted it for himself here and now: a wrestler's nimble art of overcoming weight by lightness; of lifting a heavy antagonist off his feet into thin air where his heaviness would be against him. His small, trim grandfather had it, in good degree; was using it now. Would it were his own in this issue, where the senator held in his hand the folded petition, having already vainly proffered it to the commodore, who had as vainly motioned him to hand it to Hugh. Would the art were his! But he felt quite helpless to command it, lacking the joyous goodness of heart which in the young lady so irresistibly redeemed what the senator, the bishop, and the judge's sister, to themselves, called her amazing – and the Gilmores to each other called her American – bad manners. It made Hugh inwardly bad-mannered just to feel in himself this lack, and tempted him to thinkwhat a comfort it would be to apply the wrestler's art physically and heave the senator overboard.

Said that gentleman – "For you saw I wouldn't let the matter come up at the table. A lot of those men who signed this paper – which your grandson suggested last night, you know – " He smiled at Hugh. "Now, I am never touchy, and I know, commodore, that you're not. But, Lord, so many of us – maybe Democrats a little more than Whigs – are! We take our politics, like our bread, smokin' hot." He put away his smile. " My dear sir, to us the foreigner – as you saw last night at supper – has become a political problem, a burning question. Yet I propose to keep this whole subject so unmenacing to you personally, you owners of this boat, that I won't let a word be risked where any one might take even a tone of voice unkindly."

"So, then, Hugh can take care of it."

The senator tossed a hand in amiable protest: "Oh, sir, you see it much too small! My half of it is large enough for me, with forty times this young gentleman's experience. I don't see just this one boat and trip and these few hundred native-American citizens in deadly contact with a few hundred of Europe's refuse. I see – your passengers see – we view with alarm – a state of affairs – and a test case!"

The old commodore's eyes flashed to retort, but the senator forced a propitiative smile, adding: "However, let that pass just now, here's something else."

"Is it also in that paper?"

"It is."

"Tell it to Hugh – or let him read it."

But as the old gentleman would have moved away, the senator, ignoring the suggestion, stepped across his path: –

"Last night, commodore, this matchless new boat" – he paused to let the compliment sink in, his eye wandering to Watson, who had sauntered down from the texas roof – "this *Votaress,* swept past everything that had backed out at New Orleans ahead of her."

"Built to do it," put in Hugh while the commodore, by a look, drew Watson to them and the senator flowed on.

14

SECTION 14

XXIV

A SENATOR ENLIGHTENED

"Bur, lying at Bayou Sara this morning," said the senator, "everything worth count-ing left us behind again."

"For the time being," said Hugh.

" Good for you," said the senator. " Mr. pilot, this paper, of a hundred signatures, petitions this boat to put off her foreigners at Natchez Island. If that is refused, when and where are we likely to overhaul the *Antelope* ?"

"*Antelope?* Let's see. We'd still be a-many a bend behind the *Antelope* at sundown but fo' one thing. At Natchez she's got to discharge an all-fired lot o' casting an' boilers, things she can't put ashore 'ithout han'- spikes, block-an'-taickle an' all han's a-cuss'n' to oncet. Like as not we'll catch her right there."

"Good again; sundown!" said the senator. "Now, commodore, this petition begs "

The commodore tried to wave him to Hugh but the senator's big hand gently prevented. "It begs," he went on, "and every friend of Gideon Hayle and John Courteney on this boat insists, that Madame Hayle be required to leave this suicidal work she's doing and with her daughter and youngest son be put aboard the*Antelope* to join her husband ahead of all bad news." With his under lip pushed out he smiled into the commodore's serene face.

Hugh spoke. "The *Votaress* being slow?" he inquired.

"Not at all! But, my young friend, the *Votaress* can't hold funerals and outrun the *Antelope* at the same time."

The commodore had turned to Watson: "Want to see me?" The two moved a few paces aft.

"Then it isn't," Hugh asked the senator,"that your hundred signers of this thing are afraid madame will get the cholera?" He took the petition's free end between thumb and finger and softly pulled. But its holder held on.

"Why, yes," said the holder-on, "we fear that, too. Good Lord, she may have the contagion now!" It gave him grim amusement to note that the grandson's face was as quiet as the old man's, yet as hard and heavy as any of the *Antelope's* big castings. He thought how much better it were to have this chap for an adherent than opponent.

" Yet you're all willing," slowly pressed Hugh, while – with their pull on the paper increasing – they here the commodore and Watson yonder returned the bow of the bishop as he came from below and passed on up to the sick-room – "you're willing to send the cholera aboard the *Antelope?"*

"Willing, my God, no, sir! compelled! – to risk it – for the sake of Gideon Hayle and his people and of youand yours, in a great public interest centring in you and them." The speaker smilingly tapped the hard- pulled document so lately urged upon the grandfather. "We couldn't *write* that – in this paper. When I've explained *that* I'll hand you *this* – don't pull it."

"Well, then, let go of it," said Hugh, with a light jerk which put it wholly into his possession.

The senator's eyes blazed, but when he saw that Hugh's, though as much too wide as his own, looked out of a face as set and hard as ever, he recovered his suavity, puffed his cigar, waved it abroad, and said: "That's all right. Take that to the captain at once, will you?"

"No," replied Hugh, the wrestler's nimble art being as far, far away from him as the "happy land" of the children's hymn, which the cornet was essaying below.

"No?" questioned the tolerant senator.

" No." Small knots of passengers, the squire in one, the general in another, had drawn within eavesdropping range and Hugh lowered his voice. "Not till I hear what you couldn't write," he said. "When you've explained *that* I'll hand him *this*. No one's in his room, come there."

As they reached its door and the senator passed in, Hugh was joined by the grandfather and Watson and detained some moments in private council, with Watson as chief speaker. Then the commodore returned leisurely forward toward the captain's chair while Watson sought the texas roof and pilot-house, and Hugh shut himself in with the senator.

They sat with the writing-table between them. "I wish," said the senator, "I had a son like you. I'd say: 'My son, the worst notion in this land to-day is that always the first thing to do is fight, and that the only thing to fight with is hot shot. Don't you believe it! Don't think every man's your enemy the moment he differs with you.

He may be your best friend. And don't think every enemy wants to stab you in the back.' But, Lord! I needn't offer a father's advice to you, with such a father – and grandfather – as you've got.

"Now, here we are. It's idle for me to tell you what we wanted to put in that paper and couldn't, if you can't believe that maybe, after all, I'm a peacemaker and your friend, hunh? I don't set up to be your only friend or only your friend or your friend only for your sake. Frankly, my ruling passion is for the community as a whole; the old Jacksonian passion for the people, sir. If I'm meddling it's because I see a situation that right on its surface threatens one misfortune, and at bottom another and bigger one, to them, the people – a public misfortune. I don't want to avert just the cholera, here to-day, gone to-morrow; I want to avert the lasting public misfortune of a Courteney-Hayle feud. There, sir! That's my hand! Cards right down on the table! Oh, I'm nothing if not outspoken, flat-footed! A lot of those signers don't see that bottom meaning. They don't need to. But, sir, *you* know – your grandfather's always known – that by every instinct the Hayles, even to the sons-in-law, are fighters. They don't know any way to succeed, in anything, but to fight. It's the Old Hickory in them. Old Hickory always fought, your Harry of the West has always compromised. The Hayles loathe tact. They don't know the power of concession as you Courteneys do. And that's why your only way to succeed with them is to concede something. Not everything, not principle – good Lord, not principle! yet something definite, visible, conciliatory, hunh?

" Mind you, I hold no brief for them. I know those twins haven't behaved right a minute. But no Hayle's been let into this affair, from first to last."

The falsehood was so rash a slip that its author paused, but when Hugh's face showed no change he resumed: " Sir, it is in your interest we ask you to put those foreigners off. If you don't you'll rouse public resentment up and down this river a hundred miles wide for a thousand miles. And if, keeping them aboard, you don't put Madam Hayle and her daughter on some other boat, and anything happens to them on this one, you'll have Gideon Hayle and his sons – and his sons-in-law – for your mortal enemies the rest of your lives, long or short – and with public sympathy all on their side. Oh, I'm nothing if not outspoken! Why, my dear boy, if you don't think I'm telling you

this in friendship "

"Call it so. But stop it, at once." " Why – you say that – to me? "

"I do. Stop it, at once, or we'll call it "

"Ridiculous! What will you call it, sir?"

"Mutiny. The captain has so ordered – and arranged."

The inquirer drew breath, leaned forward on an elbow, and stared. The stare was returned. The senator began to smile. Hugh did not. The smile grew. Hugh's gaze was fixed. The smiler smiled yet more, but in vain. Abruptly he ha-haed.

" We'll call it that till you prove it's not," said Hugh.

"Did you ever hear of a poker face?" asked the senator.

"No, sir."

"You've got one, now; youngest I ever saw. I wish I had it – haw, haw! Where'd you find it? I doubt if ever in your life you've had any real contact with any real guile."

"I have," said Hugh, very quiet, very angry, yet with a joy of disclosure, communicative at last by sheer stress of so much kept unsaid. " And I've never got over it."

" Well, well! When was that?"

"All through the most important ten years of my life."

"Of your life ! Good gracious! Which were they?"

"The first ten. A guile seemingly so guileless that yours, compared with it, is botch work."

The two were still looking into each other's eyes when the latch clicked and John Courteney stepped in.

15

SECTION 15

XXV
"PLEASE ASSEMBLE"

Out from behind Fritz Island the *Votaress* swept northward into a deluge of light from a sun just finishing the first half of his afternoon decline.

Before her lay, far and wide, an expanse of river and shore so fair, without a noticeable sign of man's touch, that one traveller of exceptional moral daring – conversing with the Gilmores and Ramsey – personified the scene as "Nature in siesta." At the steamer's approach the picture – or, as the daring traveller might have insisted, the basking sleeper – seemed to awaken and in a repletion of smiling content to stir and stretch and every here and there to darken and lighten by turns as though closing and opening upon the intruder a multitude of eyes as unnumbered as those of a human sort that looked on the scene,- the sleeper, from the beautiful boat.

So for several minutes. Then the *Votaress* curved into the west till the great twin shadows of her chimneys crept athwart the pilot-house and texas, while more than one passenger of the kind who tell all they know to whoever will hear said that yonder bright mass of cottonwoods and willows, bathing in sunlight directly up the stream, with open water shimmering allround it, was Glasscock Island; that Glasscock Tow-head lay hidden behind it just above, and that a tow- head was an island in the making.

The whole view was such a stimulus to the outpouring of sentiment as well as of information, that one young pair, each succeeding flutter of whose heart-strings was more tenderly entangling them, agreed in undertone that the river's incessant bendings were steps of a Jacob's ladder with these resplendent white steamers for ascending and descending angels.

"Yonder comes another now," said both at once. They pressed forward to the foremost boiler-deck guards, among the many sitters and standers who were trying to determine, by the ornamental form of the stranger's chimney-tops or the peculiar note of her scape-pipes, before her name might show out on paddle-box or pilot-house, whether she was the *Chancellor,* the *Aleck Scott,* the *Belle Key,* or the *Magnolia.* To be either was to be famous. The next moment she swept into view on the island's sunward side, as pre-eminent in all the scene as though the sun were gone and she were the rising moon. The moon was not her equal in the eyes of those beholders. On every deck, from forecastle to after hurricane roof, there were big spots of vivid color, red, green, blue, never seen in the moon and which were quickly made out to be a high-piled freight of ploughs, harrows, horse-mills, carts, and wagons, destined for the ever-widening Southern fields of corn and cotton, sugar and rice. The passenger with the pocket spy-glass – there is always one – proclaimedthat her boiler deck was hung full – as no deck of the moon ever is – of the finest spoils of the hunt: geese, swan, venison, and bear; while the nakedest eye could see at a glance that from forward gangway to stern- most guard her bull railings were up, and a closer scrutiny revealed that the main load of her freight deck was every farm-bred sort of living four-footed beast: horses, mules, beeves, cows, swine, and sheep. She did not pass near though unaware of the distress she avoided; but in courtly exaggeration she sent across the intervening mile a double salute, white plumes of sunlit steam from her whistle – the new mode – and the gentler voice of her bell, the older form. The course of the *Votaress* lay on the island's eastern side, and the hail and response of the two crafts had hardly ceased to echo from the various shores, or hats to wave and handkerchiefs to flutter, when the flood between them began to widen, a thousand feet to the half minute, and they parted.

At the same time, from the middle of the boiler deck floated a sound ordinarily most welcome but at this time a distasteful surprise: the dinner-bell again. Not with festal din, however, it called, but with each solitary note drawn out through a full second or more, church-steeple fashion, and with a silken veil tied on its tongue to give each stroke a solemn softness and illusion of distance. Small wonder that the most of the company, just risen from "a plumb bait," turned that way and stared, seeing old Joy, with joyless face, tolling out the notes in persistent monotone while infront of her stood the Gilmores at either side of a chair, and on the chair, also standing, the daughter of Gideon Hayle. With her hands and eyes fastened upon a written notice and with the bell tolling steadily at her back she tremblingly read aloud:

"Fellow travellers: Please assemble at once in the ladies' cabin to supplicate the divine mercy for a stay of the scourge on this boat, and in concerted worship to seek spiritual preparation for whatever awaits us in the further hours of our voyage. In the absence of Bishop So-and-So, who is ministering to the sick, and at his request, the meeting will be conducted by the celebrated comedians Mr. and Mrs. Gilmore, late of Placide's Varieties, New Orleans."

The art of advertising being then in its swaddling- bands, this specimen of it struck its hearers as really creditable. While it was being read two or three men rose, and one, uncommonly shaggy and of towering height, could hardly wait for the last word before he was responding with the voice of a hound on the trail: " By the Lord Harry, sis', amen! says I, that's jest my size! I'm a Babtis' exhorteh an' I know the theatre air the mouth o' hell, but ef you play-acto's good enough to run a prah-meet'n' I'm bad enough to go to it. Come on, gentleman, the whole k'boodle of us, come on."

Some brightly, some darkly, a good halfdozen followed him into the cabin; but the most remained seated, staring at Ramsey from head to foot and back again, some brightly, some darkly, while the bell perseveredbehind her. She sunk to her knees in the chair. Gil- more addressed that half of the company on his side of her: "Please assemble at once, will you, all, in the ladies' cabin."

And his wife, on her side, repeated: "Will you all please assemble at once in the ladies' cabin."

A few more rose, but still the many, brightly or darkly, only stared on, the bell persisting. The kneeling Ramsey again began to read:

"Fellow travellers: Please assemble at once in the ladies' cabin to supplicate the divine mercy for a stay of the scourge on this boat, and in concerted worship "

"Oh, well!" some one laughingly broke in, "if that's your game – " and the whole company, in good-natured surrender, arose and went in. But the "ball- ringers," as they were promptly nicknamed, passed on to further conquests.

When at length they turned to join the assemblage the four had doubled their number. With Ramsey was the commodore. With the actor was Watson. With Mrs. Gilmore came old Joy, and, strange to tell, due to some magic in the tact of the senior Courteneys, the senator, no longer making botch work of his guile, walked with Hugh, displaying a good-natured loquacity which he was glad to have every one notice and from which he ceased reluctantly as they parted, finding no place to sit together. The player and his wife, overlooking the throng, complacently discovered standing- room only, and the meeting which Hayle's daughterhad pledged herself and them to "run" was running itself. For hardly had they entered the saloon when, from a front seat and without warning, the exhorter exploded the stalwart old hymn-tune of "Kentucky," and soon all but a scant dozen of the company followed in full cry, though hardly with the fulness of the leader's voice, that rolled through the cabin like tropical thunder:

"'Whedn I cadn read my ti-tle cle-ah
Toe madn-shudns idn the-e ske-ies
I'll bid fah-wedl toe ev'-rye fe-ah
Adn wipe my weep-ign eyes.'"

From the chairman's seat the actor kept a corner of one eye on Ramsey and as the hymn's last line rolled away he stood up. She had not sung, but neither had she laughed. No one could have seen the moment's huge grotesqueness larger, yet to the relief of many she had kept her poise. In her mind was the bishop, overhead in the texas, consciously imperilling his life to save her brother's soul, and in the face of all drolleries she strenuously kept her ardor centred on the gravest significancies of the hour, as if the bishop's success up there hung on the efficiency with which this work of his earlier appointment should be done, down here, in his absence. She saw in the exhorter a tragic as well as comic problem. Nor was he her only perplexity. Another, she feared, might easily arise through some clash of any two kinds of worshippers each devoted to its own set forms. Certain main features, she knew, had been carefully prearranged, yet as the actor stood silent about to ask the Vicksburger to lead in prayer she tingled with all the exhilaration a ruder soul might have felt in hunting ferocious game or in fighting fire. Her soul rose a-tiptoe for the moment when the Presbyterians, who also had not sung, should stand up to pray, while the few Episcopalians, kneeling forward, and the many Baptists and Methodists, kneeling to the rear, should find themselves face to face – nose to nose, anxiously thought Ramsey – with only the open backs of the chairs between. She was herself the last to kneel, kneeling forward but doubting if she ought not to face the other way, hardly knowing whether she was a Catholic or a Methodist; and she was much the last to close her eyes. But the various postures were taken without a jar and the modest Vicksburger prayed. His words were neither impromptu nor printed, but, as every one quickly perceived and Ramsey had known beforehand, were memorized and were fresh from the pen of the actor. Diffidence warped the first phrase or two, but soon each word came clear, warm from the heart, and reaching all hearts, however borne back by the rapturous yells with which the exhorter broke in at every pause.

"And though to our own sight," pleaded the supplicant, " we are but atoms in thy boundless creation, we yet believe that prayer offered thee in love, humility, and trust cannot offend. Wherefore in this extremity of grief and disaster we implore thee for deliverance."

Close at Ramsey's back, in the only seat whose occupant her diligent eye had failed to light on, a kneeler heaved a sigh so piteous that it startled her like an alarum.

But the prayer went on: "Drive from us, O Lord, this pestilence. Allow it no more toll of life or agony. Have mercy on us all, both the sick and the sound."

"Have mercy," moaned the suffering voice behind, and Ramsey, suffering with it, wished she had been Methodist enough to kneel with her face that way.

"Spare not our earthly lives alone," continued the supplicant, "but save our immortal souls. Pardon in us every error of the present moment and of all our past. Forgive us every fault of character inherited or acquired."

"God, forgive!" sighed the voice behind, in so keen a contrition that Ramsey, while the supplication in front pressed on, found herself in tears of her own penitence. The mourner at her back began responsively to repeat each word of the prayer as it came and presently Ramsey was doing likewise, striving the while, with all her powers, to determine whose might be the voice which distress so evidently disguised even from its owner.

"Enable us, our Maker," she pleaded in time with the voice behind, that followed the voice in front, " henceforth to grow in thy likeness, and in thy strength to devote ourselves joyfully to the true and diligent service of the world wherein thou hast set us. Grant us, moreover, we pray, such faith in thee and to thee that in every peril or woe, to-day, to-morrow, or inyears to come, we may without doubt or fear commit all we have, are, and hope for, temporal or immortal, alike unto thee. And, finally, we beg thee to grant us in this immediate issue a courage for ourselves and compassion for all others which, come what may, living or dying, will gird us so to acquit ourselves that in the end we may stand before thee unashamed and by thy mercy and thy love be welcomed into thine own eternal joy."

"Amen!" cried the exhorter and burst anew into song:

" 'Chidl-dredn of the-e heabm-lye kiggn,

As we jour-nye sweet-lye siggn.

Siggn '"

He ceased and flashed a glance, first up to Hugh, whose hand lay on his shoulder, and then over to the standing player. A hush was on the reseated company, and its united gaze on Ramsey and the mourner who with her had been audibly following the prayer. Two seats from her Mrs. Gilmore vainly tried to catch her eye. The penitent was in his seat again. He bent low forward, his face in his hands, and face and hands hid in his thick fair locks. Ramsey had turned toward him with a knee in her chair, a handkerchief pressed fiercely against her lips, and her drowned eyes gazing down on him. But as the actor was about to speak she wheeled toward him and stood with an arm beseechingly thrown out, her voice breaking in her throat.

16

SECTION 16

XXVI
ALARM AND DISTRESS

"it's Basilel" she cried. Then, one after another, to the exhorter, to Hugh, to each of the two Gilmores separately: "This is wrong, all wrong ! You said we mustn't alarm or distress any one – and we mustn't!" She tried to face her chair round to the bowed head, and Hugh, at a touch from his grandfather, moved to her aid. Mrs. Gilmore too had started but was kept back by others, whispering with her on the edges of their seats.

"It's all wrong," insisted Ramsey to Hugh close at hand, "and we mustn't do it! You said we mustn't!"

The exhorter was gratified, not to say flattered. "H-it ain't none of it wrong, my young sisteh," he called across. " Ef yo' bretheh's distress ah the fear o' damnation it's all right and Gawd's name be pra-ised!"

"Amen!" groaned one or two of the undistressed majority, while old Joy modestly pressed up from the rear.

"Rease, good ladies an' gen'lemens," she said as she came, "will you please fo' to lem-me thoo, ef you please? Dat's my young mahsteh, what I done nu's' f'om a baby. Ef you please'm, will you please suh, fo' to lem-me pass, ef you please?" In gentle hasteshe made her way, many eyes following, and heads swinging right and left to see around the heads that came between. The goal was reached just as Ramsey, in her turned seat, leaned to lay fond hands on her brother's locks. But Hugh interposed an arm.

"No," he said, "we mustn't do that either."

"No!" said Joy, "dat's right! Fo' de Lawd's sake tek heh clean away – ef you kin. An' ef you please, good ladies an' gen'lemens, fo' to squeeze back a leetle mite ?"

They squeezed the mite and she knelt by the boy. The sister knelt too, but as she left her chair Hugh, taking it, put himself between her and her brother. The actor was the only one left standing.

"Sing, will you, please," he said – "and will you all sing

" 'There is a land of pure delight – '

Mrs. Gilmore, will you raise the tune?"

But the exhorter was too quick for them and "riz" it before the request was fairly uttered. All sang, and over all easily soared the voice of the zealot:

"Thah is a ladnd o' pyo' de-light
Whah saidnts ib-maw-tudl reigdn.
Idn-fidn-ite day dis-pedls the-e night
Adn pleas-u'es badn-ish paidn.'"

Now he rolled his enraptured eyes and now his quid, spat freely on the rich carpet, beat time on one big palm with the other and on the floor with one vastfoot, while through the song like a lifeboat through waves, undisturbed and undisturbing, cleft the steady speech of the nurse to the boy. Regardless of the precaution just urged for Ramsey, her arm fell over his bowed form.

Thah eveh-last-ign sprign a-bi-dns
Adn nev-eh with-'rign flow-ehs – ' "

– ran the hymn, and straight through it, heard everywhere, pressed mammy Joy's tearful inquiry:

" Is you got religion, honey boy, aw is you on'y got de sickness? Tell me, honey, which you got? Is you gotbofe?"

The lad moaned, shook his head, and suddenly sat up, and cried to his kneeling and gazing sister: "Neither! Great God, I'm not ready for either!" – his words, like old Joy's, cutting squarely across the hymn as it continued:

" 'Death like a nor-rah streabm di-vi-dns
This heab'-mly ladnd frobm ow-ehs.'"

Ramsey stood. "Well, don't be alarmed or distressed !" she half laughed, half wept, while the nurse crooned:

"Honey boy, ef you ain't yit got de sickness "

"I don't know!" he cried, so loudly that only the Methodists and Baptists sang on. He sprang up and glanced round to the judge, the general, the squire, the senator, exclaiming: "I've been right in it! – to getback that infernal petition of yours when I dropped it! I've all but touched the dying and the dead! I've been handled all over by men who'd been handling them! Whatever I've caught from them I'll know is a judgment! For at last I've got a sense of sin! Right down under here behind this boat's engines I got it! I want you-all people to pray for me ! I've been an awful sinner for years!"

"So have I!" wept Ramsey aloud.

"Praise de Lawd!" said Joy, from her knees.

Mrs. Gilmore drew Ramsey backward and shared a chair with her. The exhorter and a stout few hung to the hymn –

'"Whi-dle Jur-dan rolled be-tweedn,'"

– and the terrified boy talked on through everything, no one edging away from him as the wise might in these days.

" I'm not fitt'n' to die, Mr. Gilmore," he said. "That petition's not my worst sin – by half – by quarter. But it's opened my eyes. You-all that got it up, and you-all that signed it, it would open yours, one look below; and I want you-all, right here, now, to tell God you take it back, before he lays his curse on me! You can manage that somehow, Mr. manager, can't you? Can't somebody pray it? Or – or can't – can't you vote on it?"

"Yes," broke in Ramsey, clung to by the player's wife but standing and glancing from the player sodirectly to the senator that all looked at him, "vote! vote!"

He gave the player the sort of nod one gives an auctioneer, and the singers stopped. "I think we can," said the actor, "and that if the senator votes yea so will every one. All in favor of withdrawing the petition raise the right hand. It is unanimous."

The exhorter was up. " Mr. play-actoh, 'that's all right. I neveh signed that trick, nohow. So fah so good, fo' a play-acto's church – ef you kin git sich a church into the imagination o' yo' mind! But vot'n' ain't enough!" He pointed to Ramsey, fast in Mrs. Gilmore's arms, and to her brother, in old Joy's. "Vot'n' don't take heh – naw him – out'n the gall o' bittehness naw the bounds o' iniquity. Oh, my young silk-an'-satin sisteh, don't you want us to pray fo' you?"

Ramsey's courage was tried. Many gazers, but particularly the judge's sister, seemed, by their eyes, crouching to pounce on her whether she answered yea or nay. "I know," she said, in tears again, and unconsciously wringing her hands, "I know I ought to, but – but I – I'm afraid there isn't time. For I want – oh, I – I want to vote again! I want to vote to take up a collection, and a big one, for those people down-stairs that mom-a's with. And then we can pray for her – and for Captain Courteney. Mom-a's a Catholic but it's in her Bible the same as in any: 'Blessed are the merciful, for they shall obtain mercy.'" The last word was but a breath on her quivering lip. Facing theactor she stood and waited. Joy was getting Basile away.

" It is moved by the last speaker," said the player, "and seconded by" – he glanced inquiringly about – "by several – that we make an immediate contribution for the benefit of our deck passengers, who are in dire need, and that "

"That we make it a big one!" repeated Ramsey.

"All in favor – " he said. "Unanimous. I will ask Mr. Courteney and Miss Hayle to take up the collection."

The dispersal of the meeting found the lady of Mil- liken's Bend with the judge's sister. The judge, joining them, reported that the laughing Ramsey's collection was double that of the solemn Hugh. The sister's eyes snapped as she put in: "She made me double my contribution." Ramsey passed at a distance. " It's a shame to keep short dresses on a girl of that age and of her – her "

"Spontaneity?" asked the judge. "I like spontaneity, even exuberance, at times."

"Well, I don't," said the sister.

"No," murmured the judge. These two, who were to get off at Natchez, were just beginning to be enjoyed – as types. The sister was one who had all her life complained of "enlargement of the spleen" and even oftener of a "bitter mouth." On which the judge's only comment was: "Hmm!" Just now, as to Ramsey, he grew daring.

"Her dress," he said, "is longer than it was yesterday."

"It's a mile too short."

"As much as that?"

"I wish you were not going to leave us so soon," said the lady of the Bends, and then bravely added, of Ramsey: "Her dresses are short by her own choice, old Joy says."

"Shouldn't doubt it a moment."

"Yes, she keeps them short to keep her mother young. I think that's right sweet of her, don't you?"

"No," replied the sister, and went to lock her trunks.

17

SECTION 17

XXVII

PILOTS' EYES

Once more the hurricane deck. What space! What freedom! Again from the airy, sun-beaten roof, that felt as thin underfoot as the levelled wing of an eagle, the eye dropped far below to where the tawny waters glided to meet the cleaving prow or foamed away from the smiting wheels. Again the dazzled vision rose into the infinite blue beyond clouds and sun, or rested on the green fringes of half-drowned shores forever passing in slow recessional.

Four in the afternoon. Esperance Point rounded and left astern in the east. Ellis Cliffs there too, whitening back to the western sun. Saint Catherine's Bend next ahead, gleaming a mile and a quarter wide where it swung down from the north. And the *Votaress* herself ! Once again that perfect grace in the faint up- curve, at stem and stern, of the low white rail that rimmed the deck. Again, above the stained-glass skylights of the cabin, the long white texas, repeating the deck's and cabin's lines in what Ramsey called a "higher octave," its narrow doors overhung with gay scrollwork, and above its own roof, like a coronet, the pilot house, with Watson just returned to the wheel. Once more the colossal, hot-breathing twin chimneys, their slender iron braces holding them so uprightly together and apart, the golden globe – emblem of the Courteney fleet – hanging between them, and their far- stretched iron guys softly harping to one another in the breeze. All these again, and away out beyond the front rail, with a hundred feet depth of empty air between, the jack-staff, high as a pine and as slim for its height as a cane from the brake, its halyards whipping cheerily, the black night-hawk at its middle, a golden arrow at its peak.

John Courteney, coming up into this scene, laid a hand on his solitary chair at the forward rail but then paused. Between the chair and the skylights behind it stood the squire's sister and brother-in-law and Ramsey. Yes, they eagerly agreed with him, the view ahead was certainly dazzling. Ramsey would have asked a question, but the husband remembered the contagion from whose field below the captain had just come, the wife noticed that the presence of ladies would keep the captain standing, and the three, remarking that such a scene was too brilliant to confront, moved aft. As they went, Watson, up at the wheel, and Ned, his partner, lingering by him, had a half-length view of them, their lower half being hid by the cabin roof, close under whose edge their feet passed, where its shadow kept the deck cool. The wife still had her embroidery, the husband his De Bow. By certain changes about Ramsey's throat and shoulders Ned noticed that she was in yet another dress, whose skirt – such part as showed above the cabin roof – was inflounces almost to the waist. He would tell that at home to his wife and daughter, who now and then depended on him for fashions, with striking results. Watson, too, noticed Ramsey, yet his chief attention remained, as steadily as his gaze, on his steering-mark far up in the bight of the sunlit bend, at the same time including, here below, his seated commander.

"Cap' ought to be pootty tol'able tired, Ned."

"Well, now, he jest ought!" The partner dropped back and perched on the visitor's bench, whence he could still see the river though not the closely intervening cabin – and texas roofs; and all the two said later was without an exchange of glances. Watson thought the captain would " rest more now, on watch, than what he did before, off," having got matters running so much smoother down below; though the cholera was "a-growin", straight along."

Ned told of his pleasure in seeing Hugh conduct the senator down to the devotional services: "Lard, they hev done him brown, ain't they? – atween 'em, Hugh and Hayle's girl?"

"With some help," said Watson, modestly. "That petition – ef th's anything else aboard this boat as dead as what it is" – he ran into inelegancies.

Ned offered to bet it was not dead inside the senator, and Watson admitted that the statesman would probably never forgive the "genteel" way he had been euchred; though like euchre, he said, a lot of it was luck.

"But, man! the bluff he *kin* put up! Couldn't believe my eyes when we'd passed the hat an' adjourned an' I see him a-standin' at the fork o' the for'a'd stairs, ag'in the trunk room, same ole bell-wether as ever, a-makin' a *bully* speech to Madame Hayle an' that Marburg chap down in the gangway, foot o' the steps, an' a-present'n' him our 'oblations' – says he – meanin' the swag!"

"An' her a-translat'n' for him!" said Ned, fancying the scene, with the senator, under his mask, " a-gritt'n' his tushes!" and Watson, to heighten it, told of Hugh and

the actor at one head of the double stair, and Mrs. Gilmore and Ramsey at the other – "a-chirpin' him on, an' the whole b'iler deck, ladies and gents, takin' it in, solid!"

The senator was long-headed. "Yes, an' yit Hugh's throwed him fair jest by main strength an' awk'ard- ness."

"I dunno!" said Ned. "It wuz long-headed, too, fo' Hugh an' the play-acto's to give him the job."

"It wuz long-headed in her who put 'em up to it."

"Oh, look here! *She* didn't do that, did she?"

"'Less'n I'm a liar," replied Watson, eyes front.

"Hunh! Wonder which! Say, Wats'; on the b'iler deck – did she have on this gownd she's a-wearin' now?" ,

" No," said Watson, tardily, with eyes still up-stream.

"Not wast'n' yo' words," said the inquirer.

"No."

"A short answer turneth away wrath, I s'pose."

"It turneth away discussion o' ladies' gownds."

"Lard! I don't discuss 'em to excess. Noticed hern – its upper works – an' a flounce or two – an' sort o' wondered as to the rest of it, how much water it's a-drawin'. Anything li-bell-ious about that?"

"No, considerin' the source."

Ned slipped from the bench to go, but Watson looked back with a light beckon of the head and he turned to the wheel. Thence he glanced down over the breast-board, over the forward eaves of the texas, down to the skylight roof and upon several persons. First, the boat's commander. He was leaving his seat at the approach, from the head of a boiler-deck stair, of Madame Hayle and the doctor. On the skylight roof, near the bell, were the two players, just greeting Hugh as from the other side he reached the deck and stepped up to their level. On the same roof, midway between these and the front of the texas, were the squire's sister and her husband returning from their search for shade. And lastly, close after them, came Ramsey, a source of general astonishment. For the gown she was in and whose lower possibilities had aroused Ned's avowed and Watson's concealed interest was her mother's and swept the deck.

Madame Hayle grew more beautiful as with a play of indignation which wholly failed to disguise her pleasure she cried: "By what per-mission? by what permission have you pud – my – clothes? "

The girl would have flown to her arms but the doctor forbade, and for second choice she set up a dainty tripping to and fro athwartships; dipping, rising, skipping, swaying, bridling, like a mocking-bird on a garden wall. It made Ned and Watson themselves worth seeing. Professional dignity set their faces like granite though every vein seethed with a riot of laughter. But the laughter's chief cause was not Ramsey.

" Look at Hugh," muttered Watson, gently drawing down the wheel for the *Votaress* to sweep round into a northward reach at whose head Natchez Island would presently show itself. To look at Hugh took nerve, but in a moment

"Look at her," said Ned. . . . "There! she tipped her nose at him!"

"She didn't!"

"She did. Wats', yo' game ain't never goin' to work."

"Ned, y'ain't got the sense of a loon."

"Well, I swear I've got more'n Hugh – or her." XXVIII

WORDS AND THE " WESTWOOD "

Down on the roof, while Ramsey's mother started with the physician around the skylights for the texas, and Hugh and Gilmore conversed with the captain, Mrs. Gilmore, her hands on Ramsey, said to madame:

"I want her now, to begin to make ready for tomorrow evening. My dear" – to the girl – "I've a dozen dresses that will become you better than this one."

"Long?" cried Ramsey. "I'll take the lot!" She felt Hugh distantly looking and listening.

"We won't trade on Sunday," laughed Mrs. Gilmore; "but you mustn't" – scanning her approvingly – "ever put on a short dress again."

"Ho-oh, I never will!" said Ramsey, with a toss meant for Hugh, who went by, hurrying aft to meet a newcomer. She started after him. Madame Hayle, in that direction, had gone into the sick-room, whence Ramsey's brother Julian, with barely a word to his mother, had come out. Stepping down into the narrow walk between the roofs of cabin and pantry and glancing over his shoulder upon the company about the bell, he winced at sight of his sister's attire. Yet he kept his course and was well started aft before he saw that hewas being met by some one in the narrow way, and by whom but Marburg. It was that alien whom Hugh was hastening to reach and on whom Ramsey was staring. He had come up'from the engine room through the steward's department, by the unguarded route which Basile's ascent had revealed, and now came face to face with a foe where there was room only for friends to meet and pass. So said the eyes of each to each, but just then a quick footfall on the cabin roof, behind and somewhat above him, caused Julian to face round and he confronted Hugh.

"Mr. Hayle," was Hugh's word, "what will you have, sir? "

"Nothing, sir, of you! What will *you* have of *me,* sir?"

Ramsey glided by both and halted before the exile, whose scowl vanished in a look so grateful and supplicating that her words, clearly meant to justify his presence, caught in her throat: "What will you – have, sir? My mother? – back again? – and the doctor?"

"Yes," he replied, and then added in German with an anguish of gesture which was ample interpretation, "yes, for *my* mother! for my little brother! Ah, God! he is not dead! He is yet alive! His arms are as supple as *these.* There is color still in his cheeks!"

She stood dumb with horror. Yet she woke to action as, close beside her, she heard her brother snarl at Hugh:

"I'll go where I please! Who stops me, God pity him!"

She dropped nimbly from the skylights' overhang to the alien's level and with looks as beseeching as his waved him back a step. Then with the same mute entreaty she faced Julian and Hugh. But there was a ludicrous contrast, visible to all, between Hugh's phlegm and her brother's pomp, and by a flash of feminine instinct she divined the best mood with which to match it. Grimly elated, Hugh saw what was coming. Julian saw, and groaned a wearied wrath. The captain, the commodore – for the

commodore had returned – the Gilmores, the Yazoo couple, the pilots overhead, all waited with lively and knowing gaze. She went limp, hid her face, swayed, sank to one knee, and filled the whole width of the narrow passage with arms and draperies, the meanwhile breaking into a laugh so wholly soliloqual that the two players became learners. But again she sprang erect and had hardly thrown her curls back from her blushing face when her mother, the bishop, and the doctor stepped from the sick-room, and madame addressed the immigrant:

"Ah, ritturn, if you ple-ease. Me, I am ritturning!"

"Yes," chimed the bishop and the doctor; "yes, at once!" and the exile, with pleading looks to Ramsey, to the others by turn and to her again, went below. Madame and the physician began to follow.

"How's Lucian?" called Ramsey after them.

"Getting well," replied both. They passed behind the wheel-house and only the pilots knew that at its corner Madame Hayle stopped where she could still see and hear. All others kept their eyes on Julian, who was in a redder heat than ever, and on Hugh, who was addressing him in a depth of tone that amused the Gilmores almost as keenly as it did Ramsey, who had rejoined them at his back. Suddenly he faced around.

"If Miss Hayle," he said, "would as soon go below "

Miss Hayle sang her reply, bugled it: "She would no-ot."

Hugh stepped down into her brother's path and faced him again: "You have written your father a letter "

Julian's head flew up but bent in slow avowal.

" To be put aboard the *Antelope,*" pursued Hugh

The head went higher: "Well, sir?"

"To outrun this boat."

"And – if – I – have, sir?"

"Why, yes," murmured the squire's brother-in-law and sister, to the Gilmores, "suppose he has?"

"So have I," said Hugh to Julian. He glanced up to the Yazoo couple and then to the bishop self-isolated near the sick-room door. Ramsey and the couple laughed. Hugh turned her way again: "If Miss Hayle "

"She wouldn't," said Ramsey, laughing more.

"Well, sir!" drawled the waiting Julian, to Hugh.

Hugh waved a hand toward the bishop: "That gentleman has risked his life for your sick brother."

"Yes," said Ramsey. The bishop scowled up the river. Julian scowled at Hugh.

"Well, sir?" he once more challenged.

"He was told he was wanted as a minister," said Hugh.

"Well, sir?"

"He was wanted merely to get your letter off secretly."

"You lie!"

"Oh!" sighed the Yazoo pair. Ramsey shrank upon Mrs. Gilmore.

"Not at all," said a quiet voice overhead and the eyes of Julian, blazing upward, met Watson's blazing down.

"Come," said the player's wife to Ramsey, "come away."

" I won't," tearfully laughed Ramsey, and Mrs. Gil- more and the squire's sister had to laugh with her.

"The lie," said Hugh, "will keep. Your letter is such that the bishop declines to touch it."

The bishop swelled. Julian recoiled and, glancing behind him, confronted his mother.

"My son," she began, but he whirled back to Hugh.

"You keyhole spy!" he wailed; "you eavesdropping viper!"

Ramsey came tiptoeing along the edge of the pantry roof to light down between them but he imperiously motioned her off, still glaring at Hugh and gnawing his lip with chagrin. " Oh, never mind!" was all he could choke out; "never you mind!" He ceased again, to catch what Hugh was replying to him. Said Hugh:

" I'll take your letter and send it with my own."

"No, sir! No, you grovelling sneak!"

"Mais, yass!" called Madame Hayle from her place, and Ramsey laughed from hers, but a new voice arrested every one's attention. The bishop wheeled round to it with an exclamation of dismay that was echoed even by Julian. In the sick-room door stood Lucian, half dressed and feebly clinging to the jamb.

"Let him do it, Jule!" he cried in a tremulous thin voice. "Take the whelp at his word! Don't you see? Don't you see, Jule? We'll have him in a nine hole. It'll be hell for him if he puts it through and worse if he slinks it!" He tried to put off the bishop's sustaining arm.

A light of discernment filled Julian's face. There was no time to ponder. He had always trusted Lucian for the cunninger insight and did it now though Lucian lay in the bishop's arms limp and senseless. He drew forth the letter. Gayly stooping over the skylights Ramsey reached for it and passed it to Hugh. Julian sprang up to the bishop, who had borne Lucian into the sick-room and now filled its door again, waving a cheerful reassurance.

"A mere swoon," said the bishop; "all right again."

"It may be all right up there," the squire's sister began to say to the actor's wife – and hushed. But Ramsey had heard, as she watched her mother hurry below to the young Marburg brother lying as limp and faintly pink in death as her brother up here in life; heard, and thought of the perils in store for Hugh and his kin andher and hers unless this sweet, wise mother could charm them away as sunlight charms away pestilence. Mr. Gilmore called her:

" Come, we've lots to do."

But how could one come just then? A slight turn of the boat's head was putting Natchez Island close on her larboard bow and, seven miles away, bringing hazily into sight Natchez herself, both on her bluffs and "under-the-hill." Nay, more; abreast the *Votaress* was another fine boat. The *Westwood,* she was named. Her going was beautiful, yet the *Votaress* was gradually passing her. The Yazoo pair knew her well. When they made salute toward two men who stood near her forward skylights, one of them returned it.

"Why should he be so solemn?" asked the wife.

"Why shouldn't he?" laughed Ramsey.

"Because he's a mere passenger, on his wedding tour."

"Humph!" said Ramsey. "Weddings are solemn things. Is that other man the captain?" she asked the husband.

"No, I regret to say, he's only her first clerk."

"Why should you regret to say it?" inquired the girl; but the wife, too, had a question:

" Do you think there's anything wrong? "

"N-no, oh, no."

The *Westwood's* clerk made a sign to Captain Cour- teney. The captain glanced up to Watson, and the two boats, still at full speed, began to draw sidewise together. But Ramsey's liveliest interest was in the *Westwood's* crew, who, far below about her capstan, were paying their compliments to the newer, larger, speedier boat in song and refrain with stately wavings and dippings of ragged hats and naked black arms. Now the boats' guards almost touched and their commanders spoke so quietly together that she did not hear their words. But she noted the regretful air with which John Courteney shook his head to the *Westwood's* clerk and then to the passenger, and the *Westwood* began again to drop behind. Hugh came near, paused, and glanced around.

"Looking for the commodore?" she asked.

" I thought you went down with Mrs. Gilmore," he replied, "to rehearse your part in the play."

"Commodore's down on the lower deck," she said; "freight deck – with mom-a – and the bishop."

Hugh showed astonishment. "The bishop?"

" Yes, mom-a made him go." She laughed. "Some of the sick folks down there are Protestants and were threatening to turn Catholic. Is anybody sick aboard the *Westwood?"*

"No."

" Then where's her captain? "

Hugh made no reply but to meet her steady gaze with his own till she asked in a subdued voice: "Cholera?"

Hugh nodded. Each knew the other was aware of the song that floated up after them from the boat behind.

"What did the bridegroom want?" asked the girl.

"Wanted to give us a thousand dollars to take his bride – with him or without him – aboard the *Votaress."*

"But when he heard how much worse off we are – " prompted she.

"Yes."

"But, Mr. Hugh "

"Yes?"

"Anyhow, this boat hasn't got that boat's trouble!"

"No," said Hugh, and knew they were both thinking of his father. Together they stood hearkening to the last of the *Westwood's* song:

"' Ef you git dah befo' I do –

0, high-low! –

Jest tell "em I'm a-comin" too –
John's gone to high-low !'" XXIX
STUDYING THE RIVER – TOGETHER

They did not tie to the wharf-boat at Natchez. At that stage of water there was good landing a few yards below, where the sandy bank was not too wet to walk across to a higher one which floods never reached, close under the bluff. Here had left the boat half a dozen passengers including the judge and his sister. So good-by to that lady. Never would *she* have set foot on the *Votaress* had she dreamed she was to be " dumped off" on such a spot. She believed that girl of Gideon Hayle's had laughed as she went up the perilous stage plank. And really there is no proof to the contrary.

Another incident awoke in Ramsey no mirth. Yet she never forgot it. It occurred on the upper, greener level that overlooked, across the river, a great sweep of Louisiana lowlands at that moment bathed in a golden sunset. The same light fell upon the incident itself – the Marburg lad's burial; fell upon the bent mother standing behind the priest and between her elder son and Madame Hayle, surrounded by her fellow exiles, many of whom, with faces hidden like hers, wept more for her bereavement than they had earlier done for their own. So the rude pine coffin descended into theunhallowed ground. From the hurricane-deck Ramsey looked down with wet eyes to the meek mourner returning aboard on the arm of her Otto. Thinking how easily in the play of chance the lost brother might have been saved and her saved brother lost, and recalling the plight of the *Westwood,* she suddenly realized that no one could tell who might go next – "to high-low." Otto Marburg, glancing up, saw her tears, and would have paused but for the sacred burden on his arm.

At the same time, for eyes, even wet eyes, as lively as Ramsey's there were livelier things to see. Hugh had gone ashore and up to the wharf-boat, crossed it, and boarded the busy *Antelope* with several letters in hand, the twins' letter among them. Said the squire's brother-in-law:

" That boy must know the danger to him there is in that document," and the planter of Milliken's Bend agreed.

So did their wives. There was " everything in it he wouldn't want there and nothing he would want."

He was doing the "brave thing," they all said, and the wives called it too brave. The brave thing, they thought, "ran a slim chance against Hayle's twins."

"My dear ladies," said the planter, "it runs the only chance he has. The brave thing is the only thing those two young fire-eaters have any respect for." He stopped short; Ramsey had overheard. Yet she kept a pretty front.

"Why do you call him 'that boy'?" she laughingly asked.

"Well, really, because," replied the planter, twinkling, " he's so much more than a boy. Don't you think so?" .

She gave him a sidelong glance, twitched her curls, and looked down ashore. Her mother was there with the "boy's" grandfather. They were getting into a rickety hack. Now Hugh joined them from the *Antelope,* and they went whipping up the steep road across the face of the bluff and into the "stuck-up" Natchez atop the hill. She guessed their errand.

Meantime the *Westwood* had reached the wharf-boat, put her bridal pair aboard the *Antelope,* and backed out again so promptly that as the *Antelope* cast off and started after her she had rounded Marengo Bend and was showing only her smoke across Cowpen Point. And now reappeared Madame Hayle, the commodore, and Hugh, bringing with them – welcome sight – two sisters of charity. The moment they touched the lower deck the *Votaress,* with John Courteney on her roof, backed away, and soon, in the first bend above, any eye could plainly see the *Westwood,* still less than four miles off across country though eight by the river, with the *Antelope* four miles behind her and four ahead of the *Votaress.* Said the pilot, Ned, to Ramsey, pulling the wheel down to head into the crimson west:

"Four'n'four's eight, ain't it? Used to be. Can't tell what'll change on this river. When Lake Concor- dia, over here in Louisiana, was part o' the river, an' Vidal's Island, in its middle, was in the river, this bend wa'n't jest eight mile' round, it wuz twenty. These are*the* bends. F'om here to Cairo we got to run one etar- nal wriggle o' six hund'd 'n' eighty mile' to make three hund'd 'n' seventy."

"Oh, I'm glad of it! At least – ain't – ain't you?" He shook his head: "Not this run." The supper bell rang and Ramsey fled, but he repeated: "No, not this run!" He turned and looked back upon Natchez bluff far behind the steamer's wake. " I wished every last Hayle on this blessed boat wuz off o' her an' 'top o' you!"

On that bluff, in colonial days, had stood Fort Rosalie, whose dire tragedy Ramsey, down in the cabin, found Gilmore, at table, recounting to Hugh and others: murder of its French settlers by Natchez Indians and the extermination of the Natchez tribe by the French from New Orleans. He was brief, and for a good ending went on to recall his own first sight of the spot, before the time of steamboats, when Natchez was a village; how, as his low broadhorn came drifting down around this point close above it, the bold rise swung into view, crowned with pines, its lower parts evergreen with the bay magnolia, and its precipitous front lighted up, as now, with the last beams of day. He made it seem so fair and important that Ramsey's native pride and a shame of her previous blindness almost drove her from the board to take a last look at it from the stern guards; but she was again in her mother's seat and again very hungry. He was good company to every one, the actor; always acting, yet always as natural as if acting and nature were one; a quiet education to Hugh, an unfailing joy to his wife, and both to Ramsey.

After supper the players got out an old two-act play for the next evening's enter- tainment. They cast Hugh and Ramsey for two small roles, and for two larger ones found a young brother and sister – of Napoleon – at the mouth of the Arkansas – who would have just time to act them before leaving the boat. Supper had prevented its guests from seeing the *Votaress* turn Giles's Bend and Rifle Point and meet another boat as glittering as she and pass Lake Saint John and Fair- child's Bend – where the river widened to three miles about Fairchild's double island. Wherefore the in- dulgent Gilmores, on Ramsey's pleading, elected to coach first the brother and sister – of Napoleon – letting Hugh ascend to the starlight of the roof and Ramsey follow attended once more by old Joy.

She met Hugh at the foot of the pilot-house steps. "We are postponed!" she said, "you and me – I!"

"Yes. Do you know for what?"

"Yes, because those other two parts are so much bigger than ours, and because – I d'n' know – I believe they think I'm sleepy – ha, ha! I'm glad, for 7 want to study this *river,* all I can, day and night. And you – must, mustn't you? "

"Yes," he said, which was all he was to say in the

Play-

Half-way up the steps she halted: "You're to be a

captain on it yourself as soon as you're fit, ain't you?" " If that time ever comes."

"Phew! how modest!" She stared an instant, turned her back, clasped the rail, and with her forehead on her arms laughed till Hugh was weary – not necessarily long.

He spoke: " Here come the *Weatwood* and the *Antelope.*"

"Where?" She glanced round, sprang up the steps, and soon was making room for him beside her at a larboard window behind Watson. Looking thence across the long, slim neck of Cole's Point they saw the two boats coming back westward in the upper reach of the fourteen-mile eastern loop they were running to make two miles into the north. Now the *Westwood* passed and now the *Antelope,* their skylights glinting like fireflies through the intervening tree tops, and Watson showed how to tell them apart by night. Presently they turned north again and vanished, leaving the mighty stream to its three students.

"It'll cut off this whole fourteen mile' some day," said Watson; but the other two, in their dim nook, remained silent. He knew that sort of silence. When Ramsey by and by spoke, her words were to Hugh exclusively and in undertone.

"The *Quakeress* – Oh, I didn't mean !"

"That's all right," said Hugh. "The *Quakeress* – -?"

"Oh, I meant *the Antelope!* She'll soon be in the lead again?"

"Yes."

"With both those letters." "Both."

"Ain't you glad I didn't mean the *Quakeress?"*

"No."

"Well, you're glad I didn't mean Phyllis, ain't you?"

"No."

"Would you really be willing to tell me about Phyllis?"

"I would."

"You wasn't willing – before – was you? – were you?"

"No."

"What's changed your mind?"

"Lawd, missy!" sighed the forgotten Joy.

But Ramsey insisted: " What's changed it? "

"You, chiefly."

" I haven't," very quietly said the girl.

"You have."

Ramsey glanced cautiously at Watson, but the pilot's eyes were a league ahead. Hers returned to Hugh. "Wasn't it my brothers changed your mind – the twins?"

"They helped."

She looked him over absently: " I love my brothers."

"I don't," said Hugh.

She stared again and slowly remarked: "You haven't got to ... You're powerful queer, ain't you?"

"Not by choice."

"I'm queer. Wish I wasn't – wa'n't – weren't – but I am."

"Yes," said Hugh, "you are."

She tilted her chin, stepped to Watson's side, and called down over the breast-board to the Gilmores, who had finished with their two pupils for a time and had taken chairs with a newly found young married pair on the texas roof:

"Oho, down there!"

"Oho!" the group answered.

"Do you want us to stay up here?" asked Ramsey. " 'Cause if you do we'll come right down. Or if you'd rather we'd come down we'll stay up here!" It was a new note.

The players laughed. " It's the long dress says that," they observed to the other pair.

"It certain'y is," replied they; which is Southern form for "probably." XXX
PHYLLIS AGAIN

About eleven o'clock that same Sunday evening the *Votaress,* at full speed, was in a part of the river whose remarkable character sustained the son of John Cour- teney and the daughter of Gideo. i Hayle in the theory that their interest in it was all that had brought them to – all that detained them in – the unlighted pilothouse, on the visitors' bench, beside Watson. Below, the passengers were for the most part once more in slumber. The exhorter had loudly sung himself to sleep:

Mahch-ign thoo Im-madn-uedl's groudnd

Toe fahr-eh wordlds odn high.' "

Madame Hayle was in her stateroom and berth, deep in sleep under the weight of her toils and assured by the players that Ramsey should go to bed when they did. Basile, too, slept, but talked and tossed in his sleep, while old Joy, sent to him by Ramsey and the Gilmores, crouched outside his door and dozed with an ear against it. The Yazoo squire, his children, his sister, her husband, the Vicksburgers, and they of Milli- ken's Bend, purposing to be called up an hour before day to leave the boat at their proper landings, had"retired" early, saying fond good-bys and hoping to meet every one again. The ladies had astonished Ramsey with kisses, given, doubtless, she thought, because her father was a hero and her mother a saint. The squire's brother-in-law had assured her that her brothers, all three – as Southern boys always, or almost always, did – would come out all right – every way; but on being asked for details he had slipped away to give his De Bow to the commodore and his last good-by to Hugh.

The actor and his wife, however, were as broad awake as Watson. Loving the lone starry hours for the hours' own starry sake and having for Hugh and Ramsey a certain zeal unconfessed even to each other, they were yet in view from the pilot's wheel and visitors' bench at this hour of eleven, staying up as willingly as nightingales with the young husband and wife who had agreed with them that somebody's mental radius " cer- tain'y had" lengthened as suddenly as her gown.

This young pair were expecting to go ashore within the next half-hour at "New Carthage," a city of seven houses, nearly opposite another of equal pride called Palmyra, and some four miles above the head of Hurricane Island, whose foot the *Votaress* was then passing. They and the Gilmores were still down at the forward edge of the texas roof, the players finding the Carthaginians very attractive: fluent on morals, cuisine, manners, steamboats, the turf, fashions, the chase; voluble on the burdensomeness of the slave to his master, the blessedness of the master to his slave; but soreto the touch on politics and religion – with their religion quite innocently adjusted to their politics – and promptly going hard aground on any allusion to history, travel, the poets, statistics, architecture, ornithology, art, music, myths, memoirs, Europe, Asia, Africa, homoeopathy, or phrenology. It entertained the players just to see how many things the happy lovers knew nothing about and to hear them state in some new form, each time they backed off a sand-bar of their own ignorance, that they had seen the world, sucked the orange, yet found no spot of earth so perfect to live in as New Carthage.

The briefest sittings at such entertainment had been enough for Hugh, too much for Ramsey, and had driven them back, twice and thrice, to that fairer world on high in the pilot-house, where they could study the river undistracted. There and thence, now together, now apart, they had gone and come all through Watson's watch, moved by Hugh's duties or her caprice. Their each new meeting had been by accident, but it is odd how often accidents can occur – " at that stage o' the game," thought the kind pilot, and on each recurrence he noticed that they had got a bit farther on in the story of Phyllis.

"How long is this island, Mr. Watson?" inquired Ramsey, as if islands were all she was sitting up for.

"Two mile' 'n' a half. D'd you ask me that before? I don't hear much behind me if it ain't hove right at me." Stalest device of the sentimentalist – the self-sacrificing lie! But Watson cared not for itsstaleness if it might promote the game. And the game, though as wanderingly as the river, went on. Without strict order of time, now on the bench, now on the roof, early and late, here is how it went:

"You're not afraid of my brothers, are you? I'm not."

"I'm afraid for them. And for my father and grandfather. And for your father and your mother."

"Good gracious!" laughed Ramsey, then mused, and then asked: "Ain't you afraid for me?"

Hugh said nothing, and thenceforth her tone grew more maidenly though her words remained childlike enough.

"I know why you want to tell me about Phyllis," she added more softly. "You think if you don't my brothers will."

"They don't know the facts," murmured Hugh.

"Don't they think they do? And ain't that the trouble?"

"Yes." Hugh thought her insight surprising, while she enjoyed the spiritual largeness she fancied she saw in his immobile features. "Yes," he repeated, "they think they do; that's the trouble, much of it."

"How do you know they don't?"

"By what they believe and by what I know."

"How do you know you know?"

" By my own eyes and Phyllis's own lips."

"Would she tell you things she never told any one else?"

"Yes, things she never dared tell any one else."

Ramsey pondered, laughed, and pondered and laughed again: "Why, most of that time you was – you were – nothing but a little toddler. Didn't she love you?"

"She hated me."

Ramsey flinched but quickly laughed a bright unbelief to the youth's face, a face which might as well have been a wood-carving. "Oh," she cried, "how ridiculous!"

" She used to flog me, cruelly."

Ramsey gasped: "And you never told? Oh, why – why – ?"

"She said she'd kill me – and my mother. And she'd have done it, somehow."

"But she's been dead ten years!"

"Has she?"

"Why, of course! Wasn't she on the *Quakeress* when ?"

"So was I."

Ramsey flinched worse and stared away with lips apart, wondering if that was what gave him that look.

"But Phyllis," she resumed, "was lost."

"Was she?"

"Why . . . wasn't she? Mammy Joy says my uncle – in the blazing pilot-house – did you know my uncle Dan?"

"Yes. That night, half an hour before the burning "

"Oh! was it at night?"

"Yes. I was sitting with Phyllis, behind him, with him at the wheel, as we're sitting now behind Mr. Watson."

"Uncle Dan didn't hate you, did he?"

"No, indeed."

"Then why didn't you tell him about Phyllis? He was her master, you know."

" I did. He wormed it out of me. He was like you – in some things."

The questioner flashed and stared but then dropped her eyes. "Did he – have red curls?"

"Yes, redder than yours."

"Humph!" ... She mused. . . . "I'm tired here. Let's go down by the Gilmores and walk – 'thort- ships!"

They went. "Well? – about Phyllis? What did she whip you for? Being bad?"

"Bad or good was all one to Phyllis."

"Wasn't – weren't – weren't you ever bad, Mr. Hugh?"

"Frequently."

"How were you bad? – steal jam? – eat green plums?"

"Yes; had fights, went in swimming – in snake holes "

"D'd you tease your sisters? – pull their hair? – let the sawdust out o' their dolls?"

"Yes, yes, all that."

"Hmm! that's nothing. Basile and I – Ain't you going on? Of course, if you don't want to I – I shan't worm. Why did Phyllis – oh, pshaw!"

With the exclamation came such one-sided mirth that Mrs. Gilmore looked round. But her husband said there would never be anything to look round for while "that laugh" kept its quality.

Presently Hugh found himself murmurously "going on" and Ramsey listening. It was a great moment in both lives. If we cannot see it so, no matter; but in still depths of perception below all formulated thought both the youth and the girl were aware, separately, that the story of Phyllis was not the largest fruit of the hour.

Phyllis, Hugh said, had not hated him alone. In her heart had burned a pure flame of wrath against every member – save one – of the fair race to which she belonged by three-fourths of her blood but by not one word of human law. Wronged for the race she disclaimed, she hated the race that disclaimed her. Hated even the mothers of Hugh and Ramsey, who abhorred slavery, a slavery enthralling men, women, children in whose veins ran not four only but eight and sixteen times as much masters' blood as slaves'. She hated them because all their sweet abhorrence found no deliverance or revenge for her. Mitigations there were, but mitigations she loathed. The uncompromising quality of her hatred was one thing that had made dissimulation easy, and through all Hugh's childhood she had practised it perfectly in every relation and direction on every one but him. Another easement had been her indomitable, unflagging triple purpose to be free, to be reunited to her master, and to be revenged. And a third, craftily won through the trustfulness of Hugh's Quaker mother, had been the opportunity to wreak the frequent overflow of her resentments on him. The fact that he was almost of the exact age of her own lost offspring had forever goaded her, and to him, with each maltreatment, she had told again her heart's whole burden, outermost wrong, innermost rage, thus recovering poise to treat his sisters and brother with exemplary care and tenderly to discuss with their mother Hugh's precocious reticence and gravity. Always she had held a self-command cunningly tempered in the fire of her triple resolve and fitted to the desperate chances with which she unceasingly crossed daggers. She never tired of telling her little white slave that, having herself once got the lash, she was only paying interest on it through him. Him, at least, she would teach to hate slavery as she hated it.

Hugh's listener moved as if to touch him. A boat was coming by. They paused in their "thort-ships" walk and with a slight choke in her voice Ramsey asked: "You know what I hope?" Her voice went lower. "I hope you learned."

"That's the strangest part," said Hugh. " I did."

The boat passed, a cloud of burning gems. "Go on," said Ramsey, "I can see that and hear you at the same time."

But Hugh's mind was too masculine for such legerdemain and though she sighed and sighed again he waited until the vision grew dim astern. Then, as he was about to resume, she interrupted.

18

SECTION 18

XXXI

THE BURNING BOAT

"where was the commodore all that time?" she asked.

" In Europe. We did business there too. It wasn't all river and boats those days."

"Humph!" She preferred it to be all river and boats.

"But at length," said Hugh

"What length?"

"Ten years. Grandfather was coming home, to stay. We were all to go up to Saint Louis on the *Quakeress.*"

"Phyllis too?"

"Yes, to meet him there and bring him back with us."

"Ten years!" marvelled Ramsey. "Hadn't Phyllis ever heard from my – from Walnut Hills? "

"Now and then, yes; and when those ten years seemed to have worn her, body and soul, to the breaking point "

"You're strange. You feel tender to her yet."

"Perhaps I do. One day – night – she got word – I heard it from my nursery bed – she got news; news that to her was as good and as bad as news could be.""That *he* was on the river again!" guessed Ramsey.

"Yes, relearning it – it changes so fast, you know – and that your father had asked my father to employ him; for he didn't want to go with your father."

"No, Hayles will *fight* for Hayles, pop-a says, but they won't work for them."

"Also that he was going to be married. But Phyllis told my mother so meekly that the past was all past "

"And she'd seemed so good for so long, I suppose."

"Yes – that even my father thought it *was* past, and when we went aboard the boat and it started up the river, there at the wheel was your uncle Dan."

"You didn't dare tell on her? – Oh, you were only ten years old!"

"It wasn't that. I was older than I am to-day. But if I told a word I'd have to tell all, and by that time she'd made me believe that about all the guilt was mine."

"Yours! Well, and then? Was his lady-love on the boat?"

"No, but a passenger who came aboard at Natchez turned out to be the overseer Phyllis had once run away from."

"Oh! oh! the man who lost the child! What a difference that must have made!"

"Difference a wind makes to a fire. And yet for a time things ran along as smoothly as the old boat."

"She wasn't any older than you."

"For a boat she was, several times. Mr. Watson," asked Hugh from the roof between the Gilmores and the pilot, "what's the average age of a boat on this river?"

"Average age? Well, it varies! Say about five year'."

Hugh's voice dropped again. "The overseer being aboard, Phyllis and I, to be clear of him, were allowed free run of the roofs, and I being the captain's son it was so natural to see us often in the pilot-house "

"And she was so wary, and you were so silent "

"Yes – that no one noticed anything and the past still seemed past. One day your uncle Dan told me of your twin brothers. They'd spent half a year with him."

"Which mom-a's sorry for to this day. They worship him yet, she says. Go on; skip their visit."

"Well, when we reached Saint Louis I knew that he and Phyllis had agreed on something perfectly joyful to her. I don't know even now – what it was. She was to be set free, but that was only a small part."

"Skip again. The commodore joined you?"

"No, he failed us. We had to turn back without him."

"But with Uncle Dan, of course?"

"Yes, in wedding clothes. And with the overseer and with Phyllis. She'd tried to run away again, in Saint Louis, but she couldn't do it without my mother's help, and my mother, though she declared the laws were shameful, wouldn't break them."

"I'd 've broken them!" whispered Ramsey. "Well, you turned back?"

"Yes, and I saw at once there was something horribly wrong. Day and night Phyllis was frantic. She hid her feelings from others, wonderfully, but she poured them out on your uncle Dan. It was then he suspected how she'd been treating me, and coaxed me to tell him; and when he told her I'd told him and that he would tell she saw she was at the end of everything and I thought that now she would whip me to death."

"Stop! Stop!" The two were again in the pilothouse, but Watson, just then jingling his engine bells, was too busy to heed anything not "hove at him." His big bell had sounded for New Carthage, and John Courteney had appeared down forward of it, but neither Hugh nor Ramsey was enough diverted to answer the parting hail of the town's two residents joyfully going ashore. "I can't stand it!" she ran on. "I won't hear it!"

"But I must tell you," murmured Hugh.

"Why must you?"

"Because of what you have already heard and will hear and because you are you; who you are; what you are."

"Mr. Hugh, I'm the same I was last night when you and your father were talking poetry and trying to get rid of me !"

"Not quite."

"Well, go on; they quarrelled and you thought your hour had come – it seems it hadn't. Go on – if you 'must.'"

"I must," he said, and went on. "I had picked up, that day – -it was the third day out and we were down in these bends and had taken on nearly half a load of cotton – I'd picked up, where your uncle Dan had dropped it, a small paper box of fusees – you know? – matches that you can't blow out. Childlike, guiltily, I kept them. In their quarrel, that night, Phyllis ended by imploring your uncle Dan not to tell on her. I never knew what supplication was till then. She wept on her knees, clinging to his. When she had to leave him, to put me to bed, he made her promise never again to do me the least hurt, and swore that if she did he'd sell her to the overseer.

"We went. I was afraid that down in the stateroom she'd find the fusees in my pocket and that I should go to jail as a public thief. But she stood me in the middle of the room, threw herself on my berth, and writhed and hid her face and beat her head and looked at me a hundredfold more murderously than your uncle Dan had ever looked at her. So once, while she lay still a moment, I slipped out onto the guards, and as I lifted my hand to throw the fusees into the river she caught it in hers, it and them. Then for the first time in my life I resisted her. I fought. Do you know what a cow-eat is? "

Ramsey stared. " No. Is it a way of fighting? "

It was not a way of fighting. Cattle often eat deep holes into cotton bales. " Ah, yes!" The tale went on.

"I fought her, and somehow the fusees, the whole box, got lighted and were dropped. Whether she dropped them purposely or not, or I dropped them, I'll never know; but they fell just over the rail, among the cotton bales, and we saw the lint in a cow-eat about three tiers down flash like gunpowder. She snatched me back into the stateroom, shut the door, and stood clutching me wildly and listening. 'Say your prayers," she said, and knelt with me. She'd never knelt with me before. When I finished she had me go over them again. She did not say them with me, only whimpered and whispered, and fluttered her hands on my head and back. She made me begin once more, but before I was half through we heard the watchman run along the roof close over us and cry: 'Fire!' She lifted me to my feet, whispering, 'Now! Now!' and began to put a life-preserver on me, still saying over and over nothing but 'Now! Now! Now!' until the sounds of alarm were everywhere, and just as she sprang into the next stateroom to rouse the other children my mother came into it from the main cabin. I got my little brother into my room and was dressing him there while my mother dressed one sister and Phyllis the other, when your father's overseer, who had once followed the river himself, came down the cabin shouting to every one to come out and go forward and was kicking in every door he found locked. At ours he told my mother not to mind the smoke-which had grown thick and choking – but to rush us all straight through it to the boiler deck and down the forwardstairs, and on her life not to stop for life-preservers but to go at once. So she and Phyllis ran with the three little ones; but I, childlike again, had got the notion that life-preservers were forbidden and was so long getting mine off that Phyllis turned back for me.

"That delay saved my life, for, as we ran out into the cabin together, the smoke in front of us, forward, turned red and then went all to flame, and right in the midst of it, hurrying toward us, we saw the overseer. He tripped on a hassock or something and fell and the flame literally swallowed him alive. We sprang through an open stateroom and climbed a wheel- house stair to the hurricane deck. There we saw no one, but through the crackle and roar of the flame, which a light breeze behind us sent straight up into the darkness, I heard the voice of my father, twice, at his post in front of the skylights, and the answer of the engine bells showed that your uncle Dan and the engineers were sticking to their places. We were landing in a strong eddy under a point and didn't have to round to. The boat was wonderfully quiet. I even heard – probably because the shore was. so close ahead of us – the first mate – same that's with us here now – heard him ordering the stage run out over the water, as always when about to land. I heard the clerks and others telling the passengers to 'keep cool' and 'not crowd,' saying there was room and time for every one.

"The pilot-house was burning brightly on one side but it was so wrapped in smoke that your uncle Dan was hid from Phyllis and me till the boat hit the bank. Then the breeze gave us a glimpse of him as it curled the whole blaze forward so that it overarched the people who filled the front stairs and gangway, waiting to swarm off across the stage. That brought panic and the panic brought death. Some male passengers – we couldn't see, but our hearing was like sight – had got all the women and children to the front of the crowd and a few even partly out on the stage, over the water, to be the first put ashore.

"When the boat's nose struck the shore the back part of the crowd thought the landing was made and began to push, and there were no men in front to push back – for some of the boat's family, missing Phyllis and me, had run aft to find us – and when that smoke rolled down on every one the push became a rush and suddenly two or three women were screaming at one edge of the stage, with nothing to lay hold on but one another.

"We heard their cries and the cry of the crowd, through the crackling of the fire. My mother tried to save them, with her three children clinging to her, and the whole-six fell into the black shadow of the freight guards and the swift eddy drew them under the boat's hull before a thing could be done except that two of our men jumped in and sank with them."

Ramsey covered her face. "What did your father do?"

"He let himself down by one of the derrick posts. As he did so, and when they who had tried to rescue us had failed, the mate, who is a famous swimmer, sprang overboard, as near the larboard wheel as the fire would let him, struck out round it, climbed up on it into the paddle-box, and tried to reach the cabin deck by the kitchen stair. But a sweep of the flames drove him back into the river, and he was just sinking when Mr. Gilmore, you know, drew him into his skiff.

"At the same time your uncle Dan came tumbling down from a pilot-house window and staggered with us back to the stern rail, for all the stairs were burning. It was idle to call for help. The whole thing had lasted but a minute or two. Phyllis didn't want help and we had just that instant to get down in.

" Those who had gone ashore could not see us. The smoke hid us. So did the texas. Your uncle Dan dragged a mattress out of it and dropped it over the stern, away down onto the fantail, scores of feet below. The flames made the boat's shadow as black as ink. We thought the yawl was down there, but some of the crew had swum out from the shore and pulled away in it to pick up the mate – and us, of course, if we were with him.

"Your uncle, though fearfully burnt, took me on his back and showed Phyllis how to climb down beside him by the bracket work and posts and balustrades of the guards, as I could have done, but he wouldn't let me.

" If the wind had been the other way we should have perished right there. But the guards of the ladies' cabin ran round the stern, as they do on this boat, and her fantail, below, stretched still farther aft. So we gotdown to those guards easily. But in the ladies' cabin the fire had worked aft faster than outside, and on those guards the heat was torture. We could only hang from them and drop. Your uncle went first, then Phyllis and then I, he catching us, for down there he had light enough, looking up, and as we fell the flames shot through the cabin stern windows. He caught us, but then he said, 'I'm gone, Phyllis,' and crumpled down at her feet. Then I cried for help but Phyllis said we didn't need to call, and we didn't. We'd been seen at last, on the guards as we climbed down. They called to us to stick to the boat till swimmers could reach us. But we couldn't. The wind had turned, the heat was worse than ever, the fire had parted the boat's lines and she was being blown out into the current. Then your uncle struggled half up again and helped Phyllis get the mattress outside the bull railings, where I climbed out and held it. He asked if I could swim and when I said yes he warned me not to swim to the shore as the river was falling and the bank caving, but to float with the mattress and call till I was picked up. So I went over with it. But it twisted away from me. I swam to a floating cotton bale, one with a flicker of fire still on it, as it drifted up-stream in the eddy. At the same time I'd heard your uncle and Phyllis strike the water together, and a moment later I saw them – their heads. She was holding to the mattress with one hand and to him with the other. But presently I heard her give a low wail and saw him slip from her and sink. Then thesmoke came down between us, and by and by the returning yawl, whose men had heard my calls and had seen Mr. Gillmore's skiff pick up the mate, found me on the cotton bale and had barely lifted me in when I fainted away."

Ramsey covered her face again. It would have been joy to her to let one of the drops that melted through her fingers fall on Hugh's hand.

Watson cleared his throat. "Sort o' inquirin' fo" one o' you, down on the roof," he said without looking back. He was a man not above repeating himself for a good end. "Third time they've sung out to me, but – up here I off'm don't notice much f'om anywheres 'at ain't hove right at me."

Ned entered and silently took the wheel.

19

SECTION 19

XXXII

A PROPHET IN THE WILDERNESS

Through all the middle watch of Sunday night, with her Ned quite alone in the pilot-house, the *Votaress* came and passed from crossing to crossing, up reaches, through chutes, around points and bends, a meteor in harness. Such she seemed from the dim shores. So came, so passed, before the drowsy gaze of that strange attenuated fraction of humanity which scantily peopled the waters and margins of the great river to win from it the bare elements of livelihood or transit, winning them at a death-rate not far below the immigrant's and in a vagabondage often as wild as that of the water-fowl passing unseen in the upper darkness.

If to the contemplation of the Courteneys, father and son, the fair craft, "with all her light and life, speeding, twinkling on and on through the night," was "a swarm of stars," or "one little whole world," how shall we see her – with what sense of wonder and splendor – through the eyes of the flatboatman or the swamper, the raftsman, the island squatter, the trading-scow man, the runaway slave in the canebrake, the woodyard man, or the "pirooter" – that degenerate heir, dwarfed to a parasite, of the terrible, earlier-day land-pirates and river-wolves of Plum Pointand Crow's Nest Island ? To such sorts, self-described as human snapping-turtles and alligators, her peacock show of innumerable lights was the jewelled crown of the only civilization they knew, knowing it only with the same aloofness with which they knew the stars. She woke them with the flutter of her wheels as of winged feet and passed like a goddess using the river's points and islands for stepping-stones, her bosom wrapped in a self-communion that gave no least hint of its intolerable load of grief and strife.

Not until she entered the great bend of Vicksburg did she once come into contrast with anything that could in any degree diminish her regal supremacy. There, as day was breaking, she entered the deep shadow of the southernmost "Walnut Hill." The town on its crest was two hundred feet above her lower deck, and the stiff Yazoo squire, his kindly brother-in-law and sister and the Vicksburg merchant and his wife, waiting down there while she slowed up to the wharf-boat at its foot to let them and others off, were proud of the bluff and of the two miles of sister hills hid by it and the night. Even overproud they were. The two husbands and wives silently wished for that lover of wonders, the sleeping Ramsey, that they might enjoy her enjoyment of the sight, who, though from exalted Natchez, never had beheld so vast an eminence or a city stuck up quite so high.

But Ramsey, far removed in her new, sweet-smelling berth, did not stir from a slumber into which she was throwing all the weight of an overloaded experience. She was paying large back taxes to sleep and had become so immersed in the transaction that her mother's rising, dressing, and stealing away lifted, this time, not one of her eyelashes. In not a sigh or motion did she respond to the long, quaking, world-filling roar of the *Votaress's* whistle, nor to John Courteney's tolling of her great bell, nor to the jingle of lesser bells below, nor to any stopping or reversing or new going ahead of her wheels either for landing or for backing out and straightening up the river again. She slept on though these were the very Walnut Hills of her uncle Dan's and Phyllis's dark story; persevered in sleep though John Courteney's son, her profoundest marvel, was once more up and out, with the story still on his heart and "a-happmin' yit." It was one of its happenings that, very naturally, though quite unreasonably, he begrudged the sleeper's absence from texas roof and pilot-house.

The *Votaress* was under full headway, with Vicks- burg astern, Watson again at the wheel and the captain in his chair. The most northerly of the Walnut Hills were on the starboard bow. Beyond them the sun, rising into thunder-clouds, poured a dusty-yellow light over the tops of their almost unbroken woods, here and there brightening with a strange vividness the tilled fields and white homestead and slave quarters of some noted plantation. Between the hills and the river lay a mile's breadth or more of densely forested swamp, or " bottom," swarming with reptiles great and small, abounding in deer, bear, and panther, and from which, though the buffalo had been long banished, the wolf was not yet gone. On the skylight roof, close "abaft the bell," as Ramsey would have said, stood the commodore and Hugh. They had just met there and after a casual word or so Hugh was about to say something requiring an effort, when they were joined by the exhorter.

"Mawnin', gentle-mn," he said. "Now, what you reckon them-ah po' Gawd-fo'-saken'd Eu-rope-ians down-stahs air a-thinkin' to theyse'v's whilst they view this-yeh lan'scape o'? D'you reckon they eveh, ev'm in they dreams o' heav'm, see sich

"' Sweet fiel's beyond the swellin' flood

Stand deck' in livin' green' ?

" I tell you, gentle-men, as sho' as man made the city an' Gawd made the country, he made this-yeh country last, when he'd got his hand in! You see that-ah house an' cedah grove on yan rise? Well, that's the old' Good Luck Plantation.' Gid Hayle 'uz bawn thah. His fatheh went to Gawd f'om thah an' lef ' it to Dan, the pilot, what 'uz lost on the *Qua'* – Hell! listen at me! As ef *you* didn't know *that,* which ev'y sight o' you stahts folks a-talkin' about it! But, Lawd! what a country this-yeh 'Azoo Delta is, to be sho'! Fo' craps! All this-yeh Mis'sippi Riveh, you mowt say, fo'm Cairo down, an' th' 'Azoo fo' the top-rail! Fo' craps – an' the money-makin'est craps ! An' jest as much fo' game! Not pokeh but wile game; fo'-footen beasts afteh they kind an' fowl afteh they kind. An'ef a country's great fo' craps *an'* game, what mo' kin it be great faw what ain't pyo' Babylonian vanity an' Eu-rope-ian stinch?"

The commodore admitted that game was a good thing and that crops were even better.

"No, sir-ee! Game comes fust! Man makes the craps but Gawd made the game! It come fust when it fust come an'it comes fust yit! Lawd A'mighty! who wouldn't drutheh hunt than plough, ef he could hev his druthehs? But the game ain't what it wuz, not ev'm in this-yeh 'Azoo country an' not ev'm o' the feathe'd kind. Oh, wile turkey, o' co'se, they here yit, by thousan's, an' wile goose, an' duck, an' teal, by hun- d'eds o' thousan's, an' wile pigeon, clouds of 'em, 'at dahkened the noonday sun. Reckon you see' 'em do that, ain't you? I see' it this ve'y season. But, now, take the pelikin! if game is a fah' name fo' him – aw heh, as the case may be; which that bird – nine foot f'm tip to tip, the white ones – use' to be as common on this riveh as cuckle-burrs in a sheep's tail!" The jester laughed, or, more strictly, exhaled his mirth from the roof of a wide-spread mouth in a long hiss that would have been more like an angered alligator's if alligators used fine-cut tobacco. It was addressed to the commodore; for Hugh, his grandfather's conscious inferior in human charity, had turned the squarest back – for its height – aboard the *Votaress,* to gaze on a wonderful sight in the eastern sky. The exhorter resumed:

"Why, I ain't see' a pelikin sence I use' to flatboat down to Orleans – f'om Honey Islan' an' th' 'AzooCity. ' Pelikin in the *-wildeh-ness,'* says the holy book, but they 'can't stan' the wildeh-ness/' They plumb gone! – vamoost! – down to the Gulf! – what few ain't been shot!" He grew indignant. " An' whahfo' shot? Fawnoth'n'! Jeemany-crackies! *gentle-men,* it makes my blood bile an' my bile go sour! Ain't no bounty on pelikins. Dead pelikins ain't useful – naw awnamental – naw instructive, an' much less they don't tas'e good. No, suh, they jess shot in pyo' devil-men by awn- gawdly damn fools – same as them on this boat all day 'istiddy a-poppin' they pistols at ev'y live thing they see' – fo' no damn' reason in the heab'ms above aw the earth beneath aw the watehs undeh the earth – Lawd! it mighty nigh makes me swah! An' I feel the heab'mly call – seein' as that-ah tub-shape' Methodis' bishop *h-ain't* feel it – fo' to tell you, commodo', you- all hadn't ought allowed that hell-fi'ud nonsense on Gawd's holy day."

Even to his grandfather's response Hugh paid no visible attention. The eastern sky had become such a picture that down forward at the break of the deck John Courteney rose eagerly from his chair and looked back and up to be sure that his son was one of its spectators. Yes, Hugh was just casting a like glance to him and now turned to invite the notice of his grandfather. The thunder-clouds had so encompassed the sun that its rays burst through them almost exclusively in one wide crater, crimsoning, bronzing, and gilding their vaporous and ever-changing walls. Thence they spread earthward, heavenward, leaving remotermasses to writhe darkly on each other and themselves, in and out, in and in, cloaking this hill in blue shadow, bathing that one in green light, while from a watery fastness somewhere hid in the depth of the forested swamp under the hills – some long-lost bend of the Mississippi or cut-off of the Yazoo – rose into the flood of beams an innumerable immaculate swarm of giant cranes. Half were white as silver, half were black as jet, and from moment to moment each jet magically turned to silver, each silver to jet, as on slowly pulsing wings they wove a labyrinthian way through their own multitude with never a clash of pinion on pinion, up, down, athwart and around, up, down, and around again, now raven black across the sun and now silver and snow against the cloud.

An awed voice broke the stillness and old Joy stood a modest step back from Hugh's side with rapt gaze on hill and sky.

20

SECTION 20

XXXIII

TWINS AND TEXAS TENDER

" Sign f'om de Lawd!" droned the old woman. " It's de souls o' de saints in de tribilatioms o' de worl' !"

But explanation was poor tribute to such beauty. Hugh glanced away to his father, then around to the commodore, up to Watson, and back again upon the spectacle. In a tone of remote allusion the grandfather spoke: "One wants a choice partnership for a sight like that."

Hugh cast back a sudden frown but it softened promptly to a smile which old Joy thought wonderfully sweet.

"Late sleepers," persisted the commodore, "know what they gain but not what they lose."

"Naw yit," audibly soliloquized the nurse, "what dey makes de early riseh lose." She added a soft high- treble "humph!" and gave herself a smile at least as sweet as Hugh's, which he repeated to her as he said:

"Good morning, auntie."

She courtesied. " Mawnin', suh." They need not have been more cordial had they just signed a great treaty.

The *Votaress,* swinging westward, left the picture behind, and the neglected exhorter, caring far less forcranes and clouds than for pelicans and sinners, reopened,
this time on Hugh: "But that's anotheh thing 'at rises my bristles, ev'm ef it don't the
bishop's."

"What rises them?" asked the solemn Hugh, the commodore's attention wandering.

"Shell I spit it out? Wall, it's folks a-proj-eckin' togetheh – church membehs
an' non-membehs *a.-proj-* eckin' *togetheh – to'* to drownd Gawd A'mighty's chas-
tse-ments in the devil's delights. *You* know they a-layin' fo' to do that on this boat
this ve'y evenin'. You know they a-pny-eckin' fo' to raise filthy lucre by fiddlin' an'
play-actin' an' a-singin' o' worl'ly songs an', to top all, a-dayncin'! – right oveh the
heads o' the sick an' dyin', my Gawd! You know that, don't you?"

"Yes, I'm mixed up in it."

"An' they a-doin' it fo' what? Fo' no betteh reason 'an to he'p them-ah damn'
ovehwhelmin' furrinehs to escape the righteous judg-menfe o' the Lawd! Young
brotheh, my name is Jawn. Jawn the Babtiss, I am, an' as sich I p'otess! An' also an'
mo'oveh I p'otess ag'in' any mo' leadin's f'om them-ah 'Piscopaliam play- actohs, an'
still mo' f'om that-ah bodacious brick-top gal o' Gid Hayle's. Which she made opem
spote o' *my* leadin's in 'istiddy's meet'n'! An' o' co'se! havin' a popish motheh."

"Oh! – my! – Lawd!" gasped Joy, and the commodore had begun to meet protest
with protest, when Hugh touched him.

"This is too small for you. May I ?"

"Take it," said the grandfather and turned inquiringly to the nurse.

"Yaas, suh," she hurried to say, "my mist'ess ax de honoh to see you at de stateroom
o' Mahs' Basile."

Meantime Hugh answered the complainant: "My friend, that young lady – you
mustn't call her anything else again – made no sport of you whatever."

"Oh, dat she didn't, boss!" put in old Joy, breaking off from her talk with the
commodore.

"Honestly, sir," continued Hugh, "I was afraid some one would, but I happened to
see her from first to last, and "

"Happ'm'd! The hell you happ'm'd! Yo'eyes'uz dead *sot* on heh when they'd
ought to been upraise' in prah!"

Hugh laughed – a laugh so hearty it might have been the brick-top's own. The texas
tender enjoyed it as he bore a tray of dishes from the room of the twins. Down beyond
the bell it drew the father's smile and up at the wheel the stoical gaze of Watson. Half
of it was for the exhorter and half for a newcomer at tardy sight of whom the exhorter
paled, certain that he had been overheard.

"Oh!" he cried, "I ain't meant no offence to nobody naw tuck none!" and eagerly
followed the commodore's beckon to go below with him and the nurse. Hugh, still
smiling, met the blazing stare of Julian Hayle.

" Good morning," he said, while Hayle was inquiring:" May I again ask of you a
word in private? "

"Oh, this is private enough," said Hugh. "Every private word I've had with you
so far, or with your – coterie, has been so unsatisfactory to you – and them, and so
tiresome to everybody, I can't see why you should want another. My friend "

"We are not friends, sir."

"Well, then, let's make friends. Here's my hand. I'm utterly ashamed of this miserable little spat."

Hayle folded his arms. " You'll find it life-size before we're done."

"Nonsense! it's too small for words, private or otherwise. Let's end it, for that reason if for no better."

"That's not your reason, sir. You have another."

" Yes, I simply can't quarrel with you."

" You – crawling – poltroon!"

Hugh's smile vanished at last. He gulped as though a wave had gone over him. But he remembered his father. Beyond doubt his father had heard. He glanced down to him, and what he saw was worth a year of commonplace experience. The father had heard, yet he sat at ease, his knees crossed and his gaze out forward on the boat's course. Watson – but what could Watson matter then? Hugh's eyes burned big on Hayle, his voice deepened, his words came slow. "We can't fight here and now. I can only put you ashore. Don't make me do that. There's trouble enough on this boat as it is. You're having your share. Mr. Hayle, I fear – though I don't know – that Basile has the cholera."

"Damn him and it! You wouldn't fight me if you could."

"True."

"Why? On your father's account – and his father's?"

" On everybody's. Your own father's. Your mother's."

"My sister's?" The question was a threatening sneer.

"Yes, sir." The breakfast bell rang merrily below and Hugh turned to leave. Julian blazed out in curses:

"I forbid you 'that young lady's' company henceforth!"

"And that's the private word you had for me?"

"Yes, damn you! I know who sat up late last night. If you do it again I'll shoot you right on this boat!"

" My private word for you, Mr. Hayle, isn't as public as that. Only I and the texas tender know it."

"Most fitting partnership!"

" No, it was entirely his own enterprise. While you and your brother were getting your information from him he got your weapons from both of you. I have them in the clerk's safe." XXXIV

THE PEACEMAKERS

Some four of the *Votaress's* "family," one seated, three standing at ease, were allowing their mild, slow conversation its haphazard way under barely enough constraint to hold it in the channel of discretion. It drifted as unpretentiously as a raft or flatboat, now and then merely floating without progress, like a floating alligator; that is, with one small eye imperceptibly open to every point of the compass.

He who sat was the first clerk, a man of thirty- seven or so, and therefore, as age then counted, fairly started on the decline of life. He occupied the high stool in the clerk's office, his limp back against its standing desk. Nearest him the second clerk, standing, leaned on an elbow thrown out upon the desk and rested one foot on a rung of the stool. A second clerk might do that; a third or "mud" clerk would hardly have made so free. The youthful mud clerk, with his hat under his folded arms, leaned on the jamb of a door that let back into the clerks' stateroom. Opposite him the youngest of the four, latest come among them, stood out in the cabin and hung in over the broad window counter, across which the office did business with the world. Watson's "cub pilot" he was, on the sick list, thin and weak with swamp-fever.

The forenoon watch was half gone. The boat was fluttering along at high speed under a bright but fickle sky, and the clerks and the "cub" hardly needed to glance out the nearest larboard window to know that she was already turning northward into a pleasant piece of river called Nine Mile Reach. A certain Point Lookout was some five miles behind in the east, and the town of Providence, negligibly small, with Lake Providence, an old cut-off, hid in the woods behind it, was close ahead. One of the number mentioned the boat's failure during the night to make the miles expected of her, but the four agreed that the cause was not any lack of speed power but an overplus of landings below Vicksburg – two being for burials – and a long delay at Vicksburg itself, providing for the sick.

This explanation, the second clerk said, had been as gratifying to the planter of Milliken's Bend and his "lady" as their not having to be called up before day. They had taken breakfast in the general company, which, with the commodore at one end of the cabin and Hugh at the other, had sat down when Old River and the mouth of the Yazoo were on the starboard bow, and had risen while passing My Wife's Island. Finally they had gone ashore in great elation, thanking Hugh with high voices and fervent hand-shakings, and his father with wavings from the bank to the roof, for the "most delightful trip anybody ever made"; careless as infants of the hundreds of strangers gazing on them, both native and alien, both woe-stricken and self-content, and, even when the great wheels were backing the boat away, calling fond messages to Hugh for the still invisible "Miss Ramsey" as if she were in his exclusive keeping and all those strangers were trees.

So recounted the second clerk, not to criticise such innocent disdain of the public eye and ear – to him an every-day sight – but with a feeling for the picturesque and in mild humor making the point that such messages, so given, were hardly calculated to make life easier for Hugh. The mud clerk and the cub pilot grunted their accord yet privately envied Hugh. To be message bearer to that young lady would have been rapture to either of them under whatever hardness or peril of life, the more the better. Oddly enough, with Milli- ken's Bend now forty miles astern the messages had not been delivered.

"No fault of his," said the first clerk, the second said no, and the mud clerk and the cub loyally echoed them. For they knew, at least the three clerks knew, always knew, not by flat inquiry but by trained perceptions and the alligator's eye, whatever was going on in each and every part of the boat. Indeed, the boat's news naturally flowed to them; flowed to and ran forth again from them, aerated and cleansed, as normally as blood to and from the breast of a strong man. By the sound of the steam they knew the water was right in the boilers. By the rhythm of the machinery they knewall was right in the engine room. They could have said, nearly enough, how soon the boat would have to stop again for wood. To them the quiet of the populous boiler deck, where nearly every man sat reading some stale newspaper of Louisville, Saint Louis, or Cincinnati – brought aboard from the Vicksburg wharf-boat – was informational, witnessing a general resigned admission that there was already "trouble enough." Of three notables not there they knew that one, the bishop, was in his berth, very weary, and that the senator and the general had been for some time with Hayle's twins. They could have greeted every cabin passenger by name. They knew who were filling the places lately vacated at the ladies' table, whose was each ubiquitous child selling tickets for the appointed "show," and whose each private servant, however rarely seen: not such as old Joy merely, but the senator's black Cato, the general's yellow Tom, Mrs. Gilmore's theatrically handsome Harriet, or the nearly as white Dora of the young lady from Napoleon. And they knew well that the non-delivery of those messages was no fault of Hugh's.

Miss Ramsey was up, yes; but she had breakfasted in seclusion and was then in a small under-cabin for ladies' maids, close beneath the main one, rehearsing with Mrs. Gilmore and others. Gilmore had been coaching them but was now momentarily out on the boiler deck. Through the extensive glass of the cabin's front they could see him standing before a knot of men: John the Baptist and the man with the eagle eye andthe man with the eye of a stallion and the man who knew so slap-bang that the Hayles and Courteneys had all but locked horns when the *Quakeress* burned. They were the only exponents of unrest out there and only the actor wore an air both spirited and kind. No one in the office openly kept an eye on the outer group. In there the gossip lingered on Hugh. Hugh had plenty, it was agreed, of the Courteney stuff and something besides which these four hoped was the very thing with which to meet this new phase so plainly at hand in the Hayle-Courteney contest.

Suddenly the first clerk looked straight out on Gil- more, so obviously at bay, and murmured to the cub pilot: "Go, bring him." While the cub went, the clerk spoke on. Hugh, he said, would one day be the best- liked of his name.

In kindly dissent the second clerk shook his head, but the first would have it so. The liking might be slow coming, he allowed, because of Hugh's oddities, but in the end men would like even the oddities.

The mud clerk named one as if he liked it: "When he's by himself he's got the iron-est phiz "

The second clerk laughed his appreciation. "And when he's poked up," he said, "it gets ironer and
ironer."

"It'll need to mighty soon," observed the first clerk.

"When he runs into Gid Hayle," said the second.

The actor came. His pleased manner was more thankful than inquiring and he insisted on remaining outside the window shelf with the cub.

"Mr. Gilmore," said the first clerk gravely, "we thought you might condescend to inspect our ceiling decorations through fresh foliage."

The player looked puzzled an instant but a smell of mint from the bar cleared his mental vision. Yet again he declined. Later in the day he shouldn't be so coy, he admitted, but one oughtn't to take too long a running start for his jump into bed.

"No, he *might* get there too soon," said the clerk. "My boys, sir, want to ask you a riddle. You know Gid Hayle. How can his daughter, here, be just like him for all the world and yet those twins be just like him for all the same identical world, too?"

"Well put !" was the prompt rejoinder. "My wife and I have been toying with that riddle these twenty- four hours. Those brothers are Gideon Hayle's sons if ever a man had sons; that daughter is his from the ground up; yet the two and the one are as unlike as night and noon."

The clerks-and cub pilot agreed so approvingly that the actor, lover of lines, was inspired to go on at more length. He remarked, in effect, that he had never seen so striking an instance of a parent's natural traits growing into – blemishes – in one inheritor and into graces in another. Yet to know Gideon Hayle was to read the riddle. As quick to anger as his sons, as full of mirth as his daughter; open-hearted, wrong-headed, generous, tyrannous, valorous, contemptuous of all book wisdom yet an incessant, keen inquirer with a fantastical explanation of his own for everything innature, science, politics, or religion. Implacable in his prejudices, he

"Yes," interrupted the first clerk, with amazing irrelevancy, "but a man of Henry Clay's experience ought to have known better. Kossuth is a gentleman who – well, general, how are you now? Mr. Gilmore, you know the general? Senator, you know Mr. Gil- more?"

"Assuredly!" The condescending senator had known Mr. Gilmore, "a day by contact but long by fame."

The general was civil but not suave. He remembered the player's hard names for the committee's dead scheme. "Taking care of Henry Clay, too, sir?" he asked him. "With so many pleasanter cares" – that meant Ramsey – "you might let Henry Clay take care of himself."

"That's something," put in the second clerk, flushing defensively, while the senator, with cigar cocked one way and his silk hat another, drew Gilmore aside, "that's something Henry Clay never does,"

" Right, young man. He merely tries. Th-there's no one in the nation has t-tried harder or f-failed worse!"

The youth turned to his work at the high desk. "Sir," said the general to the first clerk, who rose, "the senator and I have been up to your texas "

"Contrary to orders," mildly said the first clerk.

" I admit it, sir, but our intentions were only th-the k-kindest. It seems to us, sir, or to me – us or me, sir, as you will – that th-those sons of our old friend Hayle are not getting justice."

"They ought to be mighty glad of that, general."

"S-s-sir, they'd rather have it! We admit, of course, – we or I – I, if you prefer, sir, or if the senator prefers – I admit they are not unbiassed."

"No, I admit they're not."

"Th-they are supe-perbly stiff-necked and illogical young barons from four centuries back, sir, without a f-f-fault that isn't a v-v-virtue overdrawn – or out of date."

The speaker turned to the actor and senator and they to him: " If those boys have the pride of L-1-lucifer, Mr. Gilmore, they have also his intrep-idity. Th-they may be as high-headed as giraffes, sir, but they're as s-s-straightf-f-forward as a charging bull! Mr. clerk, the splendid surge of their imp-pulses should excuse their f-f-foibles even if their s-s-souls were *not* wr-wri- writhing under the lash of a new whip on old sores, sir."

"Will you just make that a little clearer, general?"

"I will," softly put in the senator – "by your leave, general?"

With limp majesty the general waved permission.

"All for peace, however," said the senator smilingly to the clerk. "There's been enough strife."

"Never saw so much aboard boat," said the clerk.

"Well," – statesman and clerk laid elbows on the shelf and dropped their voices while the actor and the general drew a step aside, – "this thing can be settled only by the right friends and it's now or never." The two exchanged a look but the clerk was mute and thesenator spoke on: "You've heard of Dan Hayle – and the girl Phyllis, hmm?"

"I was first clerk on the *Quakeress* when she burned." "Why, so you *was.* These twins believe, bitterly, that in that mysterious disaster all due search for their uncle was neglected to save the captain's son and that the girl and Dan Hayle were never fully accounted for."

"Shucks! Why – Dan – it was I found Dan's body." "Yes, but they call it an outrage for him to have been there at all; to give him the wheel and take her aboard on the same trip."

"Law'! what did she count, with him about to marry?"

"Why, they think that for that very reason John Courteney let his wife – from Philadelphia, you know – abolitionist – bring the girl and Dan together, hoping he'd either set her free or else skip the wedding and somehow disgrace the whole Hayle family. Just those boys' guess but – they believe it. What they *see* is a Hayle killed and no one killed for him."

"Oh, we settled that with their dad ten years ago." "They say not. And, really, you know, some of the liveliest feuds along this river are founded on less cause. Gid Hayle, they claim, couldn't bring the Courteneys to taw at the time because the only men he had to back him were his two in-laws. Now these twins are men and they feel honor-bound to throw down – no, to take up – the gage, thrown down to them every hour they've been on this boat."

"Shoo! They've been treated only too well."

"Tactfully, do you think?"

" Depends on what you call tact. Ordinary tact's the worst thing you could throw at 'em." The clerk spoke with both eyes on the general and the actor. His fellow clerk, second clerk, had nudged him. The general was raising his voice to the actor.

"They f-forbid your lady to chaperon their sister, since you both, last evening, all-llowed young Courte- ney to give her his account of the b-urning of the *Quakeress."*

"General!" the smiling senator cautioned him, "privately, if you please! more privately!"

But the soldier persisted. "Th-they even suspect you, sir, of s-s-piriting off to Canada their s-s-lave p-roperty, missing after that event."

"Why, gentlemen," began the player, looking very professional but also very hand-some, and with a flash of annoyance only when he noticed that the exhorter had joined the group, "I never in my – nonsense! fantastical nonsense! Why, I'll be – I'll see you later! At present, as I've already said, I'm overdue at that rehearsal."

"Yes, Mr. Gilmore," said the first clerk, "you are."

"A moment," interposed the senator. "Purely in the interest of peace, Mr. Gilmore "

"Oh, senator," the actor amiably laughed, "I don't question your good-will, or the general's; but you don't know, either of you, the interest of peace when you run against it – pardon! I take that back. My annoyance, at quite another thing, flew off the handle. I take it back. Excuse me, I'll make it a point to see you later." The three bowed. As he started away the exhorter blocked his path.

"Excuse *me,*" said the zealot. "Fust tell us: Ef ye *jnowt spent* a niggeh off to Canady would ye aw wouldn't ye?"

For an instant the player stood mute and then he said only, in a preoccupied tone: "Please let me pass." But at the same time he laid his unexpected left hand lightly on the questioner and by some stage trick sent him stumbling aside along a line of chairs and toppling to the floor. The cub and the younger clerks had him up in a twinkling, while a dozen men appeared from the boiler deck as if by magic, and the player walked away down the cabin.

" Now, no more noise here, said the second clerk to the lifted man, restraining both his arms. "No, you stay right here. He didn't do a thing to you, you just stepped a little too spry and sort o' tripped up."

From his window shelf the first clerk, in the tail of his eye, saw the zealot and his group disperse while he, the clerk, talked laughingly to the soldier on one subject and gravely to the statesman on another.

"You can't challenge a man, general," he said, "who apologizes for calling you a poor peacemaker."

"By – ! s-sir, I can and I sh-shall!" was the retort.

The clerk ignored it. He and the senator bent heads together again. " No," he said, " Hugh only told him he *feared* it was Basile. In fact, it wasn't. It isn't.""Who is it, then? It's a passenger and a bad case."

"Will you keep it dark – by the patient's own request – till the show's over to-night?"

The senator nodded. The two heads came closer. The general scorned to listen. The name did not reach him.

"Jove!" gasped the senator. "Come, general." They went.

The first clerk turned to the second clerk's elbow at the high desk, saying dryly: "They came to demand those shooting-irons and couldn't muster the brass." XXXV

UNSETTLED WEATHER

Again the *Votaress* was passing the *Westwood* and again was but a short mile behind the *Antelope.*

Led by Ramsey, the amateur players, including Hugh, had stopped rehearsing and were on the skylight roof, gathered about the commodore, the Gil- mores, and the bell. In their company, though below them on the forward hurricane deck, the first mate leaned bulkily against the roof on which they stood. It was his watch. Ned was up at the wheel.

As early as the evening before, a good hundred and fifty miles back down the river, the *Antelope,* it will be remembered, had been close on the *Westwood's* heels. So Gilmore reminded his wife. So Hugh needlessly reminded Ramsey. From the mate it was further learned that the pursuer had overhauled the pursued between Petit Goufre – which he and the whole company called Petty Gulf – and Grand Gulf; places named before the days of steam for their dangerous eddies. Yet, he went on to tell Ramsey, the swifter boat, with more freight to put ashore and with a larger appetite for cord-wood, had never got clean away. Even now, in full view ahead, she was down at half speed, wooding up from a barge in tow alongside. You could hear hercrew singing as they trotted under their great shoulder loads of wood. The amateurs, except Hugh but including Ramsey, caught up their song and were promptly joined by a group around the bell of the *Westwood* as that gallant loser foamed along between the *Votaress* and the shore:

"Oh, if I had a scolding wife,

As sure as you are born

I'd take her down to Noo Orleans

And trade her off for corn."

Presently the *Antelope* cast off the emptied flat in midstream, and a redoubled whiteness behind her paddle-boxes showed full speed.

"Now we can give her a square deal!" said a youth.

"And pass her inside of an hour!" declared another.

"In Bunch's Cut-off!" ventured one to the commodore, but the commodore said the *Votaress* herself was hungry for wood, and the mate confirmed him by a nod.

"How much wood," some one asked the mate, "will a boat like this use up in twenty-four hours?" It quickened the blood to be up here midway between these turbid waters and yonder passionate sky so joyous in one quarter, so angry in another; particularly to be here while steadily distancing one beautiful boat and overtaking another "amid green islands," as Mrs. Gilmore quoted – one of which, still in sight astern, was that old haunt of flatboat robbers, called Island Ninety-four, Stack's Island, or Crow's Nest. One half forgot the sad state of affairs below. Conversation glided as swiftly as a flock of swallows and in as many directions.

"How much wood?" said the mate. "Well, that sort o' depends. I once part owned a boat that fo' one whole month didn't burn enough wood to dry the sheriff's shoes, but that 'uz 'cause he kep' her tied up to the bank."

Ramsey did not hear this and cared nothing for the laugh it won. She had seen the doctor and the priest slip from the twins' room in the texas and go below aft. "How's mom-a?" she eagerly asked the commodore.

"Very well."

" How's Lucian?"

Lucian was so much better, he told her, that both brothers had been returned to their cabin stateroom.

"Then you've just put a new case into the texas!"

The commodore smiled. "Yes, from the freight deck."

"Freight – humph! That's the lower deck," she reminiscently said, turning to Hugh. "Who is it? Is it – Otto?"

But Hugh's face wore its absurd iron look, which had its usual effect on her. The old man spoke: " Will Miss Ramsey do us all a favor; one that will help the play?"

"Whew, yes! That'll help everything. What is it?"

"It's to make no mention of the new case to any one."

"Till the close of the evening," put in the Gilmores,

and Ramsey saw that they knew. Yet

"All right," she said. "Oh, I know who it is." She tossed her curls. "It's Otto's mother." But both tone and glance lacked conviction. The commodore left them.

Meantime the mate was amusing his half of the company.

"How much wood," he was repeating. "I as't that myself once 'pon a time. D'dy'ever hear the answer? They tell the yarn on lots o' loons but I 'uz the real one 'n' I got the answer f'm Gid Hayle aboard the old *Admiral.*"

The names caught Ramsey's ear and drew her gaze. "That *Admiral,*" continued the mate, "could eat wood like a harrikin. Says Hayle to me: 'Well, that depends on yo' boat 'n' yo' wood. With the right boat 'n' the right wood – oak, ash, hickory – y'ought to burn f'm sixty to sevemty cord' a day. But ef yo' feed'n' this boat cottonwood, why, yo' simply shovel- lin' shavin's into hell.' "

Ramsey looked sad. Weary of contrasts unflattering to her men-folks, she glanced from the refined actor to the elegant old commodore, blushed to the player's wife and accepted her embracing arm. "Yass," pursued the mate, "s'e jest so: 'Yo' simply shovellin' shavin's ' "

It was not Hugh's motion that cut him short but Ramsey's voice as with a flash she said: "Go on. I don't care! If pop-a said it it's so!"

A raindrop wet her cheek. From the pilot-house Ned, as he pulled the wheel over to chase the hardpressed *Antelope* westward into Bunch's Cut-off, warn- ingly drawled that they were about to run into a shower. At his side Watson's cub was letting down the storm board. A blue-black cloud overhanging the green head of the cut-off had suddenly widened across all that quarter and turned leaden gray. A writhing wind struck the boat fairly in front. The waters ruffled, flattened, and seemed to run faster. On an island close abeam thousands of young cottonwoods, a mantle of unbroken verdure, bent low, paled, reeled, darkened, and whipped. Dead ahead, a flash of lightning dropped from zenith to sky-line, stood blindingly quivering, and scarcely had vanished when the thunder cracked to split the ear.

"Scoot, ladies," said the mate, "or in three shakes you'll be as wet as the river !" A single glance up the stream – though Ramsey must needs take a double one – showed the rain coming, so near and so dense that not a sign of the *Antelope* was visible. The company fled, some to a larboard stair, some to a starboard. Hugh and Ramsey suddenly missed the Gilmores, the Gilmores missed them, each pair turned to find the other, the lashing rain leaped down upon them as if they were all it had come for, and with words lost in a second thunder-clap the mate threw open the captain's room, pressed them in, and began to dry them with a whisk-broom. The captain, he said, was below. "Off watch didn't mean off watch to John Courteney."

"Nor to Gideon Hayle," prompted Ramsey, andwhile he ha-haed a cordial assent she asked: "Whereabouts below is he – Captain Courteney?" But the mate had turned away and she asked Hugh: "Where's your father? What's he doing?" Her thought was still on the unmentionable new case.

"I'll tell you," said Hugh in the low voice she liked so well. "Will you look at the river with me?"

He felt her responsive nod and smile even after they had moved to the front window farthest from their three seniors and stood gazing out into the beautiful tempest. Both wind and downpour had somewhat slackened their fury. A bit nearer than before and more to starboard they could faintly make out the *Antelope,* so white that it seemed as if she had gone down and her ghost come up wrapped and whipped in sheets of rain.

"You don't ask me about your mother," said Hugh.

21

SECTION 21

XXXVI

CAPTAIN'S ROOM

"An! – when you've been all this time with us!"

"No, once I was away, a good while."

"That's so! And while you was away – were away – '" In lively undertone Ramsey ran on to tell of Mrs. Gilmore's having in Hugh's absence called in her maid Harriet to show the young lady from Napoleon how to do a bit of stage business without a hint of the stage. At the tale's end the pair glanced round from the nearing *Antelope* to the Gilmores and back again. "Harriet's talented. You wouldn't think she could be talented. And isn't she handsome!"

"I've yet to see her face," said Hugh abstractedly.

"That's so, too! When she heard you coming back that time, she ran like a kildee." The narrator checked a laugh. "How's mom-a? Oh, she's well or you'd have told me. I just can't imagine mom-a any way but well." But again the tone betrayed incertitude.

"Yes, she's well," said the youth. " So is my father."

"Where is he?"

Hugh's queer solemnity deepened. "He's uown in a stateroom with your brothers. The senator and the general have just joined them."

What a freshet of grave information! Ramsey laughed straight at him. "You talk like a trance medium."

"Not at all."

"You do! I heard one once. You're in a trance now."

"Not at all."

" You are ! Y'always are." When Hugh laughed, her laugh redoubled. The mate and the players, though busy talking, took time to smile; the mate winked an eye. Suddenly Ramsey sobered. "Is Basile in hot water again? Tell me quick."

"Tell me first," said Hugh, "why his two broth- ji

"Are so wild? Because pop-a won't allow mom-a to hold them in. Pop-a says: 'Oh, let 'em sow their wild oats early, like me; so deep they'll never come up.' Oh, my! they're up now."

"I wasn't going to ask that."

"Well, I can't tell if you don't ask."

"Why do they keep themselves so apart from you?"

"Me? Oh, they just can't stand me! – nor even mom-a."

"That's bad, for all of us."

"All of – who? Oh! ... Humph! ... Oh, but it's worse for Basile! He goes with them till he's sick of 'ernhen tries mom-a and me till he's just as sick of – of me – and himself – and then strays off to whoever he can pick up with!"

"This time," said Hugh, "he's been picked up." "Oh, *now* what's happened?"

"He sickened of those boys and girls he was selling tickets with and to drown yesterday's recollections he took a hand at cards with two strangers."

Ramsey caught her breath but then laughed joyously. "He couldn't! He had no money !"

"Except from his sale of tickets."

" Oh!" Her tears started. " Oh, where was mammy Joy?"

"Nursing the sick."

"The new – ?" She barely escaped breaking her word. "Oh," she moaned, " he didn't use *that* money? "

"He lost it. He was wild to play on and recover it, and his brothers were as eager to have him do it."

"Why, *they* couldn't help him. They tried, yesterday, to borrow from mom-a Wait." The last

word came softly. The Gilmores and the mate drew near to see the *Antelope* overtaken. There she loomed, out on the starboard bow, shrouded in the swirling rain. How unlike the earlier passing, down below Natchez! No touching of guards, no hail by sign or sound. "Like ladies under two umbrelTs!" laughed Ramsey to the actor's wife.

Now squarely abreast, stem and stem, wheel and wheel, the two crafts seemed to stand motionless with the tempest rushing aft between them. Then fathom after fathom the *Antelope* fell behind, the mate and the Gilmores moved away, Ramsey softly bade Hugh "go on," and his first utterance drew her liveliest look.

"There's another thing makes your brothers wild," he said, "which they're not to blame for."

"What's that?"

"Our starving plantation life," said Hugh, speaking low.

"Why, they call it the only life for a gentleman!"

"That's because they're so starved, so marooned."

"It's so tasteless without high seasoning, Basile says," said Ramsey. She meditated. "Basile loves to eat."

Said Hugh, "It's a life I don't want you to live," and for an age of seconds they looked into each other's eyes.

Then Ramsey – not drooping a lash – "I love the river."

"For keeps?"

She nodded, and still they looked. At length said Hugh:

"I tried hard to make friends with the twins, but "

"They wouldn't. I know. Mr. Watson told Mrs. Gilmore."

"Yet a while ago, on the strength of it, they sent for me, to ask me to ask my father to indorse their note."

Ramsey gasped: "You declined, of course?"

"Yes, but I told those other two passengers if they cast another card with any of your brothers they'd go ashore, themselves, as quick as the boat could land."

Ramsey turned and gazed out on the subsidingstorm. "Why are the senator and the general down there?"

"For quite another matter."

"Weapons. I know. Mr. Watson told Mrs. Gil- more. I thought that was settled."

"It is."

"Then why is your father there?"

"To get the twins away from the senator and the general, and their brother away from them and back to his "

"Sister!" softly laughed Ramsey. "Oh, not to mom-a! just to me! I'll go – " She started, but Hugh said:

"To you, yes, when my father has put him in a way to cover his loss without telling your mother."

Their eyes met again. Hers were bright and wet with accusal. "Is that *your* proposition?"

"Yes, and my father's too."

She whipped round and gazed out again over the tawny waters. To gaze out beside her he came so near that they almost touched. The shores were once more a clear picture, greener than ever and unvexed by the wind. The rain was slight and fine. The boat was swinging northward toward a small blue rift in the gray. At the room's farther door the mate was leaving the Gilmores for the forecastle.

Without a stir she asked: "Why don't *you* bring Basile?"

" I must stay with our friends here."

The surprised girl glanced across at the players. Side by side they also were gazing out and speaking low. "I'd like to know why with them."

"And I must tell you."

She faintly tossed, gazing out again: "Why 'must'? "

"Because to you I *can* – tell things."

"Haven't you told your father yet – about – Phyllis? Humph! – had to practise on me first."

"Yes. But there's a better reason – for everything I've ever told you."

She slowly faced him, and he added: "I want your help."

"For what? Not the Gilmores?"

"Yes, for them too now. They're in real danger."

"Fr' – from what? Not – not from – my brothers?"

"The twins, yes, and the general, John the Baptist, and a dozen more. They've guessed it out that the Gilmores "

"Are – So have I! A, b, ab "

Hugh was mute. She glanced round at the players' backs and then again at him, asking with soft abruptness:

"Where's the bishop? With mom-a yet?"

Hugh kept silence. "No, you know he's not," she answered for him. In her steady eyes he could see, growing every moment, a new sense of the fearful plight of things and of her relation to them. Hcf young bosom rose and fell, and when her lips parted to speak again their corners twitched. "He – he's the new case! I will mention it! I've a good right. Why shouldn't I?"

" Only that he didn't want you to know. He wanted you – us – all, without knowing, to go right on with the programme. We must. Even now you will, won't you?"

She could only nod. Just then Mrs. Gilmore's maid, in a long burnoose, with umbrellas and wraps, rose into sight close below, on a stair from the passenger-guards, spread one of her umbrellas and looked eagerly about for her mistress. One glance went up to Ramsey, who beckoned through the glass, but the maid gave no sign of seeing her. The slight rain had momentarily freshened, and she was so muffled to the eyes in the light veil which was always on her head or shoulders in pretty Spanish fashion that when she started forward round the skylights for the other side of the roof Ramsey laughed to Hugh:

"Why, I know it's Harriet by her veil, don't you?"

"I know only the veil. I saw it come aboard."

"The veil of mystery I" she playfully murmured, began to hum a tune and bit her lip on noticing that it was "Gideon's Band." "Don't you think I might omit that to-night?"

"No, it's the best thing you do."

"Humph ! – mighty poor reason – Aha! I knew it was Harriet."

The Gilmores were beckoning out their window. The actor opened the door on that side and the maid came warily in. Briefly and in hurried apology under her breath while dealing out her burdens she told of the impatience of those below to resume the rehearsal

"Stop! . . . Slop! the safest place for you on this boat now is right where you are standing – Phyllis "

and of their having driven her to this errand the moment they could. Mrs. Gilmore handed Hugh a shawl for Ramsey and an umbrella for himself, her husband laid a mantle on her shoulders, and the maid reopened the door he had shut; but Hugh called from the one opposite that it was the better way and the players started for it. The younger pair gave them precedence, a breeze swept through, the maid reshut her door,

Hugh, holding his, bade her follow her mistress, she sprang to obey and the "veil of mystery," which caught in the closed door, was stripped from her like a sail from a wreck.

Instantly she crouched and with the swiftness of a wild creature flashed round and snatched open the door by which she had entered; but a form pressed between her and the opening and when she threw up her face she was looking close into the astounded eyes of Hugh Courteney. Her frame recoiled but not her eyes; his own held them. Without turning he shut the door at his back as Ramsey closed the one opposite, and still holding the maid servant's gaze, he followed her slow retreat, and in that droll depth of voice which earlier had been Ramsey's keenest amusement said to the eyes so near his own:

"Stop! . . . Stop! the safest place for you on this boat now is right where you are standing – Phyllis." XXXVII

BASILE USES A CANE

There was a gorgeous sunset that day. Many were on the uppermost decks to see or show it, amid a lively social confusion dull to Hugh but delightful to Ramsey. In fact, Hugh had begun to want her and the hurricane-deck to himself.

The actor and his wife were there. And there, indifferent to sunsets but as hungry as ever for company, was Basile. Dinner, at midday, had dissolved the group which the twins had for a time held together. The captain had squared Basile with the ticket treasurer and by some adroitness of Ramsey and Mrs. Gilmore the restless boy had been won from his brothers and given a hand at euchre with the actor, the senator, and a picturesque Kentuckian, late of California, "back East" by way of the Isthmus and about to return by the Plains.

Another of this hurricane-roof assemblage was a young gentleman whom Ramsey told Basile it was not a bit nice to speak of as Watson's cub. And there were all the amateur players, eager for the evening's performance; and there, too, the senator, the general, John the Baptist, and others with whom Ramsey had not made better acquaintance only for lack of moments! One of these was the Californian. Think of it! A man whose shirt-pin was a gold nugget of his own digging, yet a man so modest as to play euchre with Basile, and who stood thus far utterly uncate- chised save by John the Baptist. Oh, time, time! A history of this voyage must and should be written with large room given to these last ten hours: "Chronicles of a Busy Life," by "A Young Lady of Natchez."

Captain Courteney stood near the bell. Watson was up at the wheel. His cub – whose attentions to Basile, like the Californian's, only Ramsey could not fathom – told her this was the second dog-watch. He was telling her everything he knew. She was asking him everything he knew not. Indeed, among all there was great giving and getting of information on matters alow and aloft. There was, too, frequent praise of the commodore, the doctor, the priest, the sisters of charity, Madame Hayle – all those heroic ones on the immigrant deck, where the pestilence was making awful headway. But there was so perfect a silence as to the bishop that it was manifest that every one knew about him but was too discreet to tell.

Matters beyond the boat, too, far and near, were much discussed, though some actually saw the sunset they were all there to see. Nowhere within five hundred

miles the compass round, the actor said, was there a town of ten thousand souls, if of
five thousand. Nowhere within a hundred miles was there a town population of five
hundred. Since the morning thunder- shower the *Votaress* had come ninety miles, yet
thegreat Yazoo Delta was still ahead, abeam, astern, on the river's Mississippi side.
Some one told two or three, who told four or five, it was a hundred and seventy-five
miles long by an average of sixty wide, and covered seven thousand square miles.
From zenith to farthest east the clouds that Overhung it were pink and ashes-of-roses
in a sea of blue. The entire west was one splendor of crimson and saffron, scarlet
and gold, with intervals of black and green. Even the turbid river between was an
unbroken rosy glow. The vast wooded swamps over on that shore were in Arkansas.
Louisiana had been left behind in that vivid moment when Ramsey and Hugh were
making their discovery of "Harriet" and when Hugh, we may here add, was handing
back her " veil of mystery."

"When I saw you do that," Ramsey had later said to him, "I knew she was safe
– and she knew she was!" The laughing girl's mind was brimful yet of the amazing
incident, at every pause in her talk, which was now with this one, now with that, and
often with the cub.

It was interesting to note the masterful-careless air with which Watson's apprentice
more than once endeavored to make it clear to Hugh, concerning this daughter of
Gideon, that, whereas the mud clerk, at his desk below, was utterly love-bemired, his,
the cub's, liking for her was solely for her countless questions, of which he said that
"you never could tell where the next one would hit." No singed moth he! To prove it
he offered Hugh a very blase query: "What do women ever do with all the answers
we men give 'em, hey?"

Hugh could not tell him. Yet to Hugh the riddle was at least as old as his acquaintance with Ramsey. He pondered it as he and Mrs. Gilmore conversed in undertone
while gazing on the wonderful changes of the sky, and while Ramsey, near by, visibly
studied the exhorter, whom she was cross-examining together with the actor on the
lore of the river as they had known it in the days before steam. For she had actually
got those two antipodes face to face again in a sort of truce-rampant like that of the
lion and the unicorn on the *Votaress's* very thick plates and massive coffee- cups. She
was not like most girls, Hugh thought. While their interrogations were generally for
the entertainment, not to say flattery, of their masculine informants, hers were the
outreachings of an eager mind free from self-concern and athirst for knowledge to
be stored, honey-like, for future use. Some women have butterfly minds, that merely
drink the social garden's nectar. Others are more like bees. The busy bee Ramsey,
Hugh felt assured, was by every instinct a honey gatherer.

But who, at a single cast, ever netted the whole truth as to any one? Even while he
so mused – at the same time doing his best to give Mrs. Gilmore his whole attention
– Ramsey, with her back turned yet vividly aware of him, willing – preferring –
that he should hear alone from that lady what she would later draw from him, and
ardently mindful of his word that he "wanted her help," was not merely gathering facts
regarding her beloved river but was also deep in diplomacy, endeavoring with all her
youthful arts, such as they were, to help him.

Her manoeuvres were fairly good. To her it seemed as though this spirit of strife so electrically pervading the *Votaress* might yet be tranquillized through a war of wits exclusively and she was using her own with the tactical nimbleness of the feminine mind. She knew the twins were down on the boiler deck again, one faint, yet both pursuing, egged on by him of the stallion's eye and him of the eagle's, and all the more socially and dangerously active because, by strict orders to every one, cut off from the gaming-table and the bar. She could not do a hundred things at once – though she could do six or seven – and it was well to grapple this one task first. Thus she kept Hugh free to confer with the player's wife as to "Harriet."

Her husband, the wife told Hugh, had drawn "Harriet " from the water just as Dan Hayle sank, and husband and wife had concealed her on their flatboat, unable to resist her wild appeal not to be given back into slavery.

"We didn't dream she'd done anything wrong; she didn't tell us that for years. Players, Mr. Hugh, don't meddle much in politics and we'd never thought whether we were for slavery or against it until there was the whole awful question sprung on us in an instant."

"So you took her ?"

" For my maid, yes – on wages, of course – down to New Orleans – we were bound there – and kept her when we went North and ever since."

"And she's always been ?"

"Well-behaved, faithful, kind, ana wise. That one terrible deed, which she says you know all about "

"I do."

"It seemed to change the very foundations of her character, to convert her soul."

"Yes," said Hugh, as if speaking from experience.

"Yet she kept her high spirit. She would never put on a disguise. And really that was safest since she wasn't being looked for by any one. 'I'm no advertised runaway,' she said. Still she's never been foolhardy. She'd never have come – we'd never have brought her – aboard this boat could we have foreseen the mishap to her captain which decided you and your father and grandfather to come on her."

So ran the story hurriedly, but before it had got thus far Hugh's attention, in spite of him, was divided. It was wise, we have implied, for Ramsey to take the exhorter while he was in a manageable humor. He had come to the roof with an improved regard, got by his fall in the cabin, for the " Tiscopalian play-actoh," and with brute shrewdness was glad to make an outward show of good-will to Gilmore, and accepted with avidity every pretty advance of Gid Hayle's "bodacious brick-top gal." Hugh could hear him answering Ramsey's inquiries regarding various pieces of river seen or unseen during the day.

"Spanish-moss Ben'? Why, they calls it that by reason 'at when we-all used to come down the riveh in flatboats, that's whah we al'ays fus' see the moss aswingin' f ' om the trees. Yass, sawt o' like scalps f'om wigwam poles. An' that ho'pe us to know whah'- bouts we 'uz at. We knowed we 'uz at Spanish-moss Ben'. Didn' we, Mr. play-actoh?"

The actor would have said yes, but the fountain of information flowed straight on: "Yass, same as at Islan' Ten – aw Twenty – aw any numbeh, we knowed by count we

'uz that many islan's f'om whah the Ohio comes in. Ef that wah the tenth islan' we'd
seed then we knowed that 'uz Islan' Ten aw whaheveh it wah, whetheh it wah a' islan'
yit aw b'en j'inded on to the main sho' sence it got its numbeh."

They were rounding Cypress Bend and Ramsey had asked another question. "Was
this where you first used to see cypress woods?"

"Thundeh, no! This gits h-its name by reason 'at they steals mo' millions o'
dollahs wuth o' cyp'ess timbeh f'om the gove'ment out'n this ben' than any otheh on
the whole Fatheh o' Watehs, es the Injins say. You know that, Mr. play-actoh. Lawd!
all the places ain't name' alike. 'Way back down yondeh whah we met the *Troubado'*
this mawnin' "

"Oh!" moaned Ramsey, "another o' pop-a's boats!"

"Yass, whilst you-all 'uz a-temptin' *Provi-dence* a-practisin' of a play ! Down
yondeh by Islan' Ninety, Seary's Islan' – which it ain't be'n a raal islan' these fawty
year' – you 'membeh, Mr. play-actoh, that ole san'-bah jess below it, full o' snags
as my granny's mouth, which befo' the earthquake it used to be a reg-lah death-trap
fo' flatboats? Well, *you* know h-itdidn' git its name by reason 'at anybody fo' the
fust time see thah Gen'al Hull's Lef ' Leg! No; an' likewise away up yondeh pas' the
Tennessee line, at Islan' Thutty-eight, whah the current's so full o' biles an' swells
an' snags an' sawyehs 'at they calls it the Devil's Elbow! Now, nobody ain't neveh
sho' 'nough see' the devil's identical elbow – in this life. No, suh, you'd ought to
know that ef anybody. Oh, no, Devil's Elbow, *Presi-dent'a* Islan', Paddy's Hen an'
Chickens, Devil's Race-groun', Devil's Bake-ov'm, they jess sahcaystic names." He
turned to Watson's cub, who with Basile had joined the trio, and was watching to get
in a word. "You know that."

The boy assented. "But did you see," he asked Ramsey, "the swarms of birds down
around Island Eighty-eight?"

"No!" interposed the exhorter, "she wah still a- temptin' *Provi-dence* in like manneh
as afo'said!"

Basile flashed resentment. "To put it politely," he retorted. But the actor and
Ramsey laughed.

"Oh, John the Babtis' wouldn't 'a' putt it no politer. I see' the birds. We 'uz a
meetin' the *Svuthe'n Cross* "

"Anoth' – !" Ramsey began to wail.

"Anotheh o' Gid Hayle's boats, yass, an' mighty nigh his bes'. Round'n' the foot
o' the islan' our whistle bellered howdy to her an' we riz one solid squab, mile o'
wings; an' when she bellered back, a-round'n' its head, she riz anotheh. Yit them
birds wa'n't a pinch naw a patchin' to what I hev see' thah; millions an' millions an'
millions *uv* millions o' swan, pelikin, san'-hill crane, geese "

"Birds of paradise?" asked Brick-top.

"They 'uz all birds o' paradise! the whole kit an' bilin'! by reason 'at this *wah*
a paradise them days, this-yeh whole 'Azoo Delta, which you, suh" – the speaker
turned to Gilmore with reviving spleen. By opposite stairs, larboard and starboard,
the twins, each carrying a sword-cane, as Hugh saw by the double gold band around
it a finger-length from the top, had just reached the roof, and the emboldened orator
began to make it plain that despite his "bodacious" criticism of their sister, overheard

by Julian, he had at least half righted himself with both brothers and was on their side in whatever was now afoot.

"Which you, suh," he repeated, "hev tuck on yo- seff to drap hints 'at it ain't a civilize' country! – by reason 'at it ain't cityfied! Like Paris, I s'pose, my Gawd! – with thah high-heel' shoes an' low-neck" dresses!"

His voice rose as the twins, Mrs. Gilmore, and Hugh came close. "Aw Babylon with thah jeweldry! – rings on thah fingehs an' bells on thah toes! Aw Sodom an' Gomorrah! – with thah staht-neckid statutes! Well, thaynk the Lawd, yo're plumb right, we ain't! Thaynk Gawd we *air* a 'new-bawn civilization' – as says you when you didn' suspicion I wah a-listenin' " – he fell into a mincing mimicry – "'a new-bawn civilization wkh all the chahm an' all the pity o' new-bawn things," says you to yo' wife – ef she air yo' wife."

The shock of the insult ran through the group and out to a dozen hearers beyond; to the captain and a knot of young people courting his conversation; to Watson, high above; to the stallion-eyed man and the eagle-eyed, who both had come up with the twins and were adhering to the senator the general, and the Kentuckian from California.

Gilmore paled with anger. Ramsey's merriment, which had begun at the beginning, ceased for a breath and then, to the loathing of the twins, came on worse as she found herself very erect in one of Mrs. Gilmore's gentle arms. The eyes of both the wife and the girl were on the actor and their every nerve was unstrung. Beseechingly he waved them away.

"Come," the wife said, though without moving, "come on."

"Oh, not a step!" laughed Ramsey. "They – they need us! We must help!" She had turned her frank gaze to Hugh in mingled wonder, exultancy, and distress. It seemed a dream that he should be the dull boy of yesterday. He was speaking to the exhorter and appeared not to have her in sight or mind, although, in fact, her untimely levity ran him through like a dart. His absurdly deep voice was rich with a note not of mere forbearance but of veritable comradery, yet his eyes, as they held the offender's, were as big and dangerous as she had ever seen her mighty father's and she laughed on for what laughter might be worth, the only help she could furnish.

"Not that you mean the slightest offence," he prompted.

The exhorter stiffened up. The nearer few packed close. Slender Basile was just at Hugh's left between him and the twins. The exhorter opened his mouth to reply but the words hung in his throat. To help them out he gave his head a disputative tilt, but Ba- sile's hysterical treble broke in:

"Say nol You slang-whanging lick-skillet, say no!"

The man gasped. The boy whirled to his convalescent brother. "Give me that cane!" He snatched it, whipped out its keen stiletto, and with all his light force smote the empty staff, left-handed, across the exhorter's cheek and ear, yelping: "Say no! Say it!"

"Nol" said the victim, but the word was equivocal and the boy beside himself. For Hugh had wrenched the staff from him and was holding the hand that gripped the stiletto, while the lad, with streaming tears, plunged, whined and gnashed at the backwoodsman.

"Let me go!" he begged. "I see their game! Let me kill their insulter of ladies!"

The game was not hard to see. At a better moment than this blunderer had chosen, some one was to provoke the actor to an assault which the twins would make their pretext for a combined attack on that political "suspect" and common pest, using the canes as canes until Hugh should be drawn into the fray, when the canes would become swords, dirks, the actor a secondary consideration, and the game – interesting. Hugh saw it but saw it with even less sense of peril than Ramsey, who stood her ground nervously clinging to her chaperon, yet flashing and tinkling with a mirth as of some reckless sport; a mirth mildly reflected by her companion and which, for Hugh, suddenly shed a ludicrous light on every one: on himself and Basile; on the pallid Lucian as he peevishly, vainly, ordered Ramsey off the scene; on Julian as he posed in a tragical disdain more theatrical than the actor's – who also saw the game; on the captain's dumfounded young folk; on the senator, the general, and the Californian, standing agaze, and on the two men with them, whose extra – eagle-eyed, stallion-eyed – solicitude told him they were the lenders of the canes. All at once, still holding the anguished Basile, he saw, and observed that the actor saw, the heaped-up nonsense of the affair. Ramsey's mood leaped to both of them like a flame, and they laughed together while Hugh exhorted the ex- horter: "Go below! For your life, go!"

The man cast a pleading look on the twins, but when Lucian granted him only a withering smile, and Julian with his cane in his folded arms said majestically, " Go, you hopeless ass," he went – with haste.

Out of the group by the bell John Courteney, apparently as unmoved as if all this were but common routine, answered Watson's silent look with his own while the pilot, taking his ear from a speaking-tube, grasped the bell-rope.

"Wood?" asked the captain.

22

SECTION 22

XXXVIII

THE CANE AGAIN

"partly, sir."

All marked the qualifying word though at the same time all witnessed the cross-fire of challenge and retort that flashed between the three brothers. Basile had dropped his weapon and ceased to struggle, yet still showed a mental torture, the same he had betrayed at the previous afternoon's worship, and in all hearts, even those of the senator's group, it brought back for him the same tender indulgence as before. Meanwhile Ramsey and the cub pilot had caught up the cane's two parts and laid them in the hands of the actor, who quietly resheathed them while Basile mocked the twins. "So that's the way Hayles," jeered the lad, "stand by a cat's-paw friend, is it?"

"Hayles," said Julian, "never settle difficulties before ladies."

The boy resisted again as his laughing sister half knelt to lay her arms about him soothingly. "Oh, these ladies won't mind," he tearfully sneered. " Come on! Here's your man, with the steel, and three behind each of you to see fair play!" A wave of the hand indicated Lucian and the canes' owners on one side, andhimself, the cub pilot, and Hugh on the other. The latter and the players, momentarily together, gave sudden attention, but again the humor of the situation saved it. The laugh was general;

the young people about the captain, whom his equanimity and Ramsey's and Mrs. Gilmore's stay had emboldened to linger, drew near; and the three groups became one.

The twins themselves might have made fair actors, though no one ever had dared suggest it. Julian scowled on Gilmore and Hugh and half drew the other cane from his folded arms, but then looked distantly away, while Lucian with an indolent air said to the younger brother:

"Babe! Hayles never line up on two sides."

To retort, the lad had to snatch Ramsey's fingers from his lips and so lost his chance, while under her breath she futilely implored him to desist.

"I'm not!" he wailed back at her. "I'm not ridiculous! You! you'll find judgment-day ridiculous, I don't doubt – oh, good Lordy! stop your eternal titter."

The great bell thundered and he recoiled. "There! wood! 'wood, partly.' And partly what else? d'you know? Another funeral." In spite of her fond restraints he cried out to the company: "With more to follow! The bishop "

But the sister's fingers were on his lips once more and while she half whispered, half laughed her tender chidings old Joy appeared, coming from the bishop's bedside. Ramsey turned a beseeching look to Hughbut the general had halted the nurse with a private question and now proclaimed:

"Th-the bishop's doing as well's could be exxx- pected."

"Expected!" cried Basile, "yes, when he's expected to die. And then it'll be my turn."

" It won't!" exclaimed Ramsey. " It sha'n't!" The boat was rounding to at a wood-yard and most of the company were glad to turn away to the shoreward scene. The boy dropped his head on the black woman's shoulder.

"Oh, mammy, if I was the bishop, or you, or even Ramsey, I wouldn't mind, for 1 could be ready to go. Oh, God! why can't I get religion?"

" Why, 'caze you done got it, sugah boy. You done got religion 'istiddy." Only the twins smiled. The captain stepped down to the roof's forward edge as the boat neared shore.

"And you're not going to get anything else," said Ramsey, snatching the lad's hands and finding them cold.

He moaned in unbelief: "What do you know about it? Oh, sis', if I could only die doing some fine thing! – in a fight! – or an explosion! – anything but a deathbed!"

"Law'! honey," interposed old Joy, "what you want to do fine things faw? You's done got religion. You on'y ain't got peace. Come to de bishop. Gawd won't let a religious enquireh kitch noth'n'. I 'uz tellin' de bishop 'bout missy an' you, bofe gitt'n' religion 'istiddy, an' he say, s'e: 'Go, fetch yo' young missy; fetch bofe.'"

"We'll go!" said Ramsey before the willing boy could reply, though from every side came protests.

For once Hugh and the twins were in accord. "You must not!" called Hugh. " You shall not!" said Julian.

She glanced from one to the other, tinkling her prettiest, and suddenly flushed. "We will!"

The twins sent Hugh a hot look which he paid back with a cold one, while Mrs. Gilmore said:

"I'll have to go with you, Ramsey."

For one breath the girl was taken aback, but then:

"Yes," she said, "to the door, that's all."

As they turned after Basile and Joy she added: " 'Twas I, you know, that got the bishop sick in the first place."

At the corner of the texas they glanced back but were reassured to see the cub-pilot disappearing on the nearest boiler-deck stair at the outer, depopulated side of the boat, the actor and Hugh moving toward it, and the twins holding the field and scowling after their opponents. Nevertheless, the moment the sister and wife passed from view Julian sturdily, Lucian feebly, pressed after Hugh and the player. The last witness was gone; now was their time.

"Mr. Courteney," said Julian. The other two looked back and paused.

Lucian spoke: "Mr. Gilmore, you have my cane, sir."

The player smiled. "Is this really your cane?"

With a ripping oath Julian put in: "What's that to you-, you damned Gypsy? Give him the stick!"

The player let go a stage laugh. Hugh took a step forward with a grave show of self-command hardly justified. "Mr. Hayle," he said, "you don't want to be another 'hopeless ass,' do you?"

"Gawd!" Julian rose to his toes and lifted and brought down his cane. But it never reached its mark. One stride of the actor, one outflash of arm and staff, foiled the blow, and when a second was turned on him the cane flew from Julian's hand he knew not how and dropped ten feet away.

He dared not leap after it but faced the skilled fencer, blazing defiance though fully expectant of the unsheathed dirk. But no dirk was unsheathed. Lu- cian, forgetting his feebleness, sprang for the cane and had dropped to one knee to snatch it up when Hugh set foot on it.

"No!" said Hugh. The convalescent straightened up, his brow dark with an anguish of chagrin, and before he could find speech Hugh was adding: "Wait. I'll give it to you." . "Don't!" cried Gilmore. "Keep it!"

"No," wearily said Hugh, glaring on the glaring twins, "we're all belittled enough now." He caught up the cane, drew its dagger, snapped it in half on the deck, and resheathed the stump. Then tossing the point into the river he said: "Here, Mr. Gilmore, swap."

With an actor's relish for a scene the actor swapped, and the convalescent wept with rage as Hugh, having treated the second cane like the first, tendered it to him.

"Don't take it!" cried his brother; "don't touch it!" And then to Gilmore: "Don't you hand me that one, either! Don't you dare!"

Yet thereupon the actor dared, saying: "But for – others – I'd trounce you with it like a schoolmaster."

The words were half drowned by Lucian, who snatched from Hugh the cane he tendered, answering the less crafty Julian, "Take it, you fool! take any odds they'll give!" and, while Julian complied, adding to Hugh: "Oh, you'll pay for this – along with the rest of it!"

"You'll pay for this first!" put in Julian, "and with your lives – the pair of you!"

Hugh and Gilmore merely turned again toward the stair, but a voice stopped them though addressed only to the twins.

"Did you say pair?" it inquired.

The boat was at the bank; her great wheels were still. The sun's last ray tipped the oak-leaf caps of her soaring chimneys. Once more from the cook-house rose the incense of coffee, hot rolls, and beefsteak, and from her myriad lamps soft yellow gleams fell upon the wind-rippled water and, out of view on the other side, into the tops of the dense willows. Over there the senator, the general, and the company that had gone with them looked down upon two movements at once. The funeral they could not help but see; theother was the wooding-up. The mud clerk had measured the corded pile, and the entire crew, falling upon it like ants, were scurrying back and forth, outward empty-handed, inward shoulder-laden, while those who stood heaping the loads on them sang as they heaped:

"Do you belong to de *Vot'ess'* ban'?"

"You don't mean just the pair, do you?" repeated Watson. He looked down loungingly from a side window of the pilot-house. "There's anyhow five on our side," he added. "I'm in that tea party."

Julian had caught breath to retort, when from a new direction a beckon checked him and at the nearest corner of the texas he beheld again Ramsey. Mrs. Gilmore was not with her, but at her back were the nurse and Basile. The boy wore such an air of terror that the player instantly pressed toward him.

Ramsey's beckon, however, was to Hugh. Her bright smile did not hide her mental pain, which drew him to her swiftly despite the twins' deepening frown. The two brothers heard the question she asked him when he was but half-way; perhaps she meant they should. "Can you call through Mr. Watson's speaking-tube to mom-a – and the commodore?"

"Certainly."

"Tell them" – tears suddenly belied her brightness – "to come up to the bishop, quick. I'm 'fraid – afraid "

A word or two more Hugh failed to hear, but even the twins, at their distance, read them on her lips:

"The bishop's going to die."

She sprang to Gilmore. His arm was about Basile; he was trying his pulse. The twins would have followed but in between came senator – general – all that company, moved by physical foreknowledge of an invitation whose drawing power outweighed whatever else land, water, sky, or man could offer. Suddenly it pealed in their midst:

"Ringading tingalingaty, ringadang ding "

The captain stayed by his chair. "Cast off," he said to the mate beneath, and to Watson above: "Back your starboard."

A jingle sounded below. The steam roared from one scape and widened aloft like a magic white tree – twice – thrice. "Stop her." It ceased. She swung. "Go ahead on both." Two white trees shot up together and trembling she went. Down in the quivering cabin, round the shining board, every one's spirit rose with the rising speed.

"Senator, 'twas I sent you them hot rolls, suh."

"Why, thank youl But – don't disfurnish yourself."

"General, them fried bananas "

"Th-th-thank you, sir, I have a suff-fficient plenty."

Only the seats of the Courteneys, the Gilmores, Ramsey, and Basile stood vacant.

23

SECTION 23

XXXIX
FORTITUDE

"COURAGE," the slender play was called. It is to be regretted that we cannot fully set it forth, for Gil- more was himself its author.

Also because, whatever it lacked, there was in it a lucky fitness for this occasion, since, conditions being what they were on the decks above and below, the one strong apology for giving it was the need of upholding the courage of its audience.

It was even a sort of kind rejoinder to the various ferments kept up by the truculent twins, the pusillanimous exhorter, and the terrified Basile. Its preachment might well have been less obvious, though lines, its author bade Hugh notice, never overbalanced action, never came till situation called them. It was to the effect, first, that courage is human character's prime essential, without which no lightness or goodness is stable or real; and, second, that as no virtue of character can be relied on where courage is poor, so neither can courage be trusted for right conduct when unmated to other virtues of character, the chiefest being fidelity – fidelity to truth and right, of course, since fidelity to evil is but a contradiction of terms. " From courage and fidelity," it was the part of one player at a tellingmoment to say, "springs the whole arch of character," and again, "These are the Adam and Eve of all the virtues." (Adam and Eve were decided to be quite mentionable. Mention was not impersonation.)

Naturally the Gilmores knew every line of the play.

"As perfectly," ventured the two young Napoleon- ites, " as John the Baptist knows the moral law, don't you?"

"Better, I infer," said Gilmore abstractedly. They were in the ladies' cabin, awaiting its preparation as a stage, behind the curtains that screened it from the gentlemen's cabin, the auditorium. His wife smiled for him.

"Even my Harriet," she said, "knows one or two parts. She's played Miss Ramsey's in emergencies."

Her half-dozen feminine hearers flinched. Yet one said, excusingly: "That's a servant's part, anyhow."

"And Harriet's her very size and shape," said another.

And another, drolly: "They're enough alike to be kin!"

"Harriet's free, isn't she?" asked the first.

"Yes," replied Mrs. Gilmore, without a blush, looking squarely at Hugh, who stood among them silent.

"You'd never notice she was a nigrah if you wa'n't told," said another, "or didn't see her with nigrahs."

But then said a youth, cousin to one of the girls: "Yet after all a nigrah she is."

"No such thing!" said his cousin. "After all that's what she isn't. Our own laws say she isn't."

" Well, I say she is. One drop of nigrah blood makes a nigrah – for me, law or no law."

"Well, that's monstrous – for me."

"Yes, your politics being what they are."

"My pol' – I'm as good a Southerner as you, any day!"

"All right, but I shan't play if that born servant is allowed to take any but a servant's part."

To Hugh a crisis seemed to impend, but he held off for the Gilmores, who seemed to be used to crises.

They had not thought of Harriet, they said, for any part but Miss Ramsey's. Miss Ramsey might find herself too distracted by – other things. Or, even if not, the doctor, or the captain, might think Harriet's contact less contaminating than Miss Ramsey's.

Their smile was not returned. Hugh gravely nodded but the rest shook their heads. Impossible! And suppose it were possible! they were not going to shun Miss Ramsey for refusing to shun "a sacred duty." By duty they meant the bishop, aware of his illness but not of his extremity, and none but Hugh and the Gil- mores knowing that only two doors from the bishop lay Basile, also stricken, and that Ramsey and the old nurse were with the boy. The young people fell into pairs confessing their contempt for the besetting peril. Vigil is wearisome and they were almost as weary of blind precautions as, secretly, were Hugh and others. The two Napoleonites "didn't believe doctors knew a bit more than other folks – if as much!" The two cousins so unimpeachably Southern were "convinced that contagion never comes by contact," and two or three said "the cholera was in the air, that's where it was, and whoever was going to get it was going to get it!" They all agreed that "if Miss Ramsey, because of the extra strain she was under, had lost her nerve "

" She has not," put in Hugh with a very solemn voice and solid look. The girls nudged elbows. "But," he added, to Mrs. Gilmore, "for the better comfort and safety of both sick and well we must let her off."

Must! Ahem! The amateurs lifted their brows. Of which was he sole owner, Miss Hayle or the boat? "Orders!" softly commented one tall youth.

"Yes," said Hugh, facing him with a gaze so formidable, yet to the rest so comical, that the nudgings multiplied.

"Miss Hayle's songs, however," Hugh began to add.

"Yes, how about the songs?" asked some one. "They're no servant's part and they're out before the curtain."

"She must sing them," replied Hugh. "They won't keep her long and they involve no contact."

"Right!" exclaimed one. "Good!" said another, and yet another. "Without them we might as well give up the whole business." From the curtains through which he had been peering the actor glanced back. "Those footlights are capital," he said to his wife, and then, for the joy of all: "We've got a full house!"

The wife looked, turned quickly, and murmured to him: "Hayle's twins in the front row."

"Yes," he said, absently again, "with war in their eyes. . . . Now, Mr. Hugh, if you'll send for Miss Hayle "

"Harriet's gone for her," replied his wife.

"Here I am," spoke Ramsey at the door of a stateroom appropriated as a passageway. And assuredly there she was; but by the magic of dress, through the trained cunning of Mrs. Gilmore's mind and "Harriet's" hand, and even more by the imprint of her new weight of experience, she was Ramsey transformed, grown beautiful. An added year was in her face. A chastened tenderness both lighted and shaded it, half veiling yet half reasserting its innocent hardihood. The astonished amateurs hailed her with a clapping of hands, in which, it pleased her deeply to notice, Hugh Courteney, staring, took no share. Beyond the curtain the unseen audience answered with a pounding of heels and canes in good-natured impatience. Gilmore hurriedly waved away all the lads but Hugh, and Mrs. Gilmore all the girls but Ramsey. To her she glided while Hugh and her husband conferred on some last point.

"Well, dear," she said, pressing her backward into the stateroom, "are you ready?"

"No, dear Mrs. Gilmore, please, no, I'm not."

" Ah, yes, you are. You'll go on from " – they passed out and entered the next room forward – "from here. And mark ! when you find nothing between you and the people but the footlights, and their glare blinds you, don't stand close over them trying to see, or they'll make you look scared and pale, and you're not scared the least bit, are you?"

"I don't know," laughed Ramsey, softly, through tears. "I never was, before; never had sense enough, mom-a says. But, oh, I know I'm ashamed. I'm that 'shamed that I wouldn't wonder if I'm scared too. Oh, dear Mrs. Gilmore, Basile's so sick! The doctors are doing all they can for him, and mom-a and mammy Joy are with him; but he's so tortured with pain, and with fright! And the bishop – he's pow'ful weak, as mammy Joy says. One of those sweet sisters – of charity – I got her up through the speaking-tube – oh, you know what I mean – and she's there now talking to him *so* beautifully! And down on the lower deck, freight deck, Madame Marburg's sick too, and her son and the priest and the other sister are with her and with the other sick ones – there's a dozen of them!" The last words were to Gilmore as he and Hugh appeared at the outer door.

The actor stepped inquiringly into the narrow room and began a warning whisper but Ramsey spoke on to wife and husband by turns: "And in the face of all that here we are – or here I am – about to do the silliest, most heartless thing in all my silly, heartless life. No, I'm not ready."

"Tsh-sh!" whispered the husband, with both hands up. "My dear young lady, this isn't you; you've caught this mood of a moment from your brother."

It was not his words, however, that startled Ramsey to silence; the audience was again stamping and pounding. Now she resumed: "Oh, I hear! Mrs. Gilmore, the trouble's not that home song nor the spring song nor the love-song; it's that silly thing you-all say I *must* sing if I get an encore – which I can't believe I'll get!"

"My dear, you'll get several. We've arranged that."

"Arr' – ! Why, I've only that one silly thing!"

"The fate of the whole show is in that one silly thing."

"Oh, it's not! It's in you two talented, professional, famous people!"

" Ah, maybe it ought to be, but it's not. That's the way of the stage, my dear. Your silly thing has plenty of verses. Sing only two at a time."

"A sort o' Hayle's twins," laughed the girl. Then despairingly she dropped to the edge of the berth. But Hugh had been pushing in past the players and as he reached her she sprang erect again.

"This is entirely my doing," he said to her. "These two good friends mustn't urge you to sing. They're in danger, you know; greater danger than they'll believe."

Gilmore broke in: "Now, Mr. Hugh, listen to me."

But Ramsey put out a hand. "No, *you* listen – to him," and Hugh went on:

"Should it come to be known by – certain ones "

"Certain twos," said Ramsey, "go on." "It would double, or treble, that danger."

"My dear boy – " began the actor again, but his wife restrained him, and Ramsey whispered at him in turn:

"Tsh-sh!" Then she prompted Hugh: "And so ?"

"So you must sing without any urging but mine."

Her lips parted in droll repudiation, but he went on.

"And you'll give the encore."

"Oh, when did you learn to talk? I – w-i-1-1 – n-o-t!"

Once more the actor tried to break in, but his wife eagerly whispered: "Let them alone! Let – them – alone!"

"Success hangs on it," persisted Hugh, "and success here means success all over the boat. It will mean their" (the Gilmores') "safety; while failure – Think of it, Miss Ramsey. . . . Don't you see?"

She stared an instant and then with a sign of distress and aversion gasped: "Go away! Go away!" and dropping to the berth cast her face into its pillow. With gentle speed Mrs. Gilmore pressed Hugh aside and took his place. The stamping and pounding, for a moment suspended, broke forth afresh. "Send him away!" cried Ramsey, her voice muffled by the pillow, one eye fitfully glancing from it, and one arm waving backward. "All advice rejected! Send him away! Send them both."

With such dignity as they could save, the two outcasts fled, meeting and turning back half the stage company while the actor's wife shut the door.

"Is she ill?" asked the gaping girls. "Is she ill?"

"Not at all," "No," said the actor and Hugh, right and left, the one complacent, the other "ironer" than ever. "She is, eh – she, eh "

Every head was lifted to hearken. The cabin's applause ceased abruptly for a second or two, or three. Then again there was a stillness broken only by the speeding of the boat; and then, like a perfume from some wilderness garden, came the untrained notes of a song, a maiden's song of her lost German home, and leaning elatedly from the reopened door Mrs. Gilmore loudly whispered:

"She'a on!" XL

RAMSEY AT THE FOOTLIGHTS

The actor stepped to his wife. " Will she do it all? " he inquired, and Hugh, who had started to join the audience by a short cross passage, lingered to hear.

"Heaven knows," laughed the lady, shutting herself out, yet keeping the door; "I too am banished." Her

glance drew Hugh nearer. " Miss Ramsey begs us, all three

" For her to beg is to command," said Gilmore playfully.

"Yes, and so I've promised for all three "

"Promised! What?"

Mrs. Gilmore whispered: "To pray for her."

The smiling actor and the unsmiling youth looked at each other. "Why, that's," said Gilmore, "entirely "

"Practicable," said Hugh. He moved on, and into the passage. Gilmore, following, stopped at its outer end. At the inner stood Hugh, waiting, in shadow and with downcast eyes, for the song to be done. WTiat unvoiced supplication, if any, may have been behind the lips of either was not for the other to know. Yet it was an hour of formidable besetments and we may pardon the actor if an actor's self-consciousness moved him to reflect that there were thousands of healthy men, some as raw as Hugh, some as ripe as himself, who, for the sake of a promise, a wife or a maiden, or even without them, standing thus, had prayed.

He tiptoed to the youth's side and together they leaned in enough to look down the dimmed cabin, over ranks of silhouetted heads, to the bright stage front and the singer. She was in the centre of its light and the last notes of her simple song called for so little effort that they only helped the eye to give itself wholly and instantly to the mere picture of her, slender, golden, magnified by this sudden outburst into blossom, and radiant with the tenderness of her words as a flower with morning dew. The next moment she was bowing and withdrawing, aglow with gratitude for an applause that came in volume as though for the finish of a chariot-race, and Hugh saw as plainly as the experienced actor, if not with as clear a recognition of Mrs. Gilmore's attiring skill, that the tribute was at least as much to the singer as to the song.

The same perception came to Ramsey in the stateroom to which she had returned and in which she stood alone, hearkening and trembling. She noiselessly laughed for joy to be, however unworthily, the daughter of Gideon Hayle, never doubting it was for his name, his blood, his likeness, she stood thus approved. The conviction gave her better heart for the task yet before her. She glided to the rear door, Cocked it, and dropped to her knees.

"Oh, Lord 'a' mercy!" she murmured. "Oh, Basile, my brother! And oh, mom-a, dear, brave mom-a!" She did not name her father, though his figure was central in her imagination, broad, overtowering, intrepid, imperious.

The applause persisted. Now it sank but at once it rose again, easy overflow of a popular mind glad of all unrestraint and always ready – as even she discerned – for the joy of exaggeration. She sprang up and moved toward it, her eyes sparkling responsively. Yet her tremor was piteous and in mute thought she said again, at high speed:

"My brother, oh, my brother! I'll be back in a minute. This ain't for my own silly self, you know, honey. It's for them that need it; for all the people, up stairs and down, and for – for the boat! – as any of her – owners – would do for any of our boats. You said you wished *you* could do some fine thing for somebody – in a fire – or explosion, and this is just as awful only not so sudden, and I'm doing this in your place, honey boy; yes, I am, this is just as if you did it yourself!"

The applause was still summoning her as she ended. A hand, probably Mrs. Gilmore's, had tried the locked door. From the lower deck leaked up the sad "peck, peck" of the carpenter driving his nails, and close outside the door sounded sharp footsteps and the mingled voices of the pilot's cub and the actor calling with suppressed vehemence to one of the pantrymen: "Here, boy! Here! Go below like a shot and tell'Chips' to stop that pounding this instant! He can saw if he must but he mustn't hammer!"

Then as if carried there by some force not her own she found herself again in the bewildering sheen of the footlights, smiling merrily to the hushed, half-seen assemblage, and suddenly aware of every throb of the *Votaress's* bosom, every fall of her winged feet, every tinkle of her cabin's candelabra, and, most vivid of all, horribly out of time with all, the still insistent "rap, tap, tap" of the carpenter's hammer.

At the same time, unconfessedly, the eager audience took note of quite another group of facts, emphasized by the appearance of Hugh in a back row of seats, by the presence of Hayle's twins in the dusk of the front row, with war even in the back of their heads, and by the illuminated form of the singer just drawing a last breath of preparation to exhale it in melody. Hardly in the gathering was there one who had not by this time learned the whole state of affairs between all Hayles, all Courteneys, and all those others whom its schemings, aggressions, discomfitures, tirades, and prophetic threats had entangled with them. Every one thought he knew precisely both Hugh's and Ramsey's varied relations to each and all those persons, his and her effects upon them, and his and her ludicrously dissimilar ways of getting those effects. They knew this warfare was still on and was here before them now. In every phase of it in which Ramsey had taken part she had come off victor and in every instance had done so by the sheer power of what she, with fair accuracy, called nonsense. So now they were ready to see her, at any juncture the twins or accident might spring, show the same method and win an even more lustrous triumph in keeping with her own metamorphosis. Nay, they were more than ready to lend a hand toward such an outcome. Like Watson, they had sentimentally matched Hugh and Ramsey, prospectively, in their desire, and saw that Such a union must sooner or later be, if it was not already, a paramount issue in the strife. In such expectancy sat the throng, keenly aware of the twins at their front and Hugh at their back, as Ramsey's indrawn breath began to return in song, its first notes as low as her voice could sink, its time slow, its verbal inflections those of the freight-deck negro:

"Do you belong toe Gideon's ban'?"

So far it got before it was drowned in a deluge of laughter and applause. She had made, as Gilmore said to his wife behind the curtain, a "ten-strike." Her hearers did not pause an instant to determine whether the utterance was wit or humor or pure inanity. It fitted their mood; fitted it better than the actor or Hugh had believed it could. To the company's notion it was good nonsense offsetting and overpowering an otherwise invincible bad nonsense and snatching from it all right of argument, sympathy, or judicial appeal; laughing it out of court, to remain out at least until the completion of this voyage should give this jury, these hearers, an honorable discharge. The shrewd
good sense of it, in their judgment, was the most fun
of all, and while in her heart Ramsey was gratefully
giving the credit of that to the actor and Hugh, the people naturally gave it to her and laughed and clapped
and pounded again on second thought.

Now abruptly they hushed and let her resume:

"Do you belong toe Gideon's ban'?
Here's my heart an' here's my han'.
Do you belong toe Gideon's ban'?
Fight'n faw yo' home !"

Again the audience broke in.

"Fighting for your home!" they laughed to one another as they clapped. Home was the catchword of the times. Jenny Lind was singing nightly:

"Midt Measures undt balacess "

and three fourths of all the songs not of the opera were of home and its ties. What the word might exactly signify in this case made little matter; on her lips, from her breast, it meant human kindness, maiden innocence, young love; meant courage, fidelity, the right, the true, the beautiful, the good; meant anything, everything, which she herself, shining there above the footlights like a star in the sunset, their darling of the hour, could be fancied to stand for; meant, anyhow, the twins' war-song turned into a peace-and-joy song.

"Tsh-sh-sh! let her go on!" And she went on: she,- Noah's ark, and the *Votaress*, all three, together:

"Den come de buck-ram and de

"What? what's that?" They leaned and whispered right and left. "New words! new words!"

"Den come de buck-ram and de ewe "

"Why – she must 'a' made those words, herself!" Not she. She knew no better than
to believe them the improvisations of the Gilmores.

"Den come de buck-ram and de ewe

De ole niroscenos and de gnu "

Pun ! a pun! a real pun!

"Do you belong toe Gideon's ban'?"

Yes, verily ! They clapped, ha-haed, leaned around one another to see the dark
upturned heads of the twins, and stole backward glances on the immovable features
of the captain's son. At his side sat the Cali- fornian just then gravely murmuring to
him, but he remaining as motionless as a Buddha. The refrain pressed on to its close,
and the applause redoubled, but stopped as she prepared for another verse.

"Nex' come de mule and den de quail "

Laughter! Mule and quail! royal pair of the cotton field, rightly thrice heralded!

"Nex' come de mule and den de quail,

Nex' come de mule and den de quail,

Nex' come de mule and den de quail,

De monkey-wrench and de wiggletail."

The senator clapped yea, the general thumped his cane. Half-a-dozen voices began
to chime with her, "Here's my heart and – " till Julian looked round, when they stopped
so short that the laugh swelled again and Julian resumed his seat. Only two or three
saw Hugh and the Californian softly pass out together.

"No, no, no!" cried several, but that was to Ramsey for trying to get away. "No,
you don't! Another verse! sing anoth' – Tsh-sh-sh!" . . . She sang:

"Den come de man-drake and de moose,

Den come de man-drake and de moose,

Den come de man-drake and de moose,

De hickory-pottamus and de goose.

Do you belong ? "

Belong? How could they help but belong? Was ever anything such fun? Not
itself, maybe, but she! And no more could Ramsey help belonging to them, though
thoughts of the texas and of the immigrant deck – where the carpenter's saw played
an interlude to her every verse – pierced her heart at each throb of her pulse and of
the boat's pulse and at every glimpse of the scowling twins, dimly visible to her just
beyond the footlights. Silence fell once more as she moved a step forward with a light
in her eyes, a life in her poise, that made her a pure joy, albeit an instinct warned her
that her tide was at the flood and she must make her exit on this wave. So with a light
toss as if to say, "Positively last appearance," she sang:

"Den d'rattlesnake and de antidote,

De rattlesnake and de antidote,

De rattlesnake and de antidote,

De rangitang and de billy-goat.

Do you belong ? "

The applause was as lively as ever and increased with each step of her bowing retreat.
Near the stateroom door, chancing to look across the cabin to the one opposite, she saw
within two or three of the amateurs clapping and the actor approvingly waving her off.

Then finding herself alone she threw open the rear door and was in Mrs. Gilmore's embrace. "How's Basile?" she demanded – "and the bishop – and Marburg's mother? All this time "

"My dear, you've sung only six minutes."

"It seems a week," she laughed. Hugh appeared in the outer door. She listened to the insistent applause. " I can't go back, Mrs. Gilmore. I don't need to, do I?"

"No. . . . Let go of me, dear!" The applause ceased. The curtain was about to "rise." The servant who was to draw the near half of it reached in from the cabin and closed their door. " No, dear, you won't sing again till after this act, anyhow."

"Oh, not even then! I just must stay with Basile. I've sung all the verses but one, you know."

"We've got some more new ones," replied the lady, smiling to Hugh, who was moving to let her pass out.

"Got them!" cried the girl. She turned to Hugh. "They've made them! Didn't you know Mr. and Mrs. Gilmore made every line I've sung? Oh, Mr. Hugh, what can't genius do?"

Hugh solemnly dissented. "Those lines," he said, "could never have been made by mere genius!"

She stared at him a moment and then at Mrs. Gil- more, who was escaping by the outer door and who replied: "My dear, every line made for you has been made by Mr. Hugh." She vanished while the two stood dumbly face to face, but on second thought was back again just in time to see and hear Ramsey say, still gazing:

"Well, of – all – things! You! That frightful rubbish! You've got to sing the rest, yourself! Oh, Mrs. Gilmore, make him do it! It'll tickle 'em all to death – to hear *him* sing Gideon's Band! – and I can stay with Basile."

"Preposterous!" rumbled Hugh, and again, "preposterous!"

"Why – happy thought!" said Mrs. Gilmore. "Why, the very thing, Mr. Hugh, the very thing! Come. First we'll take this young lady up-stairs – " As they started the Californian appeared, laying a caressing hand on Hugh.

24

SECTION 24

XLI

QUITS

"WAIT here," slowly said Hugh in response to the gold-hunter's touch. "I'll – see you presently."

The modest adventurer waved assent, yet looked so disappointed that Mrs. Gilmore, moving to take his arm, asked:

"Can't Mr. So-and-so go with us?"

Oh, kind, quick wit! Three is a crowd, four is only twice two!

"Certainly," said Hugh, and to Ramsey added: "We'd better lead the way."

As they led she softly inquired: "Does he want to know something about the twins?"

What arrows were her questions, and how straight they struck home! Yet with that low voice for their bowstring they gave him comfort. Her forays into his confidence not only relieved the loneliness of his too secretive mind but often, as now, involved a sweet yielding of her confidence to him. Yet now a straight answer was quite impossible.

"He wants to know something about you," was the reply.

She let the palpable evasion pass. On the hurricane roof there was a new sight. The breeze was astern andmoved so evenly with the boat as to enfold her in a calm.

Looking up for the stars, one saw only the giant chimneys towering straight into the darkness and sending their smoke as straight and as far again beyond, spangled with two firefly swarms of sparks that fell at last in a perpetual, noiseless shower.

"Why do we go this way?" she asked, meaning forward around the skylight roof instead of across it.

"Because this way's longer."

"Humph!" was the soft response. Presently she added, "We get more fresh air this way," and called back to their two followers: "This is to avoid the sparks."

"Um-hmm!" thought kind Mrs. Gilmore, and, "Oh, ho!" mueed the Californian, not quite so unselfishly.

Around in front of the bell both youth and maiden observed how palely the derrick posts loomed against the spectral chimneys and their smoke, and silently recalled their first meeting, just here, in the long ago of two days earlier. The captain's chair was occupied.

"Well, father," said Hugh.

"Good evening," twittered Ramsey.

"Good evening, Miss Ramsey. Be back this way, Hugh?"

"In a moment, sir." They passed on. Ramsey looked behind at the Californian.

" What does he want to know about me? " she asked.

"He says," said Hugh, "he's nursed this sickness at sea and at Panama and hasn't the slightest fear of it."

"Humph! . . . That's not about me."

"Yes, it – was. He's taken a great fancy "

"To Basile."

"To several of us, including Basile."

"Yes, because he and Basile played cards together."

"Not entirely for that," said Hugh, looking at her so squarely that she had to smooth back her curls. "But he'd like to help take care of him if you – and your mother, of course – are willing."

"Oh, how good – and brave ! And he wants to ask me?"

"No, he's too bashful. I'm asking for him."

"Too – !" Ramsey pondered. They'stepped more slowly. The other pair turned back; the play demanded Mrs. Gilmore. The sick-room door was so near that Ramsey knew her mother was inside it, by her shadow on its glass. Suddenly, just as Hugh was about to say she need not hurry in – whereupon she would have vanished like a light blown out – she faced him. "D'you ever suffer from bashfulness – diffidence?"

He answered on a droll, deep note: "All its horrors.'

She looked him over. He barely smiled.

"You never show it," she said.

"No." To the fanciful girl the monosyllable came like one toll from a low tower. She laughed.

"Basile says there's another thing you suffer from."

" 'Suffer'? From what do I 'suffer'? "

"From everybody else on the boat having a better chance to do things – big things – than you have."

He smiled again. "If I did, no one should know it; least of all you."

She ignored the last clause. "Aha! I said so. I told him – and mammy Joy told him – there's nothing bigger than to wait your turn and *then take it.* And there ain't – there isn't, is there? "

"Well – even that can be small. Nothing a man is big enough for looks big to him."

"Hoh! – after he's done it," laughed Ramsey.

"True – " said Hugh reflectively, "or suffered it," and both of them began to see that we can rarely lift more than our one corner of the whole truth at a time. "In your way," he added, still musing, "you're larger than I."

"Oh, I'm no – such – thing!" Her speech was soft, yet she looked up warily to Watson's pilot-house window, but Watson too thoroughly approved to be looking down. "I'm not half or third or quarter as large." She eagerly turned his attention up the river. Visible only by the lights of her cabin and the sparks from her unseen chimneys, a boat was coming round the next bend. As she entered the reach and breasted the breeze which so calmly accompanied the *Votaress,* her two spangled plumes of smoke swept straight astern as if two comets raced with her, or

"The Golden Locks of Berenice," whispered Ramsey.

"Come," Hugh softly responded. The *Votaress* had signalled the usual passage to starboard and unless they went forward the shining spectacle would at once be lost. As they gained the front of the texas the distant craft, happening to open a fire-door, cast a long fan of red light ahead of her, suddenly showingevery detail of her white forecastle, illumining her pathway on the yellow waters and revealing in their daylight green the willows of an island close beyond. Then the furnace was shut and again her fair outlines were left to the imagination, except for the prismatic twinkle and glow of her cabin lights.

"That was like you when you laugh," murmured Hugh, and before she could parry she was smitten again by an innocent random shot from the darkness round the bell.

"Do you make her out, Mr. Watson?" asked Hugh's father, and she flinched as if Watson were peering down on her.

"Yes, sir," said the pilot, "she's Hayle's *Wild Girl.*"

Not waiting to hear that she was known by her "front skylights standin' so fur aft of her chimbleys," Ramsey wheeled to fly. But instantly she recovered and went with severe decorum, saying quiet nothings to Hugh as he followed, until at the sick-room door again she turned.

" I'm willing he should help us, Mr. Hugh, if mom-a and Basile are. I'll send him word by mammy Joy. Mr. Hugh – what is it he wants to know about the twins?"

Hugh was taken aback. "Why, it's nothing – now. It was as pure nonsense as those verses. Ask him. He can tell if he chooses; I can't." There was a pause. Her eyes gave him lively attention, but one ear was bent to the door.

"I hope Basile is better," he added.

"I'm sure he is; he's so much quieter." She felt a stir of conscience, loitering thus, yet – "Mr. Hugh, do you think diffidence is the same as modesty?"

" Certainly not."

"I'm – " She meditated . . . "I'm glad of that
I never was diffident a moment in my life."

"You never had need to be," said Hugh very quietly.

"They go together, don't they, diffidence and modesty?"

"Not as often as diffidence and conceitedness."

"Why, Mr. Hugh!"

"One thing that makes me so silent is my conceit."

"Oh, you! you're not conceited at all! You're modest! You little know how great you are! You're a wonder!" Her tone was candor itself till maiden craft added, while she tinkled her softest and keenest: "You're a poet!"

With a gay wave, which dismissed him so easily that she resented his going, she turned, stepped warily into the cramped room, and stood transfixed with remorse for her tardiness and appalled and heart-wrung. The foot of the berth was by the door. There old Joy stood silently weeping. At its head knelt her mother in prayer and on it lay her playmate brother peacefully gasping out his life. A flash of retrospection told her he must have had the malady long before he had confessed it and that something – something earlier than her singing – yes, and later – not twins nor Gil- mores nor river – oh, something, what was it? – had kept her – these two long, long days – blind.

"Ah, you! *you!*" she dumbly cried, all at once aflame . with the Hayle gift for invective. "You stone image! 'To help you,' indeed! *You!* As if you – as if I – I won't, you born tyrant! ' Help you' – against my own kin! I will not – ever again. We're *quits* for good and all." XLII

-AGAINST KIN

"ramset," said the boy, his voice gone to a shred, "you're good – to come back in – in time. Ain't you going – to laugh? It'd be all right. Oh, sis'" – the sunken eyes lighted up – "it's come to me, sissy, it's come. I've got religion, Ramsey. I'm going straight to the arms of Jesus. Sissy dear, I wish" – he waited for strength – "I could see the – twins – just a minute or two "

"Why, you shall, honey. I'll go bring 'em."

"Wish you would – and Hugh Courteney. It's the last "

"Honey boy, th'ain't room for so many at once. And it ain't your last anything; you' going to get well."

His eyes closed, his brows knit. The tearful mother rose and looked at her. The glance was kind, yet remorse tore the girl's heart again. "Go," said her mother. "Joy, she'll go with you. Bring the three."

"My last" – the boy whispered on – "last chance – to do some' – something worthy of" – he faintly smiled to his mother – "of Gideon's Band."

The door opened and closed and the two were alone. At his sign she knelt, took his clammy hand, and bentclose that he might flutter out his hurried words with least effort.

"She sang it finely!" he whispered. "She'd 'a' known we heard it if she'd 'a' thought. Wish you'd sing a verse of it. It's a hymn, you know – or was. The chorus is – yet. Anyhow, it's our song. Oh, I'd like to live on and be a real true Hayle – a Gideon! I hope – hope Hugh Courteney'll – live. Just think! he was on the *Quakeress* when Uncle Dan – . . . He's going to do big things some day. Mother – want to tell you something." She bent closer. He whispered on:

"I wish Hugh Courteney'd live and – marry sis'."

His eyes reclosed and the mother drew back, but he whispered on with lids unlifted:
" Sing – a verse or two – or just the chorus, won't you?"

As softly as to an infant fallen asleep she sang, in her Creole accent, with eyes streaming:

"Do you billong to Gideon' ban'?

Yere's my 'eart an' yere's my 'an'."

Outside, meantime, before old Joy had quite left the closed door, another, the second aft of it, opened and the texas tender stepped out. A fellow servant within shut it, and he started for a near-by stair, but checked up, amazed, to let Ramsey hasten on for the same point.

But Ramsey halted. " How's the bishop? " she asked him.

" Good Lawd!" he gasped, and then tittered at himself. " I ax yo' pahdon, miss, I *neveh* know de Hayles twins 'uz *double* twins, male 'n' female. You ax me ?"

"The bishop; how is he now?"

"Well, Miss Hayles – you is Miss Hayles, ain't you? Yit, my Lawd! miss, ain't I dess now see you down in de cabin a-playin' in de play, an' a hund'ed people sayin': ' *'tis* her, 'cose it is'? "

"Humph! no, I left as the curtain rose. How's the ?"

"Bishop? Oh, de bishop, he, eh – 'bout five-six minute' ago – aw it mowt be ten – whilse I 'uz down dah – de bishop – I'm bleeds to say – breave his las'."

"While I – !" She tossed both arms.

"Ummmm, hmmmm!" droned old Joy; "gone to glory!"

"Yass, de good bishop gone to his good bishop!"

"Oh, who was with him?" cried the girl.

"Why, eh" – the three moved on their way – "de doctoh, he 'uz dah, and de bofe sis' o' charity; yass'm."

"The commodore – wasn't? – Nor the senator – nor ?"

"Oh, yass'm, de commodo', he 'uz dah – faw a spell. He didn' stay till de – finish. He couldn'. He git slightly indispose', hisseff, an' have to go to his own room."

The nurse made a meek show of despair and Ramsey turned upon her. "Now, mammy, this is no time – *now – don't – cry.*"

The old woman braced up superbly. "Yass'm," persisted the waiter, "he dah now, in bed; slightly indispose'."

A rumble close below broke in upon the rhythm of the boat. "What's that?" demanded Ramsey.

"Oh, dat's on'y de aujience a-stompin' de actohs."

The next moment, a step or two down the stair, with the skylight roof still in sight as much as hidden tears would let her see it, she stopped again, to stare anxiously at another trio, coming from the bell to the captain's room.

"Da' – dat's all right," the white-jacket reassured her. "Dat's dess de cap'm, wid Mr. Hugh an' a pas- sengeh."

"Kentucky passenger?"

"Yass'm, 'zac'ly; f'om Ca'fawnia; dat's him."

She sprang back to the deck, and the servant went his way down the stair. Hugh had left his father to proceed on the arm of the Californian and was approaching. He murmured only a preoccupied greeting and would have taken the stair, but old Joy motioned eagerly to the girl. She spoke. He stopped. "Yes, Miss Ramsey?"

"Go on," she said, "we're going that way."

Down on the cabin guards the two paused at the bottom step, the old woman lingering at the top. "Mr. Hugh," said Ramsey, " mom-a's sending me for the twins." She drew a breath. "You know about the commodore? "

"Yes, Miss Ramsey."

"And the – the bishop?"

"I know, Miss Ramsey."

"Mr. Hugh, is your father – taken?"

"Yes, Miss Ramsey."

"Where are you going?"

"To bring the first clerk."

"The boat's command doesn't fall to him, does it?"

"It falls to the first mate."

"I don't see why. Who'll it fall to next? You?"

"No, the first clerk."

Double disappointment. "But you; you'll still look after us passengers and help him, too, won't you?"

"I may."

She knew it! Somehow he was to share with the mate and the clerk the command of the boat!

" Mr. Hugh" – they moved on, with Joy at a discreet distance – "you're in a hurry – so am I; but I ought to tell you, though of course it's just ridiculous for us – for me – to think I've ever helped you or can help you in any of these things or in anything – I – oh – I can't help you, or play help you, any more."

Cruel word in a cruel moment. She felt it so and expected him to show the same feeling. But instead he halted in the lamplight of a passageway to the cabin and confronted her with the widest, most formidable gaze, not her father's, she had ever met. He seemed absolutely majestic. It was very absurd for one so young and – stumpy – to seem majestic, yet there he stood, truly so. Partly for that reason she could not so much as smile; but partly, too, it was because shefelt herself so guiltily frivolous, having anything to say to him, or even standing in his gaze, gazing into it, while his father, her brother, and the bishop lay as they were lying in their several rooms so close overhead.

"You *can* help me," he said in his magisterial voice, so deep yet so soft. " You will. You must. I cannot spare you."

Did any one ever! She tossed a faint defiance: "I can't. No. I won't – can't – ever again, against my own kin."

"There are things stronger than kin."

"I'd like to know what!"

"Truth. Justice. Honor. Right. Public welfare."

She waved them all away as wholly immaterial. "Hoh!"

With a kindness far too much like magnanimity to suit her, Hugh, drawing back-ward, smiled, and replied, not as pressing the argument but as dropping it:

"One can be against one's kin, yet not against them. Basile knows that. He proved it to-day."

"Basile – oh, Mr. Hugh, Basile wants to see you. Mom-a's sent me as much for you as for the twins. Basile's asked for you. But of course if your father "

"I'll come, the moment I can be spared. Is your brother really better?"

Ramsey flinched as from pain. She leaned on the shoulder of the nurse – who had come close – and sadlyshook her head. But then she straightened smilingly

and said: "If you're coming at all "

She might have finished but for a faint sound that reached her from directly under-foot, a sound of sawing. She faced sharply about, passed into the cabin, and found the Gilmores and the amateurs in the midst of their play.

25

SECTION 25

XLIII

WHICH FROM WHICH

This world of tragic contrasts and cross-purposes, realities and fictions, this world where the many so largely find their inspiration in the performances of the few, was startlingly typified to Ramsey as, out of the upper night and the darkness of her troubles, she came in upon the show; the audience sitting in their self-imposed twilight of a few dimmed lamps, designedly forgetful of the voyage for which all were there, and the players playing their parts as though the play were the only thing real.

If the prefigurement was at any point vague it was none the less arresting. As the *Votaress* – or Gideon Hayle's *Wild Girl* – might, in full career, strike on hidden sands, so Ramsey struck on the thought – or call it the unformulated perception – that whoever would really live must, by clear choice and force of will, keep himself – herself – adjusted to this world as a whole; as one great multitudinous entity with a stronger, higher claim on each mere part's sympathy, service, sacrifice, than any mere part can ever hold on it.

In a word, Hugh Courteney, baby elephant, born tyrant, egotist – or egoist, whichever it was – self- confessed egoist, stone-faced egoist – with his big-wigairs and big-fiddle voice – was nearer right than she would *ever* submit to confess to him:

there *were* things stronger than kin, bigger every way; and other things bigger than those bigger things, and yet others still bigger than those, and so on and on to the world's circumference. Staggering discovery. Yet how infinitely old it looked the moment she clearly saw it: old, obvious, beautiful, and ugly as the man in the moon. It chanced that right there and then she was forced to accept its practical application. A white- jacket said to her in a muffled voice:

" Ef you please – to not to move up to'a'ds de stage whilse de play a-goin' on."

"Oh, but I must," she explained. "I'm on business; business that can't wait any longer. I've already been delayed – " Her last word faltered. Something occurring on the stage held her eyes, while two or three auditors who had turned on her a glance of annoyance changed it to a gaze of astonishment. The cub pilot came to her on tiptoe.

"Oh, Mr. So-and-so," she smilingly whispered as she edged on, "I want my twin brothers. Mom-a wants them, right away, up-stairs."

He nodded at each word and began softly to say that this act would be finished in a minute; but she broke in, still inching along: "I can't wait a minute. I've no right to be this late. Basile wants the twins and he's so sick that – that he can't, he mustn't wait."

"Missy," pleadingly whispered old Joy at their backs, "missy!" But neither she nor the cub pilotcould stop the messenger. Nor did she heed the growing number of those seated all about her whose attention she attracted, though now they were a dozen, a score, glancing, in a suppressed flutter, from her to the stage and from the stage to her and one another.

Yet she stopped. For on the stage, in the play, in the part that was to have been hers, she beheld " Harriet" doing that part so well, and winning such lively approval, that doing it better would have distorted the play. Rouged and coifed to reduce her apparent age as much as Ramsey's was to have been increased, she was at all points so like what Ramsey would have been that the bulk of the audience had mistaken her for Ramsey and had made her more and more a favorite at each brief reappearance.

Fearful moment. Beyond sight only to the outer eye, the bishop, whom she herself had pushed into the grapple of the pestilence, lay dead. Basile was dying. Two of the Courteneys were plague stricken, and the third, for whom she felt a special, inexplicable accountability, was, with Gilmore and Watson, in constant mortal peril from her twin brothers, and the twins therefore from them. Before her eyes, so near she could have tossed a flower to her, was Phyllis, a spectre from an awful past, the destroyer of the *Quakeress,* liable herself, within any hour, should the truth be discovered, to be burned like a witch. There she was, "the slave girl Phyllis," as the runaway advertisement would have had it, a culprit, and a property no way superior, in popular regard, to the blackestAfrican, yet by Hayle blood so near of kin – kin! kin to her ! – that with no other aid than a few touches of paint and pencil she was being enthusiastically acclaimed as Ramsey Hayle by an assemblage which has just applauded her, Ramsey, in the blaze of those same footlights. Fearful moment ! that aged her as no earlier moment ever had; yes, and for the instant, at least, threw into her face a maturity that heightened the unhappy resemblance.

She stopped because her presence seemed about to precipitate a terrible mischief, and she stood because flight would but leave that mischief to do its worst. Through this glaring show of likeness she seemed to be in the keenest danger of betraying back into slavery on the spot this poor, intrepid " Harriet," identified as the Phyllis supposed these ten years to be under the floods of the Mississippi. At that moment, on the stage, in Ramsey's role of a housemaid, the role from which Ramsey bitterly remembered she had been excused through Hugh Courteney's urging, "Harriet" chanced to be acting a ludicrous dismay before a transient dilemma in which, as in Ramsey's, staying threatened disaster yet good faith said stay – Ramsey's own present actual case except that Harriet's was comic. A hundred beholders laughed, and then turning and peering at the dim, central figure of Ramsey suddenly redoubled the laugh and presently redoubled it again.

Yet it yielded a certain relief. While there is mirth there is hope. Even now the player of the part wasrecognized only as Mrs. Gilmore's maid. Her resemblance to Ramsey was passing for pure accident. That the whole thing was visibly offensive to Hayle's twins made it all the more amusing, and Ramsey's pause in the aisle seemed the most natural thing she could do on finding herself in two places at the same time. So for a moment, in which she rejoiced that at any rate the twins had never seen Phyllis as Phyllis. But then the demonstration broke short off. At different points three men stood up at once. In the front row appeared Julian. A few seats behind him loomed the exhorter. The third rose just at Ramsey's elbow, offering her his seat, yet counting it but courtesy still to keep his attention mainly on the play. It was the first clerk, he who had once been clerk on the *Quakeress,* where he had known Phyllis as Hugh's nurse, and whose scrutiny "Harriet" had until now somehow escaped. Whether in thanking him Ramsey accepted or declined she hardly knew, for just then the gaze he still bent on "Harriet" showed a gleam of recognition. Ramsey's heart rose into her throat. She murmured a hurried word, which she had to go over a second time before it took effect on him:

"Mr. Hugh's looking for you, out forward. The commodore and the captain are both sick."

As the announcement drew his quick glance she almost waved him to go. Yet what was done was done; with Phyllis recognized, it might be far better for him to remain, and she turned her dismissing gesture into one of detention.

"I'm Miss Hayle," she whispered, while both looked again toward Julian and "Harriet." "That's my old mammy back yonder. I want my twin brothers. Mom-a wants them, up in the texas, as quick as – never mind, here they come." XLIV

FORBEARANCE

Ramsey was mistaken – her brothers were staying. The play's first act was done, there was great clapping and thumping and the curtain was falling – or closing, in two parts from opposite sides, eased over sticking- points by nimble efforts behind it; but though Julian – who evidently had been getting through the general's courtesy the indulgence denied him at the bar – had moved a step or so from his chair, Lucian remained seated. Next them sat the general and the senator, and the four were debating together. Oddly enough, the twins were in disaccord, and while Lucian had the senator's approval the general's went to his brother. The applause died out prematurely and the whole company gave its attention to the debate, Ramsey sinking into the clerk's seat and laughing merrily – since it was laugh or perish.

"No, gentlemen," she heard Julian say, "this is the last-st st-straw. A nigger wench made up to counterfeit a member of our family, and the part given her which that member of our family was to have played! . . . Overlook – oh, good God, sir, we've done nothing but overlook, every hour of day and night since we started."

From the other three came responses too quiet to be understood. Ramsey half rose toward the clerk and sank again, begging him to carry her errand on to the brothers, and he had softly moved forward as far as to the exhorter when that person, still on his feet, called to Julian:

" Yass! an' thah ah cause to believe said niggeh "

Two small interruptions came at once, provoking a general laugh: Julian, staring at him in heavy abstraction, said dreamily, "Ho – ho – hold your tongue," while the clerk, at "John the Baptist's" side, gently grasped between the shoulders a fold of his coat, mildly suggested, "Have a seat," and put him so suddenly of! his balance that he plumped heavily into his chair – quite enough to rouse the mirth of a company already a trifle nervous. And now Julian was heard again:

"No, Luce, you can stay, I'll go alone – or with – thank you, general! Oh, senator, we are not blind, sir, though every time we overlook some insult they think we are. Good Lord! do you reckon we don't see that all this laugh is at us, got up at our expense, and has been at us since the first turn of this boat's wheels at Canal Street? We saw – *and* overlooked – that vile attempt to take our two ladies up the river without us, starting the instant they got aboard and leaving us at the water's edge a laughing-stock for passengers, crew, and pantry boys !"

Both senator and general coaxed him to sit down, but the most he would concede was to drop his voices he continued: "You know, gentlemen, and they know, that any true man would as soon be slapped in the face and spit upon as to be laughed at. ... No, I – " His words became indistinguishable.

Ramsey was in anguish. She would have glided forward with her tidings and summons but for the clerk blocking the path half-way. A stir of annoyance ran through the gathering, here grave, there facetious, but it stopped short as a new figure moved quietly past Ramsey and stood beside the clerk. It was Hugh, and the general interest revived. He exchanged a word or two with the clerk, who turned and left the cabin while Hugh stayed with the exhorter.

Julian, without seeing the newcomer, once more broke forth, this time plainly intending to make every one his listener: "No, we don't interrupt and we shall not."

"Oh, no," daringly put in an ironical hearer, "Hayle's twins, they never interrupt an innocent pleasure!"

"How air it innercent?" called John the Baptist, at Hugh's side, rising again and gesticulating. "No theayter play kin be innercent an' much less this-yeh one, by reason 'at they ah cause to believe that-ah servant-gal "

He was pulled down again with even less ceremony than before, though by friendlier hands, hands of the two lenders of the sword-canes, who fell to counselling him in crafty undertones. But Julian was talking dead ahead, ignoring all distractions and not even yet discovering Hugh:

"We didn't more than whisper, general, till the curtain fell. Now, did we? When it rises again – what, sir? . . . My dear senator! it's our fellow passengers who don't see – that their kind intentions are being made part of a put-up game to torment us to leave the boat. . . . Oh, no, they – why, sir, the dastards set it a-going the moment they'd persuaded our ladies to stay and risk their priceless lives nursing those damned Dutch on the lower deck."

The senator ached to be the steamer's length removed but saw no way of dignified escape. Several listeners, remembering Ramsey's tactics and their success, gayly laughed, but two or three gasped an audible dismay; two or three men said, "Sh-sh-sh!" two or three said, "Ladies present," "Remember the ladies," and some one droned out in a mock voice: "The stage waits."

And plainly it did so; waited on the audience, with Mrs. Gilmore peeping through the curtain, whose rise would reveal "Harriet" alone; a terrible risk if the exhorter should get in the bolt he was trying to launch.

"Oh, where is Mr. Gilmore?" thought Ramsey, and, "Why don't they call again for 'Gideon's Band'? Yet who would sing it?" Her distressed lips were silently asking many such questions when she sprang up and halted the Californian, who had come in at her back on his way to Hugh.

"How's the captain?" she whispered in smiling agitation.

With low affirmative bows, so enraptured to be speaking with her as to be all but speechless, he murmured: "Get' – getting on – so far." He waved an oddly delicate hand – backward from the wrist, girlishly – "He's all – hunkadory."

"And Basile?" Anxious as she was, she yet saw while she spoke – and he saw – that Julian had at length sighted Hugh and that at least three-fourths of the audience, the whole male portion, was eying that pair with the alertness of man's primitive interest in man-to-man encounter. At her mention of the sick boy the gold hunter ceased to nod. His countenance fell.

"Oh," she whispered, "won't *you* go and tell them, all three, Mr. Courteney and both twins, how bad off he is, and that he sent me, and mom-a says come quick?"

He went. Forgetting to sit down, she watched him go and let Gilmore pass her as Hugh had done. Now, what was his errand? The actor and the Californian reached Hugh together. The three drew a step back from the exhorter and his advisers and conferred in the aisle while Julian's tirade went straight on as completely ignored by them as though it were the most normal sound of the boat's machinery. The sight so amused the audience that laughter came again and then clapping and pounding, in a succession of outbreaks, each coming so close after one of Julian's utterances that his dizzy head took it for approval, though to . every one else, and especially to Ramsey, the meaning was weariness of him and impatience of Gilmore's delay.

He spoke with his face to his associates but with his voice addressed to those other three in the aisle: "We were invited on this boat in pure cowardly malice." (Applause.) "To have our weapons stolen from us by servants and locked up by underlings and to have the boat's ordinary refreshments forbidden us." (Laughter and applause.) "To be thrust into contact with a deadly pestilence and to be insulted or assaulted by hired blackguards on one or another of every deck from forecastle gangway to pilot-house." (Long and loud applause.) "And all this, sirs, we have overlooked; but to be made a public laughing-stock we will not endure if I have to pull every Courteney's nose to stop it!" (Loud laughter and prolonged applause.) Amid the din Ramsey recognized the voice of old Joy moaning with grief and consternation in the gloom behind her, and caught the words of the cub pilot, said for his soul's relief, not dreaming she would hear: " If you two ornery cusses wa'n't Gid Hayle's boys we'd clap you in irons quicker'n you could lick out your tongue."

But amid the same din what, she laughingly, painfully wondered, were the three standers in the aisle so privately, calmly saying together – with the actor as chief speaker, Hugh grim, and the Californian mostly a nodding listener? Was Hugh – whose big eyes and stone visage so drolly fitted each other yet seemed so sadly unfitted to this big emergency – was he insisting that it would be idle for him to go to Basile without the twins, as was only too true? Or that John the Baptist and his two disciples must first be disposed of? Or was it his word that the most pressing need was for the actor, long trained to perceive just what would capture an audience in such a stress, to step between footlights and curtain, tell the people that honest facts had never been more crazily twisted into falsehood and slander, and explain the true situation in a brief, apt speech, dignified and amusing? Certainly something had to be done and done this instant. But not that, ah, no! Or if that, not done by him, the actor. She could never imagine such a manoauvre attempted on a boat of her father's, whose sole way of mastery was by pure lordship and main force. Yet here, with these Courteneys, who, he had always said, outmastered him by their clever graciousness, and dealing here not with subordinates but with passengers – a living nerve of the river's whole public – talk treatment might be the cleverest, wisest kind to give, if only Hugh – oh, if only Hugh! – could give it. But of course he could not, with that face, that visage, so much *too* lordly and forceful – and hard – and glum – for a clever task.

Julian ceased. His high head went a shade higher; the Californian was advancing straight upon him. With a pang Ramsey remembered that she had failed to charge the gold hunter not to let the twins know that their brother's summons included Hugh, lest that should keep them away. But surely he would see that necessity; and in fact he did. Hugh stood still, looking in the opposite, her, Ramsey's, direction, where the actor was coming toward her. The old nurse had stolen to her side. The player went by withouta glance at her. It was so much like asking why she stood there doing nothing that she granted the old woman's whispered prayer and sat down. Behind her he spoke busily for a second to the cub pilot and passed out by a side exit. The pilot's cub came by, had a word or two with the exhorter, and stayed there as if on guard.

Now, for all these small things to happen in the one moment and to happen in the midst of a waiting audience made its show of suspense more vivid than ever; excitement was in all eyes; every chin was lifted. The Californian seemed to tell Julian a startling thing or two. The general rose, the senator helped Lucian to his feet. The four came close about the news bearer and he told more. Ramsey could almost feel his mention of the bishop and then of Basile. Lucian asked a question or two and the five came down the aisle, one pair leading, the other following, and Julian between, alone, overpeering all sitters, with a splendid air of being commander and in the saddle.

26

SECTION 26

XLV

APPLAUSE

Diffidence! Hugh had spoken of diffidence – in himself – in the twins. Could Julian really be hiding such a thing behind such a mask? Ramsey wondered.

Every eye was on him and again the floor thundered, shaming her, flattering him. As he came on, the ex- horter began to put out an arm, to speak and to rise, but the cub pilot blandly intervened and Julian ignored him. For there both brothers came face to face with the first mate. He had entered where Gilmore went out, and now passed them with a stare like their own, fire for fire, and at close quarters began to accost the exhorter and his two adherents.

They rose, and with evident change of meaning thunder came again, though not for them. The departing twins and their triple escort; the exhorter and the four about him; Ramsey, Joy, and the returned Gil- more, who just then touched her shoulder and whispered something to which she replied with quick nods of consent – all these groups lifted their gaze, with the whole company's, to the curtained stage.

Diffidence! oh, where *was* diffidence? Hugh had stepped in behind the foot-lights and was standing andlooking out across them as foursquare and unsmiling as a gravestone.

Their light was on his brow, whose frown smote her with foreboding. Half folded he held a slip of paper as if about to give official notice of some grave matter, and his aggressive eyes, that seemed to her to look a greater distance away from a greater distance within than ever before, were fixed on one man. Absolute silence fell. And thereupon, to the open-mouthed amazement of the audience, with his stare yet on that one face, and in a voice that seemed octaves below hers, he began to sing straight at the exhorter:

" Do you belong to Gideon's ban '? "

A shout of laughter, a rain of clappings, a thunder . of canes and feet. Sitters bumped up and down. They were safe home again in nonsense and were glad. Ramsey's laugh was like a dancer's bells though under cover of the dusk she let the tears roll down. Old Joy moaned and shook her head. John the Baptist had begun to retort but withered before a ferocious muffled threat from the mate while following him into the aisle. "Bucked and gagged," was the mate's odd phrase, at which a dozen or so nearest him laughed again, a bit nervously. They looked back to see if the twins had heard it, and were just in time to catch from Julian and the general a last glare of scorn as the group of five left the cabin. Then again came silence, except behind the footlights, where the sphinx-like singerbore straight on through the refrain and came to the new lines. Sing them out, sphinx; the more senseless the better.

"Nex' come de 'coon and de cockatroo,

Nex' come de 'coon and de cockatroo,

Nex' come de 'coon and de cocki troo,

De hawg and de whoopdedoodendoo.

Do you belong ?"

The inquiry was drowned in applause, which swelled as the mate and the exhorter went out with the latter's two backers – more eagle-eyed and stallion-eyed than ever – and with Watson's cub at the rear. A number stretched up for a glimpse of Ramsey but she too – and the actor – and Joy – were gone. There was another waiting hush, and the droll singer, so droll because so granite solemn, resumed:

"Den turkle-dove an" blue-bird blue,

Den turkle-dove an' blue-bird blue,

Den turkle-dove an' blue-bird blue,

De merry-go-roun' and de hullabaloo.

Do you belong ?"

Applause! Was that the end? Not if the applauders could help it! The day was coming when a boiler- deck and pilot-house tradition, heard by many with hearty enjoyment, by many with silent disdain, would be this: that aboard the old *Votaress* on her first up trip – late spring of '52 – cholera on every deck – mutiny hotly smouldering – the unreason of fear and

of wrath were beaten in fair fight by the unreason of

mirth, and men's, women's, children's lives – no telling

how many – were saved, through the cleverness of some

play-actors and first the youngest of all the Hayles

and then the youngest of all the Courteneys singing a

nonsense song! Sing it! sing on!

He sang on:

"Den de grizzly-b'ah and den de mole,

De grizzly-b'ah and den de mole,

De grizzly-b'ah and den de mole,

De terrapintime and de wrigglemarole.

Do you belong ?"

The plaudits were at their height and Hugh still on the interrogative line when there came from behind the curtain a voice skilfully thrown to reach only him:

"Give them one verse more and we'll be ready!"

He gave it:

"Las' de cattlemaran and de curlicue,

De cattlemaran and de curlicue,

De cattlemaran and de curlicue,

De daddy-long-legs and de buggaboo.

Do you belong ?"

He stepped quickly from the "stage." The curtains drew apart. The scene revealed was a drawing-room. In it stood alone, as if playfully listening for something, the housemaid; not "Harriet" but Ramsey. (Laughter and applause.) XLVI

AFTER THE PLAY

Neither Hugh nor Ramsey slept a moment that night. And no more did the Gilmores or "Harriet" or John the Baptist or even the senator or the Cali- fornian. The play, second act, was cut without mercy and rushed to a close to let its hero and heroine off at Napoleon, which Ned called a "future city" but which, some years later, became a former city, by melting into thin air, or thick water, and leaving not so much behind as a candle-end or a broken bottle.

It was not far above there that these unsleeping passengers began to remark a fresh rise in the river's flood, which her "family" and crew had noticed much earlier by a difference in the nature and quantity of its driftwood. Near the mouth of White River, about an hour's run above Napoleon, a great floating tree stump, with all its roots, was caught on the buckets of the "labboard" wheel – "like a cur on a cow's horn," said Gilmore – and carried clear over it with a sudden hubbub in the paddle-box, tenfold what ten curs could have made, bringing to his feet every passenger not abed, and scaring awake every sleeping one. Neither Ramsey nor Hugh ever forgot it, for it evoked the last stir in the supine form of Basile, and a faint spasm in his cold grasp on Hugh's fingers. Under his freer hand, on his all but motionless breast, lay his mother's crucifix. Shortly before, while waiting for Hugh's tardy coming, he had held a hand of his sister, whose other held her mother's. On the edge of the berth, at his feet, sat Lucian, very pale, with Julian standing by him. Both betrayed deep feeling yet kept a brave look that was good to see even with eyes as prejudiced as Hugh's. Only Basile himself was without tears.

How fashions change! There are styles even in death-bed scenes. This one was of the old fashion, bearing a strong tinge of fatalism; no hopeful make- believe to the dying that death was other than death; no covert, diligent, desperate economies of the vital spark; but a frank, helpless reception of the dread angel as a royal guest, and a pious, inert consent to let the dying die. Before either Hugh or Ramsey could come from the cabin the twins had reached the bedside and had been received with a final lighting up of the boy's spent powers, which his mother made no effort to restrain. In a feeble, altered voice, without heat, scorn, or petulance, with a mind stripped of all its puerilities and full of fraternal care and faithfulness, and with a magisterial dignity far beyond his years, he slowly poured out a measured stream of arraignment and appeal which their hardened hearts were still too young to withstand unmoved.

His conversion, he told them, had come to him with a great light, "on the road to Damascus," and by that light he saw, as he implored them to see, the hideous deformity of the life he and they and the young fellows of their usual companionship had been living. Even Ramsey knew, he continued as she and their old nurse silently reappeared, that by the plainest laws of the land, they were not too good for the penitentiary. An overweening pride in their lawlessness did not justify or excuse it; the devils had that, in hell. They, the twins, were not Christian gentlemen. They were *not gentlemen at all.* They'd shoot a man down in his tracks for saying so, or for calling them liars, yet they'd turn the truth wrong side out every day in the year. These last two days they'd done it right along. At this moment they had a fixed design to kill Hugh Courteney on the first good chance and didn't care a continental whether they did it in face-to-face murder or from behind a bush. Lying at death's door, he said, and in jealousy for the same Hayle name they professed to be so jealous for, he demanded their oath to abandon that design; to stop it, drop it, "right here and now," and never to seek the life of any Courteney but in clear defence of some other life. His own seemed almost to fade out at that point, yet presently:

"Hold up your right hands," he gasped, trying to raise his. The mother lifted it for him while giving the twins a tearful flash of command. Unconsciously Ramsey put up hers as Lucian's left suddenly caught Julian's right and he held up both it and his own.

But neither the boy nor Ramsey nor the old nurse felt assured, and all three were glad when the mother asked:

"You swear?"

Julian stood mute but, "With that provision," said Lucian, "we swear."

"So help you God?" insisted the mother, and while she spoke and the twins bowed, the narrow door let some one in. .

" Is that Hugh Courteney? " asked the boy. " You're just in time, Hugh. The feud's off."

"Oh, there's no feud, Basile," tenderly murmured Hugh.

"No, it's off, thank God. I got it off. The twins have just sworn it off. Shake hands, boys. Come, you first, Jule."

But Lucian led, with a certain alacrity, Julian following with less.

"Now take my hand, Hugh." The voice was failing but once more it rallied. "Give it to him, sis'. . . . Thank you. . . . Keep it, Hugh Courteney. I love a brave man's hand. We heard you singing, Hugh. My! but you've got grit. I wish you belonged to Gideon's band yourself. You're braver than most men, though most men'll always think they're braver than you."

Hugh could only dry the damp from the cold brow. He grew fiercely ashamed not so much of his tears, which those around him were too tearful to observe, as of the boy's praises, before which he could only stand dumb.

"He's brave, sis'," Basile went on, "and he's clean, and he's square, mother, boys. You were on the *Quakeress* when she burned, wa'n't you? Ah, me! –

" My heavenly Father wouldn't 'a' had to call me in out of '

'ulian stood mute but, "With that provision," sai! I iieian, "we swear."

"So help you God?" insisted the mother, and while she spoke and the twins bowed, the narrow door let some one in.

" Is that Hugh Courteney? " asked the boy. " You're just in time, Hugh. The feud's off."

"Oh, there's no feud, Basile," tenderly murmured Hugh.

" No, it's off, thank God. I got it off. The twin have just sworn it off. Shake hands, boys. Come, you first. Jule."

But Lucian led, with a certain alacrity, Julian following with less.

" Now tak- my hand, Hugh." The voice was fail- ins but iur more it rallied. "Give it to him, sis'. . . . Thank . . mi. . . . Keep it, Hugh Courteney. 1 lo. a I-1-!.'- Man's hand. We heard you singing. Hugh. V ' l-.-t you've got grit. I wish you belonged to Gideoi.'-. band yourself. You're braver than most men, though most men'll always think they're braver than you."

Hugh could only dry the damp from the cold brow He grew fiercely ashamed not so much of his tearx which those around him were too tearful to observe. as of the boy's praises, before which he could onl stand dumb.

"He's brave, sis'," Basile went on, "and he's clear, and he's square, mother, boys. You were on the *Quakeress* when she burned, wa'n't you? Ah, me! –

" My heavenly Father wouldn't 'a' had to call me in out of'

wish I'd known you then. I'd be a different man now. I don't believe I'd be dying. My heavenly Father wouldn't 'a' had to call me in out of the storm."

His mother sank to her knees against the berth's side, covered her face, and shook with grief. The daughter sank too, weepingly caressing her, yet was still able so to divide her thought as yearningly to wish Hugh, for his own sake, well away, as she saw his hand softly endeavor to draw free from Basile's. But it was on that instant that the great tree root came thundering up through the wheel-house and the dying clasp tightened. The shock of surprise revived him. " Hugh – do something for me? . . . Thank you. Bishop's gone, you know. Read my burial service. I don't want the – play-actor – though he's fine; nor the priest, though he's fine, too. Mom-a'd be a saint in any – persuasion, and pop and us boys are Methodists, if anything, and I – I didn't get religion in Latin and I-don't want to be buried in it." He waited. Hugh was silent.

The Creole mother, still kneeling, drew closer. "Yass," she said, "he shall read that."

But plainly there was one thing more though the tired eyelids sank. "Let down your ear," murmured the lips.

Hugh knelt, bent, waited. The distressed twins watched them. The hold on his hand relaxed. He lifted and looked.

"What do he say?" tearfully asked old Joy, pressing in.

"Nothing," said Hugh; and then to the twins: "He's gone."

Out in the benign starlight and caressing breeze Hugh hastened to his father's door.

27

SECTION 27

XLVII

INSOMNIA

Down in the cabin, in one of its best staterooms, where all were choice, the senator wooed slumber.

In vain. Sounds were no obstacle. They abounded but they were normal. Except – "Peck-peck-peck" and so on, which the steady pulse of normal sounds practically obliterated. The peck-pecking was not for him.

An unwelcome odor may keep one awake, but the senator's berth was fragrant of fresh mattresses and new linen, the wash-stand of jasmine soap, and the room at large of its immaculate zinc-white walls and doors and their gilt trimmings. Nor could the cause be his supper of beefsteak and onions, black coffee, hot rolls, and bananas, for every one about him had had those, and every one about him was sound asleep. It could not be for lack of the bath; he had already slept well without it too many nights hand-running. Nor could it be a want of special nightclothes; he had won his election over a nightshirt aristocrat, as being not too pampered to sleep, like the sons of toil, in the shirt he had worn all day and would wear again to-morrow. Nor yet was it nicotine or alcohol, the putting of which into him was like feeding cottonwood to Hayle's old*Huntress.* Such, at least, was his private conviction. Oh, he knew the cause! He believed he could drop into sleep as this boat's sounding-lead could drop to the river's bottom, if for one minute he could get his mind off that singularly old, contemptibly young poker-face.

Recalling that face and the grandfather's as he had confronted them together earlier in the journey, they were a double reminder of the Franklinian maxim – he kept a store of such things for stump use – that an old young man makes a young old man. But maxims didn't bring sleep; he turned the pillow and damned the maxim and the men, with Benjamin Franklin to boot.

It tossed him from his right side to his left, to think of his own part in this two days' episode, and of the flocks of passengers stepping ashore at various landings who, as sure as – hmm! – would at every step drop that story into the public ear as corn is dropped into the furrow. It tossed him back again, to think how his adversaries in the political game, where cunning was always trumps, would light down on that story like crows behind the plough. He mixed his metaphors by habit; the people loved them mixed. Another maxim, his own invention, was, Take care of your character and your reputation will take care of itself.

The it will! You've got to take *at least* as much

care of reputation. But here both were concerned. He could not, for the sake either of his character *or* his reputation, let himself be made a fool of by anyone, however small, anywhere. He had got to recover a personal importance solemnly pilfered from him by a half-grown Shanghai still in his pin-feathers. Against Hayle's girl he was excusably helpless, but him he had got to get the upper hand of and get it quick. Memphis in the morning! More passengers to be dropped there and the whole town's attention to be attracted by the burial of the bishop. Good Lord ! That " verbatim report for the newspapers"! And of all papers the Memphis papers! *Avalanche – Appeal* – it was all one, he happening to be at the moment equally at odds with both. It, the "report," would not take a defensive attitude. Poker-face was too sharp for that. It would take the offensive from the start and it would take the start. Gentlemen of the jury, in a war of words there's just one word better than the last, and that's the first! And moreover! the brief "report's" main theme would not be he, the senator, nor his vanished committee of seven. No, sir-ee, it would be the cholera, and he would be dished up in a purely casual way; as the French say "on, pass on."

He rubbed his head and sat up. There was a chance that he might find Hugh awake and on duty. If so his cast-iron lordship might yet be browbeaten, or wheedled, into inaction. Or if sleeping he might yet be circumvented. Was he worth circumventing? How absurdly troubles magnify on a waking pillow. Despise your enemy and sleep! Well – hardly. Let *him* do that, especially when *you can't*.

He threw off the light cover, rose, and dressed. Hebegan to see a way to win. He would countermine. He would raise a counter-issue – "Harriet." Loitering by the twins' door he listened and rightly judged they were asleep, Lucian being so feeble and Julian so full. The office was open but empty. Its clock read two. The card-tables were vacant. The bar was closed. Out on the dim boiler deck he found only the two who had fleeced Basile. They sat at the very front, elbow to elbow, with their feet up on the rail. Their quiet talk ceased as he came near and stood looking out over the gliding bow and the waters beyond, which were out of their banks and stretched everywhere off into the night, a veritable deluge.

"A good forty miles wide, no doubt," he remarked to the pair, and they assured him he was right.

"What piece of river is this?" he inquired, and was told that they were in the long, winding, desolate sixty- mile stretch between White River and Horseshoe Bend; that they had just put Islands Sixty-two and Sixty- three astern and would be more than two hours yet in reaching Helena.

"Arkansas your State?" he asked. "Helena your town?"

" No," they said, they were of the " hoop-pole State," meaning Indiana. He knew better but changed the subject. "The Ohio," he remarked, "must be up on her hind legs."

"Yes, everything was up: the Saint Francis, the Tennessee, Cumberland, Illinois, Wabash, Kentucky, Miami, Scioto – " The pair did not talk like mennarrowly of the hoop-pole commonwealth. Modestly speaking on, they seemed to know the whole great valley quite by heart.

So the senator, to show how quite by heart he knew this whole little world, said affably: "The pan-fish ain't biting so very lively this trip."

The reply was as flawless for candor as though they had the same hope to use him which he had to use them. Said one:

"No, we ain't paying expenses."

And his mate: "We've caught a few little flappers."

"Captain's son make it hard to do business?"

"Oh, he – we've all got our prejudices, you know."

"Yes, you ought to have some against him by now."

"Maybe so. You've got yourn, senator, we've noticed."

"I? No! I admire him. The way he runs this cabin "

" Makes her keep up with the boat," they admitted.

"I never saw his like," laughed the statesman.

"Wouldn't want to, would you?"

"N-no, he makes big mistakes. But – he's got a future!"

"So mind his heels," said one of the pair. They were enjoying their politician. He saw that by their gravity. In their world men looked gravest when amused, and saved their smiles for emergencies. While he offered, and they accepted, cigars he spoke absently:

"The young gentleman's making a mistake right now that he ought to be saved from."

" Another?" they dryly asked as they used his cigar for a light. So far had he fallen in the general esteem.

He chose not to hear. "I wish," he insisted, "we could save him from it."

"Why, yes! – wish you could. But 'we' ain't us. We sporting men, we're mighty bashful, you know."

"Naturally," admitted the senator.

"Yes, glass, with care. But there's another mistake maker we wish you wished you could save. We ev'm might help."

"Aha!" thought the senator. He was right, after all. He had felt confident that these men, treated by Hugh as they had been, would privately "have it in for him"; that they would be glad of any safe chance to "get away with him" – not so utterly as to imperil their necks, yet not too lightly for their spiritual comfort the rest of their days – and that they saw their chance just where he saw his.

"Ye-es?" He mused. They let him muse. The exhorter, he reflected, having picked up the trail and opened the cry – trail which the headlong twins had so witlessly overrun – these older dogs were on it hot; trail of the Gilmores and "Harriet." Somewhere on that trail the captain's son would show up, and when the game should be treed they would be able, in the general mix-up, to " go and see Hugh" and " cook his goose."

The musing ceased. "You mean the actor?"

The pair warmed up. "Yes, sir-ee, him. *That* fellow's making a mistake we might help you to handle. God! sir, he's a nigger-stealer. His wife has got a stolen nigger wench with her now. Had her these ten years. Save *him.* Save *them.*"

"Our friend John the Baptist suggests that," began the senator.

"Adzac'ly!" was the facetious affirmation. "Smelt 'em out at the show. That's how come the mate has locked him up."

The senator stiffened. " Oh, you must be mistaken!"

" Want to bet? Pull out. Go you a thousand they've jugged him and them two Arkansas killers. Yes, sir, to stay jugged till they leave us, at Helena."

"Who! – have done that?"

"Same as you're thinking; they; them; him; that believes he's bossing the boat – which maybe he is."

"Where is he?"

" Up on the roof, with a select few, both sexes."

"Gentlemen, he must let them go at once!"

"Senator, not with money, but just on your word, you sort o' bail 'em out. If they cut up, nobody'll blame you."

"I'll do it! We don't want an owner of the finest boat on Southern waters to have any part in *that sort* of mistake, whatever his youth."

"Youth!" (Profanity.) "That boy's forty year' old. Oh, he's all right; if he thinks he'd ought to protect every galoot on his boat, why, maybe he'd ought. What you know is that that white nigger's *got* to be took away from them two barnstormers instanter and restored back to her own Hayle folks. That's a mistake you ain't never got to ask nobody's leaves to save nobody from."

"You don't mean to-night?" Capital disguise for eagerness – the cigar. The senator puffed. The pair puffed.

"We mean now; when the right men can be woke up and the others – and the ladies – sleep on. Now, straightaway, while the shouter's still aboard – and the two shooters. If we wa'n't sporting men we'd like to sit into that game ourselves. Maybe we can if it's kept – dignified."

"Even if there's resistance?"

"Who'll resist? The boat's people? Only thing they dassen't resist. Couldn't never run another trip on this river. Resist! Couldn't ever resist, any time; but now? Look at their fix. Sweet time to set everybody a-kicking like steers. Bishop dead, chief Dutch

woman ditto, that nice young Hayle boy that they took away from us when he wanted
to stay like a man, ditto "

"Oh, not dead? My God! I hadn't heard that."

"No, it ain't been properly advertised. But Hamlet knows it – I mean your actor.
The way him and his wife – or lady – are buzzing around, you'd think they was the
undertakers. Maybe they are. *He* won't resist. He knows how well resistance would
suit you – oh, not yourself, no more'n us, but – the crowd; men like them three that's
locked up and must be turned loose first thing. He knows if he lifts a finger, or so
much as gives anybody any of his lip – and maybeanyhow – he'll be took ashore and
lost in the woods, first time we stop to bury some more Dutch; say daybreak."

"Ah, but we mustn't let that happen, either." "Oh, no! we mustn't let that happen,
either." "Well" – the senator put on a bustling frown – "I'll see Hugh. I wish – I wonder
if that Californian
    has "

"Put up his shutters? No, he's on the roof. Why?"

" He might help wake up the right men, as you say."

One of the pair, without rising, tapped the senator
caressingly. "You – let – California – sweat. Trust in
Providence. The right men'll get woke up somehow,
beginning with the general. That right? ... All gay,
but don't you take no California in yourn to-night."

" No? Very well. But – I wonder if you gentlemen really recognize the seriousness
of this affair."

"Look a-here, senator, you go up-stairs and save Mr. Innocence from running his
boat into this mistake." The sleek pair rose, evidently to begin their part.

The senator rummaged his mind for a word that would give him creditable exit but
had to hurry off without it. Turning, the two exchanged a calm gaze and one luxurious
puff, which meant that the "old sucker's" use of them would suit them exactly. They
rummaged for no words; had no more need for words than two leopards.

Before falling to work they glanced out over the flood. This was Horseshoe Cut-
off. Kangaroo Point was just astern in the west. Yonder ahead, under theold moon,
came Friar's Point. In these hundred miles between Napoleon and Helena they were
meeting one by one the Saturday evening boats out of Saint Louis. Now one came
round the upper bend, four days from Cincinnati. They knew her; the Courteneys'
fine old *Marchioness*. The young *Votaress* swept by her saluting and saluted like the
belle of a ball, a flying vision of luxury, innocence, and joy.

28

SECTION 28

XLVIII

"CALIFORNIA"

Under the benign stars, as we have said, Hugh hastened from Basile to his father.

Those were the same heavenly lights with which only two nights earlier he and that father had so tranquilly – and the dead boy's sister so airily – communed. With a hand yet on the door that he was leaving, and while his distress for what had befallen in this room brought a foreboding of what might impend in the other, he felt the chiding of that celestial benignity and was dimly made to see its illimitable span and the smallness of magnifying the things we call trouble.

Ah1 the more, then, a melting heart for the tearful mother and sister, to whom no word of this could be said; but a stout heart, stouter than he knew where to find, for whatever was yet in store. Also a preoccupied good-by to sweet companionship. Nay, a mind too preoccupied for any good-by to any companionship for the remainder of this voyage, if not forever. It was humiliating to have even so much thought of such a kind at such a time; yet suppress it as he might, he could not wholly stifle it, even at his father's door.

Three hours later the senator, coming up in search of him, gradually discovered the presence of morepeople than he was looking for or cared even to find awake – being who they were. At the top of the steps he told the watchman sleeplessness had driven him up here for fresh air. It is but human to explain to a watchman.

But how was the captain? And how was the commodore?

The commodore was doing well enough, but the captain – the watchman shook his head with the wisdom of a doctor.

The seeker after fresh air, eager to move on, yet loath to imply that the air about a watchman was stale, said, with a glance at the stars, that here was quiet.

But the watchman begged to differ. Never by starlight had he seen so busy a hurricane-deck. Just now there was a lull but it was the first in three hours. Preparations here, preparations there, for the dead, for the living, the sick, the well; such a going and coming of cabin-boys, of chambermaids, of the immigrant they called Marburg, the Hayles' old black woman, the texas tender, the mud clerk, the actor and his wife, her servant girl

"And others," prompted the senator. "What doing?"

A hundred things. The actor's wife had got Miss Hayle into funeral black from her own stage "war- robe," and the young man Marburg had brought up, for Madame Hayle, one of his deceased mother's mourning gowns, "a prodigious fine one." It did notfit but the actor's wife and her maid were altering it while they kept watch where Basile lay and while Madame Hayle resumed her cares on the lower deck.

And who was caring for the commodore?

Second clerk and mud clerk answered his few needs.

But the captain ?

Ah, that was another matter. The actor was with him.

Mr. Gilmore; um-hmm. A step or so forward of the captain's room, as the senator moved toward the bell, two male figures seated on the edge of the skylight roof spoke his name in a mild greeting, and, looking closely, he found them to be Watson's cub and the Kentuckian whom the pair down on the boiler deck had just called "California."

The senator expressed surprise that these two were not abed, where he himself ought to be but – sleeplessness had driven him up here for fresh air.

"Well, here the fresh air is," said California. "Senator, we've just been wishing we could see you."

"Ah!" said the senator, grateful yet wary. "I'll just take a turn or two up forward and be right back."

" But – hold on, senator; just one question."

The three stood. "Now, this first question ain't it; this is just the cut and deal. Hayle's twins have offered to fight Hugh Courteney – any way open to gentlemen, as they say – haven't they?"

"Oh – night before last, I – believe so."

"Ancient history, yes; but it's a standing invitation and they've called him names: poltroon, coward "

"Well, really, Mr. So-and-so, while we can't justify the names, nor the invitation, we can't wonder at the givers."

"Why – I can. I think they're pretty tol'able wonderful. But so's he – to let 'em do it. Now, this ain't the question, either, but – why does he allow it? It ain't for lack of pluck, senator. I know a coward's earmarks and he ain't got 'em. It ain't for religion; less'n two hours out of Orleans he'd offered them twins, I'm told, to take 'em down to the freight deck and dish up the brace of 'em at one fell scoop. And no more is it because his people won't let him alone to do his own way. He's about the let-alone-dest fellow I ever see, for his age, if he is any particular age. No, sir, I've studied out what it's for."

"Hmm. But what's your question? What's *it* about?"

"Why, it's about this – and your friend the general. For I'll tell you, senator, why Mr. Hugh don't fight. It's for – can I tell you in confidence, strict, airtight?"

"Certainly, strict, air-tight."

"Well, then, it's for love. He's in love with their sister. Now, *that's* something I *don't* wonder at. I am, too. So are a lot of us." He smiled at the cub, who frowned away. " Now, by natural fitness, he's got ground for hope. I ain't got a square inch. She ain't on my claim. Next week my face'll be to the setting sun. So what do I do but go to him – this was before her young brother died – which I almost loved thebrother too – and s'l, 'Mr. Courteney, I've saw the sun go down and moon come up on this thing three times running, and every time and all between I've stood it, seeing you stand it. And I've studied it. And I see your fix. But most of us don't; so somebody's got to indorse you. Now, being a Kentuckian, not blue-grass but next door, I feel like doing it. You've *got* to play two hands and you *can't* play but one. Well, I'll play the one you can't. I'll fight them twins.' "

"Well, of all – and he accepted?"

"Now, you know he didn't. He said it would be absolutely impossible. But he said it the funniest way – ! It made me see the size of him for the first time. And, senator, he's life-size. But I reckon you knowed that before I did. He took me by the buttonhole, just as I'm holding you now, and talked to me as majestic as a father sending his boy off to school, and at the very same time and in the very same words as sweet as a girl sending her soldier to war."

"And he convinced you?"

"No, we was interrupted and couldn't talk it out. Well, I can't go back to him and resume, no more'n a wildcat bank. For one thing, I wouldn't take him from her."

"You don't mean they're together now?"

"Now, no, but by spells, yes. Bound to happen – so many of us so willing. I'd try to talk the thing out with this young man and Mr. Watson, but they all feel alike. Reckon it does 'em credit, but – well – I'd like to talk it out with you and the general. I think we can dispense with the boat's consent. Don't you?"

"Oh, Lord, man, what have I got to do with that?"

"Hold your horses, senator. I look at it this way: If the twins hadn't been too busy pecking at Mr. Hugh I'm just the sort o' man they'd 'a' pecked at, and hence I have a good moral right to waive their not doing it and take the will for the deed."

"Nonsense, my good friend; good joke, nothing more."

"Hold on; there's this anyhow: If Mr. Hugh *could* accept their invitation maybe he'd take me for his second; and what does second mean if it don't mean that if, after all, something should force him to drop out I could drop in?"

"Oh," laughed the senator, freeing his buttonhole by gentle force and edging away, "very well; but the twins! They're out! Look at *their* fix; *they* can't fight now."

"Senator, just so. But the general, all along he's sort o' been their second; indorsed for 'em same's I'd like to for Mr. Hugh. He'd be their second now if they could fight – as we know they'd be glad to. So, why ain't he honor bound to take their place if I take Mr. Hugh's? This young gentleman'll act for me – won't you? – yes, and the senator can act for the general. Then, senator, the first time we can get ashore we can settle the whole thing without involving Mr. Hugh and without ever letting the ladies know – or thecrowd either – that it ain't just our own affair. I can easily give the general cause, you know."

"My friend," said the cunning senator, who knew his ruling sin was tardiness and that he was tardy now, "I don't say anything could be fairer – in its right time. If you'll go to bed and to sleep "

"Senator, delays are dangerous. I might get the cholera. The general might get it. Or some other trouble might crop up and sort o' separate us."

Ah! It flashed into the senator's mind that California, though meaning all he said, had in full view the Gilmore-Harriet affair and that this was a move in that, a move to checkmate. His countermove had to be prompt; some one was coming up the nearest steps. "My dear sir, there *is* another trouble; serious, imminent, and almost sure to involve our friend Hugh in a vital mistake – Why, general, I thought you, at least, was asleep."

" Sss-enator, I was. I mmm-erely had not und-ressed. Have you fff-ound that young man?"

"Not yet, general. Let's go see him together. I want to see you, too, for just a moment, if these gentlemen will excuse me that long."

"Mr. Hugh's with the first clerk, yonder by the bell," said the gold hunter. "We'll wait here, eh?"

The general wanted to reply, but" I wish you would," responded the senator and hurried him away.

29

SECTION 29

XLIX

KANGAROO POINT

Aboard the *Votaress* was a gentle, retiring lady, large and fair, whom both Hugh and Ramsey had liked from the first, yet whose acquaintance they had made very slowly and quite separately. She was a parson's wife, who had never seen a play, a game of cards, or a ball, danced a dance, read a novel, tasted wine, or worn a jewel. She had four handsome, decorous, well-freckled children, two boys, two girls.

At table, until the married pairs of Vicksburg, Yazoo, and Milliken's Bend had gone ashore, she had not sat with the foremost- dozen, although she and the bishop spoke often together and were always "sister" and "brother." Her near neighbors at the board had been the Carthaginians and Napoleonites, and it was through them that she had met the Gilmores. To Ramsey and Hugh she had been made known by her children, one boy and girl having fallen wildly in love with the young lady's red curls, and the other two with Hugh and his frown.

The Gilmores' hearts she had won largely by the way in which her talks with them revealed the sweet charities of a soul unwarped by the tyrannous prohibitions under which she had been "born and raised"and to which she was still loyal; and she had crowned the conquest by a gentle, inflexible refusal to "brother" John the Baptist. In their lively minds she reawakened the age-old issue between artist and pietist. Said the amused Gilmore:

"Humiliate me? Not in the least. She only humbles me; she's such a beautiful example of "

"Yes, but, goodness, don't say it here!" said his wife. "Harriet" and the exhorter were already trouble enough.

Nevertheless, "What lovely types of character," insisted Gilmore, " come often, *so* often, from ugly types of faith!"

The wife flinched and looked about but he persisted: "So much better, my love – this is only my humble tribute to her – so *much* better is religion, even her religion, without the liberal arts than the liberal arts without religion. Faith is the foundation, they are the upper works."

"Dear, you should have been a preacher!"

"No, I'd always be preaching that one sermon. If I didn't tell it to you, I'd have to tell it to her, or make you tell her."

Mrs. Gilmore had not told her, but between the two women, across the gulf between them, there had grown such a commerce of silent esteem that neither Hugh nor Ramsey knew which one's modest liberalism to admire most. To Ramsey it was nothing against the matron that she was not nursing the immigrant sick. Only Madame Hayle was allowed to do that, and theparson's wife, being quite without madame's art of doing as she pleased, had had to submit conscience and compassions to the captain's forbiddal, repeated by the commodore and Hugh. But after the play she had insisted, "strict orders or none, and whether her children were four or forty-four," on entering the service of the busy Gilmores, "no matter how," and was now, with old Joy, in the pilot-house, a most timely successor to the actor's wife in the social care of Ramsey. For to Ramsey, in this first bereavement of her life, sleep was as abhorrent as if her brother's burial were already at hand. Grief was good, for grief was love. Sleep was heartlessness. Moreover, in sleep, only in sleep, there was no growth. Of course, that was not true; only yesterday and the day before she had grown consciously between evening and morning, grown wonderfully. But she had forgotten that and in every fibre of her being felt a frenzy for growth, for getting on, like the frenzy of a bird left behind by the flock. All the boat's human life, all its majestic going – led on by the stars – and especially all those by whose command or guidance it went, made for growth. So, too, did this dear Mrs. So-and-so, who could so kindly understand how one in deep sorrow may go on seeing the drollery of things. Grief, love, solace, growth, she was all of them in one. If she, Ramsey, might neither nurse the sick with her mother nor watch with Mrs. Gilmore and "Harriet," here was this dear, fair lady with the tenderest, most enlightening words of faith and comfort that ever had fallen on her ears; words never too eager or too many, but always just in time and volume to satisfy grief's fitful questionings.

For refuge they had tried every quarter of these upper decks; now paced them, now stood, now sat, and had found each best in its turn; but such open-air seclusion itself drew notice, made notice more felt, and so the dusk of the pilot-house had soon been found best of all. It remained so now – while the great chimneys out forward breathed soothingly, and a mile astern glimmered the *Westivood,* and a mile ahead glimmered the *Antelope,* and here among the few occupants of the visitors' bench there drifted a soft, alluring gossip about each newly turned bend of the most marvellous of rivers. To nestle back in its larboard corner while now some one came up and in and now some one slipped down and out, and while ever the pilot's head and shoulders and the upper spokes of his vigilant wheel stood outlined against the twinkling sky and rippling air, was like resting one's head on the *Votaress's* bosom.

And yet another reason made sleep unthinkable. He who had said, "I need you," was awake, was on watch. Now that the feud, blessed thought, was all off, sworn off, and a lingering mistrust of the twins seemed quite unsisterly, probably that need of her, or illusion of need, had passed. Well, if so he ought to say so! For here were great cares and dangers yet. The river was out of all its bounds. Most of those bounds themselves and the great plantations behindthem were under the swirling deluge. The waters of Scrubgrass Bend, for instance, were crosscutting over Scrubgrass Towhead in one league-wide sheet, and Islands Seventy-this-and-that and Islands Sixty-that-and-this were under them to their tree-tops. These things might be less fearful in fact than in show, or might be a matter wherein it was only a trifle more imbecile to think of her helping than in some others. Yet here were officers and servants of the boat busy out of turn and omitting routine duties unfortunate to omit and which she might perform if they would but let her. She noticed the presence of both pilots at once – Watson at the wheel, Ned on the bench. No wonder, with so awesome a charge; guiding a boat like this, teeming with human souls and driven pell-mell through such a war of elemental forces in desert darkness, with never a beacon light from point to point, from hour to hour; running every chute, with a chute behind nearly every point or island, and the vast bends looping on each other like the folds of a python and but little more to be trusted.

And here was this "Harriet" affair, a care and danger that as yet smouldered, but at any moment, with or without aid of the twins, might blaze. No one mentioned it, but you could smell it like smoke. And here was that supreme care and danger, the plague, with all the earlier precautions against it dropped, and with its constant triple question: Who next of the sick? Who next of the well? Who next on either of the decks below?

Two or three times Hugh came, sat awhile, spoke rarely, and went out. What a spontaneous new deference every one accorded him and with what a simple air of habitude he received it, though it seemed to mark him for bereavement as well as for command ! Why did he come? Why did he go? wondered Ramsey. Not that she would hinder him, coming or going. She could not guess that one chief object was care of her. She could only recall how lately they two had stood behind the footlights and sung their nonsense rhymes, partners in, and justified by, one brave, merciful purpose. Ought he to let care, danger, and grief, as soon as they had become acutely hers and his, drive him and her apart and strike him dumb to her, as dumb as a big ship dropping her on a desert shore and sailing away? Various subtleties of manner in others on the bench convinced her that they were thinking of him and her and thinking these same questions. What right had he to bring that upon her? Once, as he went out, somebody unwittingly stung her keenly by remarking, to no one in particular, that it was hard to see what should keep him so busy.

"D'you know," retorted Ned, "what running a boat is?"

"Why, yes, it's making things spin so smooth you can't see 'em spin, ain't it?"

"Right. Ever fly a kite? Not with yo' eyes sbet, hey? Well, a boat's a hundred kites. Ain't she, Watsy?"

"Two hundred," said Watson, at the wheel.

"But Mr. Hugh ain't actually running this boat, is be?"

"I ain't said he wuz," replied Ned, and

"He ain't a-runnin' no other," said Watson.

For an instant Ramsey was all pride for him they exalted; but in the next instant a wave of resentment went through her as if their vaunting were his; as if her pride were his own confessed, colossal vanity; as if the price of his uplift were her belittlement. Never mind, he should pay! Absurd, absurd; but she was harrowingly tired, lonely, idle, grief-burdened, and desolate, and absurdity itself was relief. He should pay, let his paying cost her double. Somehow, in some feminine, minute, pinhole way, she would deflate him, wing him, bring him down, before he should soar another round. With old Joy at her feet, in the dusk of her corner beyond Mrs. So-and-so, the parson's wife, she allowed herself a poor, bitter-sweet smile.

Each time when Hugh had come back to the bench, room had been hurriedly made for him next the parson's wife – "stabboard side" – who, speaking for all, promptly began to interrogate him, her first question always being as to his father's condition, which did not improve. Making room on the bench made room in the conversation – decoying pauses hopefully designed to lure him into saying something, anything, to Ramsey, or her to him; but always the kind trap had gone unsprung. Two or three tunes, obviously, Mrs. So-and-so's inquiries had first been Ramsey's to her; as when one of them elicited the fact that the nextturn would be Horseshoe Cut-off and Kangaroo Point; and once, at length, after twice failing to believe the ear she bent to Ramsey's murmur, she said audibly:

"Ask him, dear; ask him yourself."

Every one waited and presently Hugh remarked:

"I'll answer if lean."

"I'd rather," faltered Ramsey, "ask John the Baptist."

The unlucky mention took no evident effect on any one. If that was the snub she would have to try again.

"I can ask him for you," said Hugh. "He's up, expecting to leave us at Helena."

"No, thank you," she sighed, "you're too awfully busy. It won't make any real difference if I never find out."

"Won't sink the boat to ask," drawled Watson; but she remained silent till Hugh inquired:

"Are you sure I can't tell you?"

"Oh, you can!" came from Ramsey's dark corner. " But – with the whole boat in your care – we oughtn't to ask you things we don't have to know."

" Lard! belch it out," urged the innocent Ned, taking her in earnest; but again she was silent.

"Well? "said Hugh.

"Oh, well, are there many – ? Oh, it ain't important."

"Why, missy," muttered old Joy, "you's dess natchiully bleeds to ax it now."

"Yes, dear," said the parson's wife, "let's have it."

"Well – are there many – ? Oh, it's not – are there – are there many kangaroos on Kangaroo Point? "

At any outer edge of civilization a joke may be as hard and practical as ship's bread, yet pass. Amid the general mirth and while Hugh pulled a bell cord which made no jingle down in the engine-room and had never before been observed by Ramsey, his reply was prompt and brief but too gently solemn for her ear; and when she got Mrs. So-and-so to repeat it to her it was merely to the effect that, though kangaroos were few on Kangaroo Point, she ought to see the wealth of horseshoes in Horseshoe Cut-off.

Oh, kind answer! that excused her frivolity by sharing it. Kind beyond her utmost merit. She did not say so, but she thought it, sitting dumb, in sudden tears, and burning with shame for her blindness to the hour's fearful realities. While Ned stepped to Watson's side to speak critically of the *Antelope,* now shining on their starboard bow, Hugh, near the door, dropped a quiet request to the two or three other occupants of the bench and they followed him out.

"Why do they go?" she asked, fancying them as much appalled at her as she herself was, and when the sweet lady could not enlighten her the pilots offered a guess that two had gone to relieve Mrs. Gilmore and her maid and that Hugh would presently join the first clerk by the bell.

"There he is now," said Ned, actually expecting her to rise and look down. But she sat still and watched the *Antelope,* wishing her far better speed in view of the letters she carried. So came thoughts of the long telegraphic despatch to her father which Hugh must by this tune have written for her mother, as agreed between them, and which was to be sent, in the morning, from Memphis.

The door opened and Mrs. Gilmore and "Harriet" came in.

"Well," softly inquired the actor's wife, "how do we come on?" and Ramsey answered as softly, yet taking pains that Ned and Watson should overhear:

"I've disgraced myself."

"Mmm!" mumbled old Joy in corroboration.

"What have you done now?"

"Nothing. I don't *do* anything. Only said something, something so silly I can't even apologize."

"To whom?"

"The baby elephant," said Ramsey and laughed a note or two. The door opened again and Hugh's bell call was explained by the entrance of the texas tender and another white-jacket, each bearing a large tray of cups and plates, hot coffee, and hot toasted rolls and butter. She hadn't dreamed she was so hungry.

Watson stared back from the wheel with grim pretence of surprise. "Who sent that here?"

" Mr. Hugh Co'teney sawnt it, suh," said the tender, arranging the cups on the bench. "Yass'm," he repeated to the grateful ladies, "Mr. Hugh, yass'm."

"Oh! Mr. Hugh," replied Watson. "He must V gave you the order before he come up here this last time."

"Yass, suh, but say don't fetch it tell he ring."

"Six cups," counted the pilot, "six – You go down with Miss Hayle's compliments to Mr. Courteney, and "

"No-o-o-o!" sang Ramsey, running up the scale.

But Watson was firm. " Boy, you heard me, didn't you?"

Ned, with his eyes down on the bell, interposed: "Hold on, Wats', three into one you can't. Hugh's in a confab with the senator and the general."

Ramsey, eating like a hunter come home, suddenly stood. "Now look, everybody, at the *Antelope*. She's right . abeam. Ain't she abeam, Mr. Watson?"

Watson drawled that she wasn't anything else, and Ramsey failed to see that he saw her cast an anxious glance down to the bell and the captain's chair beyond it.

30

SECTION 30

L

"DELTA WILL DO"

In Horseshoe Cut-off the course was east. When Ned directed Ramsey's sight to its upper end, where the flood came into view from the north, she feared he would name the point it turned; but he forbore and she gazed on the thin old moon off in the southeast.

"Make out yan bunch o' sycamores?" was his nearest venture. The sycamores were on the point. Across the river where it ran concealed beyond those sycamores – he went on to tell – at the up-stream end of a low pencil stroke of forest between the head of the cut-off and the eastern stars, was another turn, Friar's Point. But her interest in points had faded, and whether friars abounded on that one or not she took pains not to inquire.

Instead, she was about to ask the cause of a strange silvering in the sky close over the black pencil stroke, when, as on Sunday, the morning star sprang into view and cast its tremulous beam on the waters. She gazed on the white splendor as genuinely enthralled as ever, though at the same time her eye easily, eagerly took in the first clerk, the senator, the general, and Hugh, standing about the captain's empty chair. They loomed as dimly as the sycamores, yet when afifth figure drew near them she knew by his fine gait that it was the actor, relieved from the captain's sickroom by "California" and the cub pilot. A gesture from Hugh stopped him some yards off and he stood leaning on the bell.

For the actor was their theme. This was plain to every one in the pilot-house, the two waiters being gone. A remnant of the food was being consumed by "Harriet" and Joy. All the others were observing, like Ramsey, the morning star and the five men under it. Among her own and Mrs. Gilmore's draperies Ramsey found that lady's hand. Except a few low words between the pilots, conversation failed. Without leave-taking Ned left. Presently here he was beneath, on the skylight roof, and now he joined the actor. Ramsey let go the caressed hand and moved nearer to Watson. While he and she gazed far up the stream, yet watched the six men below, he repeated Ned's question.

"See that clump o' big sycamores a mite to lab- board o' where we're p'inted?"

She didn't believe she did.

"Well," he persisted, "that's it."

"That's what?"

"Why," said Watson, whose only aim was to set her once more at ease, "that's the p'int you "

" Humph." She turned to the two ladies, who, with their eyes frankly below, were counselling together. "Let's go down there ourselves," she said, but they whispered on.

"Better not," put in Watson; "you can't help."

His kind intent did not keep the words from hurting. With a faint toss she said:

"I hoped we might be some hindrance."

She laughed in her old manner, dropped her glance again on the two men and the four, and hearkened. So did the two ladies beside her. They could all see who spoke below and could hear each voice in turn, though they could not catch what was said. The only sustained speeches were the senator's. The general's interpellations were little regarded. The silent pair at the bell heard everything of essential bearing.

The consciously belated senator had begun with rhetorical regrets for the captain's and the commodore's illness and with paternal enthusiasm for those on whom it had brought such grave new cares. His own sympathetic share in their anxieties, he had hurried on to say, had robbed him of sleep and driven him up here solely for this interview. On the way he had chanced upon the general in the

"Sssame ffframe of mind," the general had said, while the senator pressed as straight on as the *Votaress*.

As far as the interests involved were private to this boat, he said, her officers and owners were entitled to keep them so and to be let alone in the management of them. But when that management became by its nature a vital part of an acute public problem – a national political issue – he felt bound, both as the Courteneys' private well-wisher and as a public servant, to urge such treatment of the matter as its national importance demanded. A spark, he said, might burn a city! A question of private ownership not worth a garnishee might set a whole nation afire! The arrival of Gilmore at the bell threw him into a sudden heat:

"My God! Mr. Courteney – Mr. clerk – 7 shan't offer to lay hands on *any* man; not I. All 7 ask is that you take yours off – of three. My dear sirs, equally as your true friend and as a lover of our troubled country I *beg* you to liberate those citizens of the sovereign State of Arkansas whom you hold in unlawful duress, and to hear before witnesses the plea they regard as righteous and of national concern." i

The sight of Ned joining Gilmore heated him again: "Gentlemen, if you will do that, now, at once, you will save the fortunes of this superb boat, her honored owners, and their fleet. If you don't you wreck them forever before this day dawns. And you may – great heavens, gentlemen, you *may* see the first bloodshed of sectional strife."

"K-'tional ssstrife!" growled the general.

The clerk smiled. "Why, senator, those men don't go beyond Helena. They leave us there, before sun- up."

"Precisely, sir! And if they're not set free before you enter Helena Reach, or even pass Friar's Point, you may as well not free them at all."

Hugh glanced at the clerk as if to speak. The clerk nodded and in the pilot-house they saw Hugh begin:

" Mr. Senator, suppose we do that?"

" You would do me honor, sir, and yourselves more."

"Of course the watchmen of this boat watch."

As Hugh said this the cub pilot came from the captain's room with some word to Gilmore, who, though yearning to stay, left him and Ned and hastened back to the texas.

Meantime the senator: "I should hope so, sir. I hope every one on watch watches, sir."

" They do. And so we know that you and the general know, perfectly, that the same men who want those three released want Mr. Gilmore put ashore. Is that your wish, too?"

"It is, sssir," put in the general while the senator did some rapid thinking. Now he too replied:

"Mm – no, sir, it is not. And yet – yes, sir, it is."

"Then you would advise us to do that also?"

"I would advise you to do that also."

"Why?"

"Good Lord! my young friend, to save you! you, your father, grandfather, boats, all, and Mr. Gilmore himself!"

"How about his wife?"

"And his wife. For her to be with him may help him if he goes. It can't if he stays." The speaker had let his voice rise. The pilot-house group caught his words. Also they saw the cub pilot detain Ned when he started forward.

"Let's go down there ourselves," repeated Ramsey; but the parson's wife had whisperingly laid both handson the wife of the actor, and Ramsey chafed to no avail.

The senator's voice dropped again. "Good God, sir, you know the longer they're aboard the worse it will be for them, and they've got to go some time or at Louisville a mob will burn the *Votaress* to the water's edge with them on her."

The two stared at each other, the senator's mind bewailing the loss of each golden moment. The night was not too dark to show him the poker face fitting its nickname insufferably. But not until its owner spoke again did he frown – to hide an exultant surprise.

"They could leave their maid, you think, with Madame Hayle?" was Hugh's astonishing inquiry. The senator had expected of him nothing short of a grim defiance.

"They could – they can," replied both he and the soldier. "That'll satisfy everybody." The general saw only the surface of the proposition but the senator perceived in it all the opportunity their two modest accomplices of the boiler deck asked. That pair and their adherents – not followers – you wouldn't catch them leading – they and their gathering adherents would construe the landing of the players as an attempt to deliver them out of their hands and would undertake to seize and maltreat the actor, at least, the moment he should be off the boat. That they were likely to fail was little to the senator; there would be a tumult, so managed as to bring Hugh to the actor's rescue, and in the fracas Hugh was sure of a hammering he would not only never forget but would discern that he owed, first and last, to him, the senator.

Hugh glanced at the clerk. "You had just recommended Delta Landing." The clerk nodded and he turned back to the senator. "We'll be there inside of half an hour."

" Delta will do," said the senator, his frown growing.

Hugh nodded to the clerk. The clerk looked over to Ned.

"Think Delta's above water?"

"Oh – eyes and nose out, Watson allows."

"Delta'll be all right," persisted the senator.

The clerk glanced up to the pilot-house. "Mr. Watson, we'll stop at Delta, to put off a couple o' passengers."

"Yes, sir." The group at the pilot's back gasped at each other. Then Ramsey gasped at him.

"Oh, what does that mean?" she demanded. But his gaze remained up the river as he kindly replied:

"What it says, I reckon. Don't fret, ladies – when you don't know what to do, don't do it."

"Ho-o-oh!" cried Ramsey, whisking away, "I will!"

"Lawd 'a' massy!" Old Joy sprang for the door, but Ramsey was already out on the steps and scurrying down them. On the texas roof, however, she took a wrong direction and lost time; slipped forward round the pilot-house counting on steps which were not, and never had been, out there. Returning she lost more by meeting old Joy in the narrow way between the house and the edge of the texas roof, and when at length she sprang away for the after end of the texas and the only stair she was now sure of, whom should she espy bound thither ahead of her but Mrs. Gilmore. In that order the three hurried down to the guards of the texas and forward along them by its stateroom doors.

Meantime, out at the bell the clerk had left Hugh and privately sent Ned and the cub pilot different ways. Hugh moved a pace or two aside to observe the *Antelope* out on their larboard quarter. The senator and the general moved with him.

"She'll pass you again at Delta," remarked the senator. "You see, general – you see, Mr. Courteney, – at Delta they" (the players) "can very plausibly explain – there won't be more than two or three, if any, to explain to – that they're running from the cholera and want to hail the *Westwood,* which they won't more than just have time to do.

"She won't mind taking them," he babbled on, "already having the cholera herself. Not many up- river boats would answer a hail from Delta, but she will, for she'll see they're from this boat and that it's your wish. There she comes round the bend now. Yes, Delta's a lot safer for 'em than Helena with its wharf-boat and daylight crowd and those three red- hots going ashore with 'em. On the *Westwood* they can put up with any yarn that'll carry 'em through. They're actors and used to that sort o' thing."

Musingly Hugh broke in: "Counting all the chances, isn't there a touch of cruelty in this, to the lady at least?"

"Oh, now, my young friend – " the senator began to rejoin, but two men lounging by stopped to ask after the father and grandfather. They were the second engineer and his striker, presently to go on watch.

Mrs. Gilmore, coming along the texas guards, met the cub pilot. He perched on the railing to let her pass and a few strides farther on began to do the same for Ramsey.

31

SECTION 31

LI

LOVING-KINDNESS

Ramsey stopped and the boy's heart rose into his throat.

"Whe're you going?" she asked.

He pointed to a lighted door she had just come by.

"First mate's room," he said.

"To tell him what to do?"

"Yes'm." He slid along the rail to get by her, though hungry to linger.

"To do what?" she asked. "I know; to bring out John the Baptist and those other two men?"

"Yes'm." He backed off, but the compelling power of interrogatory, especially of hers, retarded him.

"To turn 'em loose?" she asked.

He smiled ruefully. "It looks like it."

"Not with their pistols on them?"

"Oh, no, he's got their pistols."

"How'dheget'em?"

"Oh – friendly persuasion. He's fine at that. They'll get 'em back – unloaded – when they land."

She glanced forward after Mrs. Gilmore, and he sprang away. As the actor's wife neared the captain's door it opened and Gilmore himself came out, closing it after him warily. Either the captain wasworse, Ramsey guessed, or the actor had received some startling message, so grave and hurried were the players. They moved several paces away and stepped down to the hurricane-deck. She let them converse a moment alone. At the same time the second engineer, his striker, and Ned passed close and went below. Now Ramsey advanced, addressing the pair in a smothered voice:

"It's monstrous! It shan't be! It shan't be done! You shan't go!" The signal for landing tolled. She stopped short.

But the cause of her silence was Hugh Courteney, close before her. Mrs. Gilmore tried to draw her back but she stood fast, repeating to him savagely: "It shan't be! It shan't be done! You shan't do it!"

Again she ceased, as the senator and the general appeared, not with Hugh though from his direction, but, like Ned and his fellows, bound below. With a side step she brought them to a stand, saying once more to them:

"It shan't be! It shan't be done! You shan't

Both Hugh and Gilmore lifted a hand. There was a reply on the lips of each, but Hugh's remained un- uttered. He glanced to the actor, saying: "Tell it."

The actor told. "It is not going to be done," he said. "No owner of this boat, no officer, has ever promised, ordered, or intended it."

Ludicrously, from the well of the neighboring stair, the heads of Hayle's twins rose and remained gazing. Fortunately for the dignity of the moment they escaped the eye of Ramsey, who, on highest tiptoe, while the actor still spoke, was piping incredulously:

"The clerk said it! – two passengers! – to go ashore!"

"He might have said five," Hugh gravely answered, while the senator and the general blazed with astonishment.

"Five," he repeated directly to the senator; "the three whose release you demanded and those two scamps you made league with a bit ago on the boiler deck."

The senator was a conflagration. "Sir, I cannot find !"

"Words?" Hugh softly interrupted. "That's fortunate. If you do you'll be landed on the next island."

He turned away and moved to the edge of the roof. Ramsey stared at the three and fell back to the Gil- mores, whose manner, as they returned half-way to the sick-room, was more grave and hurried than before. The engine bells were jingling, the wheels stopped. At the roof's edge, well forward of Hugh, appeared the first clerk, giving commands. The shore trees glided spectrally into the firelight of the steamer's torch baskets. A solitary man stood on the bank. The morning star was fading into the daybreak. In the pilot-house Watson pulled his bell-ropes to back and to stop again, while veiled in its lingering dusk between him and the parson's wife "Harriet" stood ata closed window, a vigilant watcher of every movement below.

With the usual deck-hand on its outer end the stage hung half its length over the narrowing water. On its inboard half, attended at one side by the first mate and at their backs by a knot of white-jackets with hands and arms full of baggage, waited the exhorter, his two champions, and the sporting pair, outwardly well content, however large or dark the retributions they were inwardly promising themselves. The twins had come up from the stair, meeting the senator and the general and holding them in a close counsel that kept the four scowling. These things the maid at Watson's side noted so intently as almost to forget him and the lady next her. She marked the actor go once more into the captain's room, the Californian come out to Mrs. Gilmore and Ramsey, and the three move toward Hugh with old Joy in their wake. Before they had quite reached him he turned and addressed the actor's wife. She drew back apologetically, the Californian doing the same, but by word and sign seemed to bid Ramsey stay and speak for her.

As if to himself, but really to the two beside him, Watson murmured: " Right you air, Mr. Hugh Courte- ney."

"How is he right?" asked the lady, though she most likely, and the maid certainly, understood.

"He's telling her," said the pilot, "that it'll simplify matters for her and her husband and this girl here to sort o' keep out o' the limelight a spell."

The surmise seemed good, for Mrs. Gilmore and "California" took stand where the great chimney on that side hid them from forecastle and shore, while they still could see Hugh and Ramsey conversing, she pleadingly, he with few words, mostly negatives. Ned came back into the pilot-house. The parsDn's wife moved from Watson toward him to ask in undertone why the landing was being made so slowly. The boat seemed to hover and hesitate. Watson, at the wheel, talked on, pretending not to notice that the maid was his only listener.

"A man," he drawled, "gets to hear a right smart chance with his eyes, in a pilot-house. Puts two an' two together a lot more'n he does when he's a-usin' his y-ears. Now she's a-beggin' him" – meaning Ramsey and Hugh – " not to drop them fellows ashore. Partly that's for the fellows' own sakes, but likewise it's also for the play-actors, because they're generous, like her, and because, no less, it's a-putt'n' the play-actors themselves in a right funny fix with the rest o' this vain world, to make five Jonahs on their account. But she's a-barkin' up the wrong stump an' she knows it. She knows there's somebody else's account they're bein' put off for; somebody she's as friendly to as what he is, and which for their sakes – his and hern – if for no other – I'm as friendly to as what they air. Pro- vid'n', however, that that somebody is as friendly to them, every way, as what I am." He turned sharply. "Is she?"

And "Harriet" looked straight into his eyes and said inaudibly: "Yes."

As the glance of both returned to the scene below she was mindful that Ned had not yet quite satisfied the query of the lady at his elbow, why the wheels of the *Votaress* were turning barely enough to keep her from drifting.

"You see the *Antelope?"* he asked.

She saw the *Antelope,* once more ahead, swan-white in the new daylight on a great breadth of water which she had earlier heard him tell Ramsey was Monte- zuma Bend.

"And you see the *Westwood* down yonder. Well, when she gets up there we'll stop killin' time. But why we're killin' it – ask the clerk – or guess. It's dead easy."

Not given to guessing, she dropped her eyes again on the various groups beneath with Hugh and Ramsey central among them and did not even see that Hugh was answering the same riddle from Ramsey.

"Because if we keep these men aboard a few minutes longer," he was saying, "there'll be no way for them to reach Helena before noon to-morrow, when we'll be "

" 'Way beyond Memphis," said the river-wise Ramsey.

"Yes."

" And they can't send any troublesome word up the river that can overtake us," she ventured on, and he assented.

"And may I tell the Gilmores that's as much for Phyllis as for them?"

" I wish you would – and then would go to your rest."

"Humph," she faintly soliloquized and with no other rejoinder remained looking down on the stage, as he did. It was so near the bank at last that the men waiting on its inner end moved a step or two forward.

"Why are all those five put off together?" she asked.

"Because," he replied in his absent manner, "the gamblers will try to keep the other three quiet."

"Mr. Hugh, you'll be off watch now soon, won't you?"

"Yes." (Still no lifting of eyes by either.)

"And then you'll nurse your father, won't you?"

"I cannot! I'm too ignorant."

"Then what will you – shall you – do?"

"Just stay – on watch."

She stood a moment more, comforted to be on watch with him and thinking sadly of all there was to be on watch for. Then she heard Julian softly call her name. Without looking his way she started back for Mrs. Gilmore and the gold hunter, but the brother overtook her.

"Ramsey." She faced him. "Ramsey" – his tone was thin – "when you were talking just now with that pusillanimous whelp, and neither of you looking at the other, did he say anything of a confidential nature?"

His scrutiny read confirmation in her fearless eyes. When she would have spoken her utterance failed and, unable to do anything else hah so well, she laughed. "You can still do that!" His hint was of Basile.

"A little," she tinkled again, though her eyes ran full.

"Ramsey, did he – over there – just now – that reptile – say anything – tender? "

She flared rose-red, gazed down ashore, dropped her voice to a key he had never heard, and said, wondering why she said it: "Mr. Courteney is a gentleman."

She tried to lift her eyes to the inquisitor, but her irrepressible twitter came again and she had to turn away to the big chimney. He clinched his teeth.

"Sis," he half whispered as she began to go, "listen." She glanced back. "Sis, you may snigger at us all day or ten days; you may listen to him for a year or for ten; but, no matter what we swore to last night, the day you accept Hugh Courteney's hand we'll kill him if we're alive."

Old Joy flinched and moaned but Ramsey stared at him benumbed. She caught no rational grasp of his meaning; only stood and with immeasurable speed and a kind of earthquake sickness, in the space of one long breath, dreamed his words over and over. She felt neither fright nor horror, as she would as soon as thought could clear. Yet one word shed light, quickened her inner vision and gave it a reach, a forward range, it had never known. " Ten years," he had said, and for the first time in her life, as one might come suddenly into some vast possession, she took the future into her present by years instead of days.

"Jule," called Lucian, from between the senator and the general. Julian glanced back and Ramsey started off. But she stopped again with a fresh shock as a high-pitched yell rose from the shore below. There the exhorter, stepping from the stage to the ground, had poured his voice into the woods and now turned to the boat and let loose his tongue:

"I'm the hewolf an' wilecat o' th' 'Azoo Delta ! I'm the alligatoh an' snappin' turkle o' the Arkansass! I'm the horn-ed an' yalleh-belly catfish o' the Missis- sip'!. Glory, hallelu'! the sunburnt, chill-an'-feveh, rip-saw, camp-meetin', buckshot, kickin'-mule civilization whah-in I got my religion is good enough fo' me, all high-steppin', niggeh-stealin' play-actohs an' flounced and friskin', beau-ketchered Natchez brick- tops to the contrary notwithstayndin'! For I'm a meek an' humble follower o' the Lawd Gawd A'mighty, which may the same eternally an' ee-sentially damn yo' cowa'dly soul, you stump-tail' little Hugh Co'te- ney up yandeh with yo' Gawd-fo'sakened, punkin face an' yo' sawed-off statu'e!"

The gamblers sprang to hush him but the two " Arkansas killers" stepped between and while the *Votaress,* backing out into the wake of the *Westwood,* left the one pair insisting and the other protesting, the exhorter settled the issue by breaking into song:

"' Though num'r-ous hosts uv migh-tye foes,
Though *an ill* an" hell, my way op-pose,
He safe-lye leadns my soudl aa-logn:
His lov-ign-kide-ness, oh, how strogn!
His lov-ign-kide-ness! lov-ign-kide-ness!
His lov-ign-ki-i-i-ide-ness, oh, how strogn!' " LII

LOVE RUNS ROUGH BUT RUNS ON

Turning east in the upper arm of Saint Francis Bend, with the mouth of Saint Francis River just swinging out of sight astern and Helena an hour's run behind, the *Votaress* faced the rising sun.

Before the eyes of Hugh and Ramsey it soared gloriously into a sky reddened not by presage of rain but by the smoke of the *Antelope* and *Westwood.* The intervening shore and waters glowed and quivered in exquisite tints that renewed the world's youth and quite ignored all human, especially all young human, troubles. Suddenly it lighted up the black chimneys and scapes and white pilot-houses of the two boats ahead, as, a league or so apart, they came doubling back northwest, up Walnut Bend, to save in Bordeaux Chute the wide circuit of Bordeaux and Whiskey Islands, to hurry on round the long north-and-south loop of Council Bend and so have done with one of the most tortuous forty miles of the Mississippi.

We mention these things because Hugh and Ramsey were students of them, now and then together but never quite comfortable so, and now and then apart but never quite comfortable so. Everywhere theboat's people were awake. On the freight deck the crew squatted in circles, eating from tubs. Away aft on the roof, from *their* quarters in the far end of the texas, the whole flock of white-jackets had risen like gulls and were down in the cook-house, pantry, and cabin rattling the crockery till it echoed in every waking stomach. Already the *Votaress's* divine breath smelt of coffee, real coffee – *chattd comme l'enfer et rurir comme le diable* – smelt of it, as, we fear, we shall never smell it again in this trust-ridden world. It was Ned's watch at the wheel. Watson and his cub had turned in. So had the first clerk. So had the twins, the senator, the general. Few of us, at that hour, not having slept, are skylarks.

Yet the actor and the Californian still held vigil by the captain's bed. Joy still hovered after her "young missy," and "Harriet" after Mrs. Gilmore and the parson's wife. Ramsey and "Harriet" betrayed a vivid interest in each other, a wonderfully generous thing on the maid's part, Ramsey thought, the two being who they were. The commodore was better, but the captain was not, and together or apart Hugh and Ramsey were more consciously the prisoners, albeit the undaunted prisoners, of care and sorrow than of anything else. When their feeling for the river's lore drew them, by a spiritual gravitation, to a common centre – to learn, for instance, that Council Bend and Council Island were named for one of those historic "confabs" between the white man and the red which shouldered the red brother once andforever away from the sunrise and across the great river – that centre of gravity was the captain's chair, their tutor the first mate.

Under the circumstances we hardly need begrudge a line or two more to tell how, as far back as Delta, the *Votaress* had begun to meet the Louisville Saturday evening packets and to receive and return their special salutes. One was a Hayle boat and one a Courteney. Such moments were refreshing. Inquiry and information flowed through them as naturally and beguilingly as a brook through a meadow and gave Hugh opportunity to contemplate incidentally the play of air and light in Ramsey's curls without her having the slightest suspicion of him! – gave her chances to ply him with questions in autobiography and social casuistry and to enjoy keenly the ridiculous majesty of his eyes and voice, while the two dear chaperons talked apart as obliviously as if she were merely asking him how deep the whiskey was in Whiskey Chute.

In the long run from Commerce to Norfolk came breakfast. Commerce was another case of infant- city still-birth, Norfolk was less. Breakfast, double- ranked, stoop-shouldered, mute: beefsteak and fried onions its solar centre, with hot rolls for planets; Hugh at the ladies' table, the first clerk at the gentlemen's. Then the boiler deck, toothpicks, cigars, breezes, armchairs, spittoons, the sad news of the two deaths upstairs, the ugly news of the five passengers set ashore and the reason thereof. Men spat straight and hardas they heard or told the latter item, yet with tacit unanimity awaited the re-emergence of the still secluded senator, general, and twins.

By Hugh's unsmiling forethought Madame Hayle, Ramsey, and the Gilmores breakfasted in the pilothouse. With "Harriet" close to her elbow, Ramsey ate at a window, standing, to watch the gliding shores and floods and privily cross-examine, again in autobiography and at printing-press speed, the willing maid-servant. At Island Fifty-Two another boat, the *Shooting Star,* streamed by. At a plantation and wood-yard the *Votaress* paused to restock with dairy and kitchen-garden supplies and to lash to her either side a thirty-cord wood flat, and now swept on with the foam twenty feet broad at the square front of each while the deck-hands trotted aboard under their great shoulder loads by one narrow hook plank and came leaping back for more, and the loaders and pilers chanted and chorussed:

"Oh, Shan-a-do'e, I loves yo' daught-eh –

Ah! ha ! roll-in' riveh! – Oh, ef she don't love me she'd ought teh – Ali! Int! . . . bound away ! . . . fawdewile . . . Mi-'ou-ree!"

The foam and the swift wooding-up gave an illusion of speed to the boat herself, and in what seemed no time at all the empty scows were dropping away astern; but it was farewell for good and all to the *Westwood,* the *Antelope.* And now Cat Island, its bend, its chute; Cow Island, its bend, its chute; HornLake, a prehistoric loop of twelve miles, reduced to three by Horn Lake Bend

"Come, Ramsey." The call smote like a buffet. Memphis was almost in sight. In the southwestern corner of Tennessee, just above Tennessee Chute and the northwestern corner of Mississippi, was the fourth of the Chickasaw Bluffs. On it sat Memphis, a city with churches, banks, and the "electromagnetic telegraph." Its twelve thousand people of that day are a hundred and thirty-five thousand now and have taken in almost out of remembrance the small settlement of Pickering, or Fort Pickering, on the downstream end of the bluff, where the *Votaress* that beautiful morning landed and laid to rest Madame Marburg, the bishop, and Basile.

Aboard the *Votaress,* as in Tennessee Chute she faced again the morning sun, two scenes were enacted at the same time. One took place below, on the forecastle; the other above and just aft of it, on the boiler deck. In the lower there was but a single pine box, in the upper there were two. In the lower stood the black-gowned priest, the two white-bonneted, gray- robed sisters, Otto Marburg alone, and here a mass of immigrants and there a majority of the crew. The upper scene included all the cabin passengers – ladies seated – and half the boat's family. In fulfilment of Basile's wish Hugh read: "I am the resurrection and the life." By Hugh's invitation, given beforehand, the senator delivered a eulogy on the bishop and added such tender praises of the boy, whom every one hadliked so early and so well, and gilded them with such delicate allusions to the heroism of his mother, that few eyes were dry. The very twins wept, though there was a touch of rage in their tears. By choice of the parson's wife and sweetly led by her, they sang: "I would not live alway." With streaming eyes Ramsey remembered how yearningly the poor lad had clung to this dear earth, and she could only sit silent and modestly wonder how anybody, under any fate that left them power to sing at all, could sit there – stand there – on that boat, that river, in the splendor of that sun, the beauty of that landscape, and call life a " few lurid mornings."

A third scene occurred as the boat, facing westward, reached the head of President's Island, fairest island in all the river, and coming into full view of Memphis, a short league beyond, tolled her solemn bell and landed at Pickering. Others on the lower deck besides Madame Marburg had passed away in the night but had either been laid under the wet sands of the water's edge in some wild grove down-stream or were not quite in time, so to speak, for this landing. Contemplated from each deck by a numerous gathering and from the pilot-house by Watson, Mrs. Gilmore, and "Harriet," a small procession followed the priest and the three boxes – borne by white-jackets –

ashore and out of sight where a small wooden church spire, inland behind the bluff, peered over its crest. Madame Hayle leaned on Julian's arm, Ramsey on Lucian's, Hugh walked with Marburg, the senator with thegeneral, the first clerk with Ned, the Californian with the cub pilot. By and by they returned, outwardly unburdened, and the moment the last tread, the Cali- fornian's, was on the stage, Watson's bells jingled and the *Votaress* swung out and moved up to the Memphis wharf-boat. But there Hugh, the first clerk, the steward, and the doctor went up into town, and it was a long hour before they reappeared and the black smoke billowed again from her chimneys and she backed out and started up and away around "Paddy's Hen and Chickens."

The "family of that name" – to quote Watson – were a group of four islands so entitled from earliest flatboat days, clustered in the river, just above the town. Since that day two of the chicks have flown, or grown, to the mainland, and the mother bird is now merely the "Old Hen" with one "Chicken Island," while "Poor Paddy," we are told, "works on the railway."

In its first forty leagues above Memphis the river went – has gone – still goes – through more violent writhings than in any like part of its whole course, running almost twenty crazy miles to make two sane ones – made finally, in the republic's hundredth year, by Centennial Cut-off. On an average there was an island for every four miles of river, or, say, three for every hour of the *Votaress's* progress, and in this high water she was running all their chutes. A great resource such incidents were, on that particular day, to Ramsey. At any moment when conversation neededto be started, stopped, or turned, here was her chance. Some of the islands covered many square miles, contained large plantations, and had names as well as numbers. Island Forty, reached about ten o'clock, was also Beef Island. Number Thirty-eight, which they began to pass half an hour later, was Brandy- wine Island. To pass Island Thirty-five on its short side at full speed took half an hour, and Forked-Deer Island, which kept the boat flying up a narrow chute from half-past two till three o'clock, was old Twenty-seven and Twenty-six grown together.

Now, these things are geography rather than history. But for at least two souls aboard the *Votaress* they were more history than geography. History – they were life! the outer frame of life so really lived that for those two souls it would be history thenceforth to life's end. And here comes in some pure philosophy from the two pilots: to wit, that if you turn any old maxim over you will always find another truth on its other side. They reached this conclusion through Ned's remarking that the course of true love never runs smooth.

"That," said Watson, "depends. It depends a lot on who they air that's a-takin' the course. Ef they're the right ones, a real for-true pair, sech as the wayfarin' man though a pilot kin see *air* a pair, like "

"Two gloves," said Ned.

"Yass, or galluses – I misdoubt ef there's anything in the world that'll run so smooth through and overand around and under so much cussed roughness as what true love will."

The remark was justified before their eyes. The two whom they contemplated, outwardly so unlike, were in their essence so of a kind that they belonged each to each as simply and patently as the first human pair. They saw it so themselves. Society about them was strangely primitive – a "clapboard civilization," the actor named it to his wife at their pilothouse point of view – and the "for-true" pair in sight below them took frank advantage of its conditions to appropriate and accept each other as simply and completely as if these weird conditions – with their Devil's Elbow, Race-ground, Island, Tea-table, and Back- oven – were a veritable Eden as Eden was before the devil got in. Without a note of courtship or coquetry love ran ever more and more smoothly, growing hourly and receiving each accession as we have seen the Mississippi receive Red River – merely by deepening its own flow – but, unlike the Mississippi, gaining in transparency as it gained in depth and power.

Sin e leaving Memphis this love without courtship or coquetry had grown under the effulgence of Madame Hayle's immediate presence like a grain-field in sunshine. On her return from the triple burial, through sheer exhaustion, she had fainted away. Borne upstairs by the physician's command and allowed the roof but forbidden the lower deck for twenty-four hours, she had let Mrs. Gilmore and "Harriet" assume her pious task'turn about, going and coming byafter stairs. And so love grew on. But so did hate, so did craft, all three, to borrow the figure, going and coming by the after stairs of general intercourse.

32

SECTION 32

LIII

TRADING FOR PHYLLIS

This afternoon was cooler than any of the three before it.

Change of latitude, assuredly; but also a sky half blue, half gray, and a brisker air. Yet for that small minority of the ladies, who rather craved than feared the sunlight, the boat's roofs – since custom debarred them from the boiler deck – were still its most inviting part. After a few modifications of dress a very pleasant refuge those roofs were, although when the boat's course led her into the wind it was good to shut a sash or two if you were in the pilot-house, or to draw your chairs into the lee of something if on the open deck. Madame Hayle, urged by all to seek repose in her stateroom, said to Hugh and the Cali- fornian, behind one of the chimneys:

"Me, I fine it mo' betteh to breathe on that deck than to bleach in that cabin."

Her presence was to the Californian's advantage also, in his desire to be near Ramsey, and indeed the same was true of the two younger clerks and the cub pilot. And this advantage was heightened by the fact that there were such definite things to be considered wherever two or three came together. The need to keep up the passengers' spirits was as real as ever anda number of resources for doing it required to be discussed. Ramsey mentioned the unidentified man with the cornet but found no seconder. His "Life on the Ocean Wave" was thought hardly convincing and his "Bounding Billow, Cease thy Motion" seemed to clash with the sentiment for an ocean life and to suggest uncomfortable symptoms. Undaunted, she tried again. Through Basile she had early discovered three striplings of the circus ring, the "Brothers Ambrosia." Their true name, her cross-examination had revealed, was Vinegar. In star-spangled tights they would give some real " acrobatics," then some " aerial globe dancing," equally star-spangled and even more up-side- down, and finally a bit of "miraculous walking" on champagne bottles set upright on the dining-table. This proposition was accepted without audible dissent, only the parson's wife not voting. Then the Californian spoke for a self-styled "young gent" and "amateur professor" who had eagerly volunteered to "take everybody's breath away" by the magic of his tricks with hats, handkerchiefs, and cards, and to "throw them into convulsions" with his "evening cat fight among the chimney-pots." But "Beware the laugh that sours overnight," Mrs. Gilmore said, and the decision was prompt, Madame Hayle voicing it, that as convulsions could be brought on and breath taken away by the cholera itself the young gent, through "California," be gratefully requested to await a situation either less desperate or more so. The gold hunter admitted the wisdom of this action, though his humble spirit felt acutely its discrediting reflection on himself, especially when – with only the kindest meaning – Ramsey laughed. He bravely kept his pain to himself and said nothing to disown the "amateur professor." With a brief aside to Hugh, to which Hugh nodded, he slipped away to the lower deck and for nearly two hours made his nursing skill so valuable to "Harriet" among the immigrants that her fearless mind overlooked the main object of his stay; which was to defend her from any stratagem of the twins and others, that Marburg might not detect in time or might be unable to cope with. At length, puzzled to know why Mrs. Gilmore did not appear, he was leaving, when at the foot of the narrow stair under the kitchen he met Lucian coming down. They stopped. He smiled. "Howdy!" he said.

Lucian stood silent.

"Can't come down here, you know," said the gold hunter, and instantly Lucian was white hot.

"Who tells you," he drawled, "what I may or may not do?"

"Who? oh – just a little black dog."

"Black – *what?*"

"You heard. He's a funny little cuss; like you, a trifle puny. Has coughin' fits. Coughs six times each fit. Spits up a chunk o' lead ev'y time he coughs. Want to see him?"

Lucian's unaffrighted eyes blazed down, though his reply was as if to himself. "Great God! if my

brother "

"Oh," kindly said the Californian, "he ain't fur off. Go, get him. I'll follow you, lock-step."

Lucian turned and went, the speaker adding as he followed close:

" Ladder's no place for scienced fighting, you know."

They found Julian, evidently waiting, on the passenger guards just forward of the pantry gangway. But before words could be exchanged the cub pilot came along by way of the main staircase, escorting the physician from the lower deck. The latter passed on up the wheel-house steps to the roof, but the "cub" hung back. "California" faced him.

"What's the fraction? The captain?"

The youth nodded. His inquirer waved him away.

"All right. I'll come. You go on." The boy complied.

Julian had swelled for encounter, but a warning look from Lucian checked him and he let the Californian speak first.

"Here," said the gold-digger, "I'm fixed. You're not. True, I could loan you the twin to mine, but "

Julian's lip curled. "'But' – you're not hungry to fight."

"Oh, other things being equal, I have an appetite! Yes, sir-ee, Bob Hoss-Fly, and a red dog under the wheelbarrow! But" – smiling again – "let's do things in scientific order. You two claim that you Hayle folks own that forty-year-old white gal downstairs which you call a runaway niggeh, and which we'll allow she is one. Well, I'll buy you two's share in her – providing I can buy the rest of her from your two ladies up-stairs – and fight you afterward or not as the case may require. Now, what'll you take for your said two shares, right here, cash down, gold; not dust but coin, New Orleans Branch Mint? Going at – what do I hear?"

The spendthrift pair stared on each other, thinking with all their might. But they failed to think that on the deck above them, in group with Mrs. Gilmore, Hugh, the parson's wife, Ramsey, and old Joy, the ownership of Phyllis was being fully set forth by their mother to their own whilom champions the senator and the general, or that Ramsey was about to be sent down to the stateroom of the mother and daughter for documentary evidence.

"What do I hear?" repeated the Californian, watching his own hands as the right drew double- eagles from his belt and stacked them in the left.

Eagerly asking themselves what might be their tempter's motive, the pair thought primarily of the white slave's well-preserved beauty and the rarity of women in the far West. With that came a stinging remembrance of her glaring Hayle likeness and then of their father's old scheme – averted by their mother – to sell the girl forever out of sight and reach. And then came the pleasanter thought that at any rate here was a chance to put this daredevil at odds with the hated Gilmores as well as with their own mother and sister, the Courteneys, and all the Courteney clan. Till now they had felt that, if only for self-respect andgood standing, they must recover their property, seize Phyllis on the spot, if they could possibly command the backing to do it. But this was now very doubtful. Something had happened to the senator's mind, while the general was but his echo and the element called "others" was strangely sluggish. And, finally, or rather, first and last, the brothers were thrilled with the prodigal's lust for ready money. So far they saw and no farther, but so far so good; here seemed to be an unguarded opening in the enemy's line – to use a phrase the great valley was one day to know by heart – and the warier of the pair ventured in. Said Lu- cian:

"We're Uncle Dan's sole legatees."

"Then name your price for her, lock, stock, and barrel."

"Want to take her only to Kentucky, or to California?"

"Californy – maybe Oregon."

"To keep house for you – single gentleman?"

"Yes, sir."

"When do you expect to come back?"

"Never."

The questioner glanced back to his brother. Both were gratified to note that the bargain would work no relief to Hugh or the Gilmores, but Julian wanted better assurance that it would not free a runaway slave or make her a lawful wife. He turned abruptly, and so it happened that all three failed to see Ramsey, in dark attire and with Joy close behind, emerge an instant from the pantry gangway and shrink again into it. On the return from her stateroom to the roof, for mere variety, she had taken this direction. Said Julian as he turned:

"You're a Kentuckian, sir. Henry Clay man?"

"No. Only don't allow anything said again' him."

"Abolitionist?"

"No, sir-ee." The emphasis was sprightly.

The twins looked at each other once more. Julian nodded.

"One thousand dollars," said Lucian. . . .

Let us go back a step or so and up to the hurricane- deck. We have named Hugh as in the group about Madame Hayle; but he went and came. In his absences the matrons debated the Phyllis matter as it involved the Gilmores, trying to find some way not to leave it an undivided burden on Hugh and the *Voiatess*. It was on one of his quiet reappearances, reporting his father "easier," that Ramsey put in:

"Mom-a, the senator's a lawyer. Send for him – and the general – and talk them over to our side. You can do it. You can talk anybody into anything! You always could!"

Madame Hayle and Hugh looked at each other very much as the twins were doing about that time on the guards next below, and Hugh said:

"I will go bring them."

"Ah, if you please, yass, go."

He brought them and they were among madame's auditors when later she said, addressing her words wherever they fitted best, so that even old Joy got her share:

"Had it not have been for Phylliz, Dan Hayle, he wouldn' neveh took that troub' to wride that wall. But I insiz' he shall wride it, biccause – Phylliz. Tha'z all. An' biccause Phylliz he wrode it. But he say to me "

"When was this?" inquired the senator.

"Tha'z when those twin' make him thad visit, Walnut Hill'. He say: 'W'ad uze to you if I make my laz' will? I give any'ow everything to those twin'.'

An' tha'z biccause" (to old Joy) "thad chile w'ad j-

"Drownded," murmured the nurse. "Ayfteh dat transpiah he take a shine to ev'y man-chile he git his ahm aroun'."

Madame resumed: "An' I say to him: 'Give all the rez' to who' you want, but Phylliz – to me.' 'No!' he say, 'you, you'll put her free!' "

"Why didn't he want her set free?" asked Ramsey.

"An' you are there – an' silend! I forgod you!"

"Why didn't he want her set free?" insisted the forgotten.

"Ah!" said the mother to the senator as though the inquiry were his, " Dan, he seem' to thing tha'z a caztigation on him. An' he say: 'Neveh mine, I figs thad so she can'd be free pretty soon.' An" me, I thoughd he leave her to those twin' till I'm reading the will."

Ramsey stood up elatedly. "I know what he did! I see it!"

But as her mother chidingly murmured her name she reflected the maternal dignity and accepted a bunch of keys.

"Go, if you please, ad my room," said madame, "open "

"Your little trunk, and pop-a's tin box inside," the girl interrupted, but deferentially caught herself again and with the corner of an eye felt about for Hugh. But Hugh had gone back to his father and thence to the deck next below.

" Yass. You fine there manny pape'. One is mark' – you'll see. Fedge me thad. 'Tis the h-only tha'z blue."

Ramsey sped away over skylights and down a back stair.

The senator spoke: "Who were that will's executors?"

"Ah, of co'se, my 'usban', Capitan Hayle, al-lone."

"The heirs, I dare say, have seen it?"

The lady smiled. "Not at all. Biccause h-anybody can see it if he want, nobody eveh want, an' leaz' of all those twin' when they are getting everything. Nobody speak abbout Phylliz, biccause Phylliz is su'pose drown', an' drown' peop' they don' count."

In the stateroom Ramsey knelt, opened the trunk, then the tin box, and then, despite old Joy's reprehending moan, the document itself.

"I knew it!" she whispered elatedly, relocking the box and trunk. "I guessed right!"

When at the forward end of the pantry gangway she came upon the twins and "California" and shrank back into hiding, the will was in her hand. In a tremble between staying and fleeing she heard the gold hunter, as he stood with his hands full of yellow coin, declare himself a Kentuckian and no abolitionist, and therefore understood instantly the significance of Lu- cian's response:

"One thousand dollars."

Too eager for speech, she glided forth and at the Californian's back halted before her brothers. But he had already smitten a fist into the hungry palm of either twin and was saying as he unburdened it there:

"A hundred on account to you – same to you – balance when you show title – she's mine!"

"She's mine !" cried the laughing girl.

The three men stared, but the twins hurried the gold into their pockets while she laughed on to them: " Hand that back. You've got no title. This is Uncle Dan's will and she's been mine for eleven years." On the stair close by them she began to step up backward but stopped to add to the Californian: "Take back your money and come trade with mom-a."

The twins showed instant conviction, but to them all dispossession was robbery and Lucian broke out, first on Ramsey, "We don't give back one dime!" then to the Californian, "You pushed it on us and we'll keep it!" then to Julian, "He hasn't the faintest right to it now in law, morals, or custom!" and thenback to the Californian: "You sha'n't ever see a copper of it!"

Ramsey was quick-witted again. She threw the gold hunter a glance which conveyed to him the realization that to leave the money with the twins was to put them at a hopeless disadvantage. Almost as quickly Lucian saw the same thing and flashed it to Julian; but in that brief interval their sister disappeared on the deck above, old Joy following, and while the brothers lost another moment in a motionless contest of impulses the Californian vanished after her. Lucian, with his breath drawn to call up the empty stair, started forward but struck his knee-cap on a light, gilded chair left there by some child. Burning with rage and trembling with nervous exhaustion, he barely saved himself from lunging into two men of slight stature who had just come from a neighboring stateroom: a slender old man leaning feebly on a thick-set youth, whom one flash of his eye identified as the commodore and Hugh, though as they passed toward the stair they betrayed no sign that they had observed him.

He gave his speechless brother a single look, caught the chair by its back, lifted it over his head, and with a long, smothered cry, half moan, half whine, crashed it down upon the balustrade – once – twice – and again, again, hurled the last fragment underfoot, and with eyes streaming stamped, stamped, and stamped, while the commodore and his supporter went on up to the roof and beyond view without a glance behind.

33

SECTION 33

LIV

"CAN'T!"

On handing the will to her mother, Ramsey found her no longer leading the conversation. The senator had the floor, the deck, and, as Ned or Watson might have said, was "drawing all the water in the river." His discourse was to madame and the general alternately, though now and then he included the parson's wife and Mrs. Gilmore.

Ramsey's talent for taking in everything at once was taxed to its limit when at the same time that she attended to him she watched an elegant steamer, one of the Saturday-evening boats out of Cincinnati, pass remotely on the Arkansas side behind Island Thirty- six; marked the return of the Californian as he followed her from his conference with the twins; noted the slow, preoccupied passing of Hugh and his grandfather to the captain's room; measured every winged stride of the *Votaress's* approach toward the Third Chickasaw Bluff; observed – as earlier bidden by the actor – the strange pink and yellow stripes of the bluff's clay face, and recognized in the great bell's landing signal the sad business which had become so half-conscious a habit in the boat's routine. Yet she caught the senator's every word.

Whether a person born in slavery, although seven eighths white, he was saying, was free by law was hardly a practical question, the matter being so nearly independent of any mere statute. For if such a slave sought liberty of an owner inclined to grant it there certainly was no law to prevent its bestowal, whereas if the owner was unwilling the burden of proof would naturally fall upon the slave, who, of course

"No," said Ramsey, drawing his and every eye and interesting everybody by a sweet maturity of tone to which her mourning dress lent emphasis. "No, it would not. The judge told me about that on Sunday."

Madame started and smiled. "You h-asked? An' fo' w'at?"

The transient air of maturity failed, and Ramsey's shoulders went up in her more usual manner.

The senator had his question: "What did the judge say?"

" The judge says, where the slave seems to be white the owner must prove she ain't – prove she isn't; but the burden, he says, of getting the case into court "

"Ah!" The senator was relieved. " Practically the same thing. For no slave can get a case into court without white help, and no decent white man will step between an owner and a slave who confesses to any African blood."

" No-c'ommunity would ssstand it," said the general.

"Now," pursued the senator, "a claim based on pure white blood and charging some palpable mistakeor fraud would be different. That would invite a community's sympathy and support. I've heard of such cases." He faced Ramsey again, whose smile implied a query in waiting.

Madame had handed the document to the senator. It was short. He read it in a glance or two and, refolding it, addressed Ramsey again: "This slave girl can neither be set free nor sold, for she's yours, and you're a minor. She seems to have been left to you just for that."

Until her mother spoke, Ramsey was mystified by her gracious bows of satisfaction to the senator and the general, but then she understood and was glad. "Verrie well," said madame, "iv Phylliz be satizfi' to billong to Ramzee "

"She is," said Mrs. Gilmore. "She's told me so."

"Verrie well, she'll juz' billong. An'" – to the senator – "you'll tell h-all those passenger' you h-are the fran" of my 'usban' an' fran' of the pewblic an' you 'ave seen thad will, an' Phylliz she's h-all those year' billong to Ramzee, an' tha'z h-all arrange' and h-every- boddie satizfi', ondly those twin' they 'ave not hear' abboud that yet, but you'll see them an' make them satizfi' "

"They know," called Ramsey and "California," and the latter added to the senator: "They've sold all claim to her, sight unseen, and have got the money; took it from me, before witnesses." Then to the astonished matron he added: "We can fix that in a jiffy, as slick as glass."

But there the immediate scene diverted every one; the whole group moved to the roof's edge to see the boat land. Then, while her bells still jingled and her wheels yeasted, the company, heart-sick of burials, fell apart. The senator and the general, promising zealous action and the best results, returned to the boiler deck, the parson's wife sought her children, Mrs. Gilmore went down to "Harriet." To shield madame from the full force of the breeze "California" moved her chair, Joy following with Ramsey's, to the shelter of the great chimney nearest the captain's door, where sympathy itself tended to draw them, and by the time this was done the commodore, again on Hugh's arm, reissued from the captain's room and, at sight of this quartet, paused, turned, and accepted a seat among them.

The first word was Ramsey's: How was the captain?

The best that could be said was that he was " holding out" – or "up" – or "on" – the commodore's voice was weak. He had come away from the captain's bedside because a convalescent was "only in the way," he said, and because Hugh felt that he belonged on deck if anywhere, though that, the old man fondly added, was less important than Hugh chose to regard it. This unimportance Ramsey recognized by diverting the conversation so far as to announce that "mom-a" had just settled the whole Phyllis business.

"Mighty nigh," the Californian admitted, answering Hugh's quiet glance, while his heart praised the daughter's failure to credit him with his share in theachievement, that being a thing still in progress, whose design he had not fully revealed. The omission seemed to him most maidenly and daughterly. He spoke on, to the two ladies:

"There's a thing or two more "

"Oh, I'll pay that two hundred dollars!" cried Ramsey.

In animated approval her mother nodded to both.

"Not if the court knows itself," said the modest man, with so winsome a smile that every one noticed how blue were his eyes. "I can trump that," he added, musingly.

"What's the other thing? You said a thing or two," asked Ramsey.

"Her wages, ain't it, for eleven years?"

"Ho, ho!" laughed madame in amiable scorn, while

"Paid!" cried Ramsey. "Mrs. Gilmore's always paid her!"

"Knowin' she was a runaway? and who' from?"

Madame bowed sweetly, yet with an aroused sparkle.

"Humph!" said Ramsey, watching the boat back out and lay her course for Island Thirty-five, "I'd have done as they did, either of them." She stepped into the freshening breeze.

The inquirer's eyes rested on her, bluer than ever.

"Don't you propose to collect?" he asked.

"Most certainly not!" sang Ramsey at full height.

"Not a sou," said madame, looking about in grand amusement. " Not a pic-ah-yune – hoh!"

"But she's going back into yo' hands?"

"My 'an's," said madame.

"And you'll never sell her?"

"Can't!" laughed Ramsey, with eyes ahead.

"You can hire her."

"Yes," said Ramsey, turning. "Oh, yes."

"Well, what'll you take, from the right bidder, for that girl's free papers dated ahead to when you come of age, bidder takin' all the resks? "

"You said down-stairs you wasn't an abolitionist!"

He twinkled. "Well, down-stairs I wa'n't, and in general I ain't. I'm a Kentuckian. But I've got an offer to make." He turned to the Courteneys: "I allowed to make it to this young gentleman first, alone, an' get his advice – an' the commodo's if he'd give it; but the' ain't anybody in this small crowd but what's welcome to hear it, even this young lady, considerin' that she's jest heard so much worse again' me – insinuated – down-stairs."

There was a pause. Old Joy murmured and Madame spoke the daughter's name, adding something in French.

"Mai," replied Ramsey, planting herself and gazing up the river, *"je prefSre* to stay right here."

The mother's smile to the Kentuckian bade him proceed, but he still addressed Hugh and the grandfather:

"You see, that girl down-stairs, 'Harriet,' 'Phyllis,' has been free – Lawdy, free's nothin', she's been white! – fo' ten years. Now, if she goes back home, there may be no place like it, but she's got to be black again. Well, think what that is. I've been weighin' that fact while I looked into her eyes and listened to her voice, an' thinks I to myself: 'If I was this girl, this goin' back to be black would mean one of two things: I'd either die myself, aw I'd kill some one, maybe sev'l.' True, I'm pyo' white an' she ain't, quite, but I don't believe her po' little drop o' low blood makes her any mo' bridlewise 'n what I'd be."

While the speaker's smile drew smiles from madame and the commodore, Ramsey turned to him a severe face and in the same glance managed to see Hugh's, but Hugh's might as well have been, to her mind, the face of a Chickasaw bluff.

"Well, what then?" she asked the gold hunter.

"Same time," said "California," still to the Courte- neys, while madame promptly discerned his covert argument and Ramsey suddenly busied herself talking up to the pilot-house, "I noticed, more'n eveh, how much she, Phyllis, favoh'd somebody I was once 'pon a time pow'ful soft on, but whose image" – his smile won smiles again – "I to'e out o' my heart – aw buried in thah – aw both – it bein' too ridiculous fo' me to aspiah that high. An' so here looked to me like a substitute, gentlemen, that ought to satisfy all concerned." His eye turned to madame but lost courage and escaped back to Hugh.

"Now, Mr. Hugh, I've got money a-plenty. It's all I have got excep' maybe a good tempeh, an' I'm goin' back to the diggin's anyhow, one man to the squa' mile is too crowded fo' me. Meantime, madam" – he turned again and this time he was invincible, although madame straightened and sparkled and Ramsey gave a staring attention, having throughout all

her pilot-house talk heard everything " Meantime,

madam, with a priest right here on boa'd, if I can buy, at any price, Phyllis's free papehs "

"You can't!" chanted Ramsey. "She can have 'em for nothing but nobody can buy 'em."

"Pries'?" asked madame, "an' free pape'! Wat you pro-ose do with those pries' an' free pape'?"

"I'll marry her; marry her an' take her to whah a woman's a woman fo' a' that an' can clean house aw cook dinneh whilst I gatheh the honeycomb bright as gold and drive the wolf to his secret hold." He cast around the group a glance of bright inquiry, but except old Joy every one silently looked at every one else. The old woman softly closed her eyes and shook her head.

"Vote!" cried Ramsey, remembering Sunday's victory. "Let's vote on it!" LV
LOVE MAKES A CUT-OFF
But the grandfather addressed the adventurer. "You'd rather not, I fancy."

"Rather not; looks too unanimous the wrong way." "Would you still like to have Hugh's advice?" "I would! I'd like to hear yo'-all's argument." Ramsey dropped into her chair with a tired sigh and up-stream gaze though with an inner ear of keenest attention.

Hugh glanced toward his father's door, whence at any moment, as every one realized, the actor might beckon.

" I have no argument," he began. "You have," breathed a voice, unmistakably Ramsey's; "you always have."

"You know," he continued to the Kentuckian, "there's something in all of us, I don't say what, or whether wise or foolish, that says : ' Don't do it.' You feel it, don't you?"

Madame interrupted: *"Mais* don't do w'at?" Ramsey faced the group as if to answer just that question. "Now we pass between Cedar Point and Pecan Point and head for the Second Chickasaw Bluffs!"

"Ah bah, *les* bloff'," murmured madame and repeated to Hugh: "Something say,'Don'do it'? *Mais* w'at it say don' do?"

"Don't mix the great races we know apart by their color."

"Umph! An' w'at is thad something w'at tell uz that?"

"Grandfather calls it race conscience."

"Grandfather!" whimpered Ramsey, while madame asked:

"Of w'at race has Phylliz the conscien'? An' you would know Phylliz' race – ad sight – by the color?"

"I'd know it!" put in the Kentuckian. "She's white, to all intents and purposes."

"No," said Hugh, "not quite to all. Not to all as organized society, in its "
Ramsey, with eyes up the river, sighed: "Mrs. Grundy?"

"Yes, but Mrs. Grundy in her best intents and purposes."

"In her race conscience," wailed Ramsey to the breeze.

" In her race conscience," assented Hugh.

Ramsey whipped around. " Thought you had no argument."

" I'm giving grandfather's," said the grandson.

"Humph! it's yours. I'd know it at sight – by the color."

"Miss Ramsey," said the old man, toying with his cane, "Hugh and I have been finding that, right or wrong, Mrs. Grundy or Mr. Grundy, race conscience is a wonderful, unaccountable thing for which men will give their life-blood by thousands." His voice failed. He waved smilingly to Hugh.

"And when," broke in Hugh to Ramsey, "when Mrs. Grundy, in her race conscience, says Phyllis is not white no one ought to snap his fingers hi even Mrs. Grundy's face merely to please himself or to relieve some private situation."

Ramsey stood up, flashing first on him and then to her mother, dropped again, and with her face in her elbow on the chair's back recited drearily – from her third reader:
"You can hear him swing his heavy sledge
With measured beat and slow,
Like the sexton ringing the village bell
When the evening sun "
"Ramzee!" exclaimed madame, while the old nurse groaned: "Oh, Lawd 'a' massy!"
The girl rose, laughed, and flashed again: "Well, if Phyllis ain't white what is she? She's got to be something !"
"Yes," said the youth, "but not everything. I know her wrongs. But none of us, with whatever rights and wrongs, can have, or do, or be "
"Oh, don't we know all that?" Ramsey turned to the grandfather and with sudden deference sprang to help him rise. He faced her and the Californian together.
"Miss Ramsey, Hugh has all your feelings in this matter."
Madame, "California," and old Joy eagerly assented.
"But poor, blundering old Mrs. Grundy, always wronging some one," the old man smilingly continued, " is really fighting hard for a better human race. That's the greatest battle she can fight, my dear young lady, and when "
"Well," rejoined Ramsey with eyes frankly tearful, "she fights it mighty badly."
"Ah, a hundred times worse than you think. Yet we who presume to fight the blunders of that battle must fight them unselfishly and to help her win."
Old Joy groaned so approvingly that he turned to her.
"What do you think, old mammy?"
"Who, me? Lawd, I thinks mighty little an' I knows less. Yit one thing I does know: Phyllis ain' gwine. She know' you cayn't make her white by takin' her to whah it make' no odds ef she ain't white. Phyllis love' folks. She love' de quality, she love' de crowd. White aw black aw octoroom free niggeh, Phyllis gwine to choose de old Hayle home and de great riveh – full o' steamboat' – sooneh'n any lan' whah de ain't mo'n one 'oman to de mile. Phyllis ain't gwine."
The closing words faded to soliloquy. For every one stood up, and even the old woman's attention was diverted to Watson's apprentice approaching from the captain's room. On his way below for the doctor hecame, in the actor's behalf, to ask if he might bring up also Mrs. Gilmore.
Assuredly he might. How was the patient?
"Very quiet," the boy hopefully replied. Whereupon madame begged leave to repair at once to the sick-room, but neither of the Courteneys would consent nor either of them allow the other to go. The steersman passed on down.
From enviously watching him do so, "California" turned to the company and in open abandonment of his amazing proposition said drolly that never before had he failed, in so many ways "hand-running," to make himself useful. He reseated Madame Hayle and would have set the daughter beside her, but the mother bade Ramsey give Joy the chair and leaned wearily on the old woman's shoulder. Both Courteneys urged their seats on the girl, and when she would not accept while either of them stood for her servant to sit, the grandfather left Hugh debating with her, took "California's" arm,

found other chairs a few paces away, and engaged him in a gentle parley which any one might see was an appeal to his sober second thought. It was Ned's shift up at the wheel, but the change of watch was near; his partner stood at his elbow. Their gaze was up a reach between the two most northern of those four groups of bluffs whose mention even Ramsey was for the moment tired of, yet they studied the three couples on the roof below.

"Runs smooth at the present writing," said Watson.

"Clair chann'l ef noth'n' else," responded Ned. The allusion was neither to boat nor stream but to a certain opportuneness of things, whose obviousness to them, looking down, was mainly what kept Ramsey standing. While she stood beside the two empty chairs cross-questioning Hugh with a fresh show of her maturer mildness and he stood inwardly taking back his late farewell to sweet companionship and softly answering in his incongruous pomp of voice with a new tenderness, and while the worn-out mother gradually let her full weight sink on the tired slave, this obvious propitiousness was embarrassingly increased by the two weary ones falling asleep.

True, the clearness of channel – this channel in the upper air – was not absolute, but its obstacles nettled mostly the pilots. To Ramsey, even to Hugh, obstacles were almost welcome, as enabling them to show to a prying world that nothing beyond the grayest commonplace was occurring between them. One such interruption was the upcoming and passing of Mrs. Gilmore and the physician to the sick-room and the cub pilot's parting with them to join the younger pair. The boy found Hugh confessing that he should not know exactly how to word Phyllis's "free papers" but adding that the first clerk would be pleased to make them out at once if Ramsey's eagerness so dictated. It did, and presently the modest intruder was hurrying away on a double errand: to bear this confidential request to the clerk and then to seek the Brothers Ambrosia and with them and the two under-clerks arrangefor the evening performance, the giving of which, however, Ramsey insisted, must depend on the captain's condition when evening should come.

" Wish it were here now," she said as they watched the messenger go. "Don't you?"

"I could," he replied, "but it will be here soon enough."

The conversation which followed remained in their memory through years of separation.

She spoke again in her new tone: "You think your father will get well, don't you?"

"No, Ramsey."

At those words her heart did two things at once:- stopped on the first, rebounded on the second. But it fell again as he added: "I fear I must lose my father to-night."

She stood mute, looking into his eyes and pondering every light and shadow of the severe young face that to her seemed so imperially unlike all others. "He's great/' she said in her heart. "And he loves with his greatness. Loves even his father that way; not as I love mine or love anybody, or ever shall or can, or could wish to, unless I were a man and as great as him – he. I never could have dreamt of any one loving me that way, but if any ever should I'd worship him." Suddenly her sympathy rose high.

"Oh, why not just think to yourself: 'He *will* live'? "

"Why should I? Should I be fit to live myself if I were not true to myself? "

"You are! You always are!"

"No one can be who isn't truthful to himself."

Ramsey gazed again. A sense of his suffering benumbed her, and for relief she asked: "Is that why you don't wish it were evening, when really you do?"

He smiled. "I can't wish the sun to get out of my way. That's what it would mean, isn't it?"

She fell to thinking what it meant. All at once she pointed: "That's the First Chickasaw Bluff. . . . Yes, I s'pose it does mean that. . . . It's terrible how thoughtless I am."

"It doesn't terrify me. I promise you it never shall."

Was he making game of her? She narrowed her lids and looked at him sidewise. No, plainly he was not; so plainly that she took refuge in another question. "Don't you like night better than day sometimes?"

"I do, often."

"Why?"

"For one thing, we can see so much farther."

"Oh, ridiculous! we can't see nearly so far!"

"We can see so much farther and wider, deeper, clearer. The day blinds us. Spoils our sense of proportion. At night we see more of what creation really is. Our sun becomes one little star among thousands of greater ones, and we are humbled into a reasonableness which is very hard not to lose in the bewilderments of daylight."

Ramsey sank to the arm of a chair, but when heremained standing she stood again. "Wasn't you saying something like that the evening we left New Orleans?" she asked.

" To my father, yes. I couldn't have said it in daylight then. I couldn't say it in daylight now to any one but you, Ramsey."

Her heart leaped again. Her eyes looked straight into his; could not look away. He spoke on:

"You're a kind of evening to me, yourself; evening star."

Her bosom pounded. She glanced up behind to the pilots. Watson had the wheel. As she strenuously pushed back her curls she felt her temples burn. She could have cried aloud for Hugh to cease, yet was mad for him to go on.

And so he did. "You are my evening star in this nightfall of affliction. I tell you so not in weakness but in strength and in defiance: in the strength I summon for the hour before me; in the defiance I fling to your brothers. I may never have another chance. If ours were the ordinary chances of ordinary life I should say nothing now. I should wait; wait and give love time; time to prove itself in me – in both of us. I *ask* nothing. I am too new to you, life is too new – to you – for pledges."

She flashed him a glance and then, looking up the river, said, with the ghost of a toss: "I'm older than you think."

He ignored the revelation. " But I will say," he went on, " – for these three days and nights have been three

" For I believe that we belong to each other from the centre of our souls, by a fitness plain even to the eyes of your brothers"

years to me and I feel a three years' right to say – I love you; love you for life; am yours for life though we never meet again. For I believe that we belong to each other from the centre of our souls, by a fitness plain even to the eyes of your brothers."

Still looking up the flood and red from brow to throat, Ramsey murmured two or three words which she saw he did not hear. Yet he stood without sound or look to ask what she had said, and presently repeated:

"I believe in God's sight we belong to each other."

"So do I," said Ramsey again, with clearer voice and with her brimming eyes looking straight into his. A footfall turned her and she faced the relieved pilot.

"Isn't this Island Thirty-three," she asked, "right here on our stabboard. bow?"

"Thirty-three," assented Ned. "Alias Flour Island; but *not* Flow-er Island. Flour-ladened flatboats wrecked there in the days o' yo' grandfather, Eliph- alet Hayle, whose own boats they might 'a' been, only Hayles ain't never been good at losin' boats. But his'n or not, *can* you suspicion they wuz flow-er- ladened? Shucks! them that spell it that-a-way air jest as bad an' no wuss than them that stick *b* onto Plum in Plum P'int an' pull the *y* out o' Hayle fo' Hayle's P'int! They jest a-airin' they ignorance. Some fellers love to air they ignorance. I do, myself."

He gave these facts of topography in reward of the grave interest that Hugh – elated interest that Ramsey – still seemed to take in all such items, as well asto allow them to infer that he had not noticed them betraying interest in anything more personal.

"Hayle's P'int – " he resumed, and when Madame Hayle and old Joy roused and glanced around on him, while the senator and the general reappeared close by, looking back down the steamer's wake with military comments on the First Chickasaw Bluff, just left behind, he addressed them all as one. Hayle's Point, he persisted, was miles away yet and comparatively unimportant "considerin' its name," but the small cluster of houses on the Arkansas side up in the next bend was Osceola, where Plum Point Bars made the "wickedest" bit of river between Saint Louis and the Gulf; a bit that "killed" at least one steamboat every year. He said they were then passing a sand-bar, under water at this stage, which had been Island Thirty-two until " swallered whole" by the " big earthquake" of 1811.

"Better'n forty year' ago, that was. Only quake ever felt in these parts, but so big that, right in the middle of all the b'ilin' an' staggerin' an' sinkin' down to Chiny, the Mis'sippi River give birth to her fust steamboat – an' saved it!" So he continued, egged on by the conviction that, over and above the intrinsic value of the facts, these conversational eddies outside the current of incident "a-happ'min' to 'em yit" helped forward his two most deeply interested hearers on that course erroneously supposed never to run smooth.

Be that as it may, the two pilots' joint theory of maxims working as well backward as forward workedhere; deep waters ran still. Love, that is, having broken intolerable bounds in one short fierce " chute" of declaration, was content to run deep and still and to give broad precedence to duties, sorrows, and courtesies. The pair noticeably drifted apart and conversed with others when others were quite willing they should drift together. Madame Hayle needed but a glance or so to perceive that something beautiful had happened in the spiritual experience of her daughter. By and by when the commodore and the Californian rejoined the group, Hugh and his grandfather spent a still moment looking into each other's eyes and when both gazes relaxed at once the story had been told and understood.

They turned to hear what was passing between the general, senator, and Californian. Said the soldier:

"Sssirs, I only insssist that *if* this region ever sees war Port Hudson, Grand Gulf, Vwicksburg, these fffour Chickasaw Bluffs, and Island Ten up here above us will be imp-regnably fffortified."

Ramsey turned to the actor's wife as she came from the texas.

"How's the captain?" asked both she and her mother. But Mrs. Gilmore was too overcome to reply.

Ramsey saw the actor at the stateroom door. He had beckoned. Hugh and the grandfather were on their way. At a quieter pace the four women followed and more slowly still the other four men. Reaching Gilmore, the Courteneys paused and spoke, then lookedback to Ramsey and madame, and beckoned – Hugh to the mother, the commodore to Ramsey. Gilmore repeated the gesture and they glided forward. At the same time the player advanced to meet his wife, and, as if some intuition had rung the call, the scene- loving twins appeared in the senator's halted group and stood with them gazing, while Madame Hayle, the commodore, Ramsey, and Hugh entered the captain's room.

34

SECTION 34

LVI

   EIGHT YEARS AFTER

   "A Hundred months," says the love-song that beguiled so many thousands of hearts throughout the Mississippi Valley in those old "Lily Dale," "Nellie Gray," "What is Home Without a Mother?" days, when the lugubrious was so blithely enjoyed at the piano. Its first wails date nearly or quite back to October, 1860.

   "A hundred months had passed" since that first upstream voyage of the *Votaress,* or, to be punctilious, something under a hundred and two. It was the opening week of that mid-autumn month in which it became evident that Abraham Lincoln would be the next president. Another new boat, new pride of the great river, the fairest yet, still in the hands of her contractors, and on her trial trip from Louisville to New Orleans, was rounding, one after another, now far in the east, now as far in the west, the bends nearest below Memphis: Cow Island. Cat Island, St. Francis, Delta – so on.

   The river was low. You would hardly have known a reach, a cut-off, a point of it by any aspect remembered from that journey of April, '52. Scantness of watersappeared to contract distances. "Paddy's Hen and Chickens," just above Memphis, were all out on dry sands and seemed closer under the "Devil's Elbow" than eight years before. Every towhead and bar and hundreds of snags were above water and as ugly as mud, age, sun bleach, and turkey-buzzards could make them. Many a chute comfortably run by the *Votaress* was now " closed for repairs," said one of the pilots of the *Enchantress*. He was the whilom steersman we knew as Watson's cub; a very capable- looking man now. At the moment, he was off watch and had come out from the bar to the boiler deck with a trim, supple man of forty, whose shirt of fine white flannel was open at the throat, where a soft neckerchief of red silk matched the sash at his waist: "California," eight years older and out of the West again despite his "never" to Hayle's twins.

"I like to change my mind sometimes," he explained. "It shows me I've got one."

A towering, massive, grizzly man several years older than the Californian, with a short, stiff, throat-latch beard and a great bush of dense, short curls, stood by the forward guards, a picture of rude force and high efficiency. At every moment, from some direction among the deck's loungers a light scrutiny ventured to rest on him, to which he seemed habituated, and the lightest was enough to reveal in him a striking union of traits coarse and fine. He wore a big cluster diamond pin, a sort of hen-and-chickens of his own, secured by a minute guard-chain on a ruffled shirt-frontof snowiest linen, where clung dry crumbs of the "fine- cut" which puffed the lower side pockets of his gray alpaca sack coat. His gold-headed cane was almost a bludgeon. He had come aboard at Memphis, having reached that city but a few hours earlier by railway train from White Sulphur Springs, Va., where he had had the good fortune to find great relief from rheumatism. The young lady in his company, now back in the ladies' cabin, was his daughter, they said, beautiful and all of twenty-two, yet unmarried! This man the pilot and the Californian approached and waited for his attention. When he gave it the pilot spoke.

" Commodore," he said, " welcome back to the river."

The big man grew bigger and his shaggy brows more severe.

"I feel welcome," he said. "Only place under God's canopy where I can breathe down into my boots."

"And you want the roof for it here, don't you? I do. Roof or wheel. Commodore Hayle, my friend Mr. So-and-so, from California. He's your brand; Kentuck' born and raised."

The two shook hands, scanning each other's countenances. The eyes of both were equally blue, equally intrepid.

"Are you the man – ?" Hayle began to ask with grim humor.

"I think so."

"Well, my boy, I've been wanting to see you for better than eight years." The speaker glanced around for privacy.

"Come up," said the pilot; "I'm just going on watch." They followed him. On the roof he continued :

"Seen Captain Hugh yet, commodore? He's sure enough captain now, you know; youngest on the river. He was looking for you a bit ago. This is a beautiful boat he's going to have, eh?"

"Humph, yes. *Votaress* over again." The critic gave her a fresh scrutiny from cutwater to stern rail, from freight guards to the oak-leaf crown on either chimney-top.

"Why, commodore, she knocks the hindsights off the old *Votaress* every way. You'll see that mighty quick."

"Humph, yes; best yet, of the Courteney type. Ridiculous, how they hang to that. I'll build a boat to beat her inside a year if old Abe ain't elected. If he is, we'll just build gunboats and raise particular hell." On the skylight the speaker amiably declined to climb any higher.

"No, us two Kentuck's will try it here." The pair found seats together, and soon the Californian was making the best of an opportunity he, no less than Gideon Hayle, had coveted for eight years. It interested him keenly, as affording a glimpse into the famous boatman's character, that the latter showed a grasp of the dreadful voyage's story as vivid and clear in each of its two versions – the mother and daughter'sand the twins' – as though the intervening months had been one instead of a hundred – and two.

They rehearsed together the arrival of the *Votaress* at Louisville in the dead of night; confessed the folly of any "outsider" seeking the grief-burdened Gideon's ear in that first hour of reunion with his family, and the equal unwisdom of his pressing, in such an hour, an acute personal question upon Hugh and his grandfather who, at Paducah, had just buried John Courte- ney.

"And you've never pressed it sence?" asked "California."

"Mm-no."

"Nor let either o' them press it?"

" No!" – a sturdy oath – " nor you nor anybody alive. Go on with your story."

The gold hunter went on unruffled; told it as he had seen it occur; recounted, among other things, how, on the final landing of the immigrants, at Cairo, Marburg and not a few besides had covered Madame Hayle's hands with kisses and tears and would have done Hugh Courteney's so could they have got at him. His hearer frowned and set his big jaw, but the narrative flowed on, describing how, like Marburg, many had waved affectionate farewells to Hugh and to Ramsey which she could guess no reason for in her case except her own wet eyes, but which "California" saw was because, through himself and Phyllis, the immigrants had found her out as another who believed in letting the oppressed go free and come free. Hetold even those irrelevant things about himself which had made him ludicrous. They imparted a needed lightness and kindled the big commodore's smile.

"They never found out," said '. California," "that the fellow who played 'Bounding Billow' and 'A Life on the Ocean Wave' was me – I – myself."

He told all as honestly, fearlessly as we might know he would. When his huge listener tried to say offhandedly that every man who knew anything knew that women and men never see things alike and that different witnesses could, quite honestly, give irreconcilable accounts of the same thing, the Californian serenely waved away all such gloss and with the seated giant hanging over him like a thunder-cloud said that the twins could never see anything straight enough to tell the truth about it if they wanted to and that just as certainly they often didn't want to. Pausing there and getting no retort, he ventured another step. Said he:

"And there you've hung the case up for eight years."

"That's my business!" Gideon smote the arm of his chair.

"California" laughed a moment like a girl, with drooping head. Then – oh, the twins had their good points, yes. One was the way they stuck to each other. And their biggest virtue, their "best holt," the one their worst enemy couldn't help liking them for, was their invincible sand.

" The devil couldn't scare 'em with his tail red-hot."

At that the father laughed gratefully.

"They'd ought to be in some trade where pluck," the Californian went on, "is the whole show. They'd ought to be soldiers. As plain up-and-down fighters for fight'n's sake, commodore, they'd hit it off as sweet as blackstrap!"

The truth smote hard but the parent feigned a jovial inappreciation. If that was so they had made a " most damnable misdeal," he laughed, having settled down in Natchez together, "too soft on each other to marry and as tame as parrakeets"; Julian as county sheriff, his brother a physician.

The Californian silently doubted the tameness. Abruptly, though in tones of worship, he inquired after Madame Hayle.

Madame just then was at home, on the plantation at Natchez. Yes, she and Ramsey often made trips with Gideon on that *Paragon* which they had gone up the river to come down on, in '52. The *Paragon,* wonderfully preserved, was still in the "Vicksburg and Bends" trade and happened then to be some forty-eight hours ahead of the *Enchantress* and nearing New Orleans. Madame and her daughter now and then spent part of the social season in the great river's great seaport, which was – "bound to be the greatest in the world, my boy," said Gideon. But Ramsey

When Ramsey became the topic, even "California," while the father boasted, had to hold on, as he would have said, with his teeth to keep from being blown away. Her "one and only love" was the river ! She "knew it like a pilot" and loved it and the whole lifeon it not merely for its excitements, variety, and outlook on the big world.

"That is to say for its poetry," prompted "California."

"Yes, not for that only but just as much for its prose, by Mike! Why, my boy, that's all that's kept her single!"

"Except!" said the Californian softly, but Gideon pressed on. "And single, now, I reckon, she'll always be. Why, sir, not a day breaks but she knows, within an hour's run, the whereabouts of every Hayle boat alive."

"Some Courteney boats too, hmm?"

"Why, eh" – a stare – "I shouldn't wonder. Yes. Humph! 'youngest captain on the river' – fact is, that's *her.* Lady as she is, and lovely as she is, she's a better steamboatman to-day than – than many a first-class one. She's nearer being my business partner than any man I ever hired."

" Partner's share of the swag? "

"No," laughed the giant, "but I'm leaving her the boats."

"Well," said "California," "all that's good preparation."

The huge man shot him a glance and the two pairs of blue eyes held each other. Then " California " smiled his winsomest and said: "Did you ever notice how much easier you can see through the ends of an iron pipe than through its sides?"

Gideon stared. "Humph! Any fool that wants to see through me may see and be – joyful. What do you think you see?"

"Oh, things you'd ought to thought of and never have."

"Why, you in' – Well, I'll be damned."

"Shouldn't wonder a bit," said "California" so amiably that the big man laughed.
"Maybe you'll tell me my oversights!"

"No, but you'll be told, shortly, if the man I think I know is the man I – think I know.
Let's pass that now, commodore. Oh, I wish you'd been with us on the *Votaress.* How
different things might 'a' turned out. You know? I don't believe any other trip on all
this big river, barring the first steamboat's first, ever made so big a turning-point in so
many lives. Why, jest two or three things in it, things and people, made me another
man."

"One not so need'n' to be hanged?"

"Yes, and not so hungry to hang other fellers. I hadn't ever met up with such
aristocratic stock as I did then but I tchuned right up to 'em and I've mighty nigh held
their pitch ever sence. Fo'most of all was this Hugh Courteney. Fo'most because, he
being a man, I wa'n't afraid of him. But a close second was yo' daughter; second
because, she being a woman, I was afraid of her. Why, even Phyllis, that's now
chambermaid on this boat "

"By Jupiter!" Gideon Hayle half started from his seat. "On this boat? our Phyllis?
that Ramsey set free?"

"Yes. Captain Hugh's nurse that was." "Look here, my boy, is that why you're
aboard?" "No, sir-ee! Don't you fret. That trip, I tell you, made another man of me.
It lifted; why, commodore, it made me a poet."

"Made you a – Oh, go 'long off!" "Yes, sir. Writ poetry ever sence. Dropped prose;
too easy. It's real poetry, commodore; rhymes as slick as grease. Show you some of
it later."

"George! if you do I'll jump into the river." "Agreed! I've got some that'll make
you do that." "You haven't got any that wouldn't." Neither smiled, neither frowned.
Obviously each knew how to like an adversary and when "California" rose and the
two, glancing aft, saw another two approaching from the pilot-house, one of whom
was Watson, Hayle touched the poet detainingly and said:

"Don't go 'way, I want some more of your prose." "Want to know why I'm here?
Not countin' the fun o' seein' Captain Hugh, half the reason's that gentleman yonder
comin' with Mr. Watson, and the other half's his lady, down below a-powwowin'
with yo' daughter. Fact is I'd struck it rich again out West and got restless and come
East, and at Saint Louis I see by a newspaper that them two was allowin' to go down
to Orleans on this boat this trip, and ree-collect- in' the pinch they got into of old on
the *Votarea,* s'l to myself, 'me too!' "

Here the other men drew near and, while "California" ran on, silently pressed the
big hand offered sidewise by Hayle.

"And with that I set down and writ a poem – took me a whole night – to the best half
dozen o' them that was on the other trip, invitin' 'em, at my expense, to jump on when
we come by – at New Carthage – Milli- ken's Bend – Vicksburg – and trustin' to luck
and fresh post stamps to find 'em. But little did we dream o' seein' you walk aboard,
at Memphis, and still less yo' daughter and her old Joy; did we, Mr. Gilmore?" LVII
FAREWELL, "VOTARESS"

Montezuma Bend. . . . Delta. . . . Delta Bend. . . . Friar's Point. . . . Kangaroo
Point. . . . Horseshoe Bend and Cut-off. Some, at least, of these we remember.

At mention of them the Gilmores and "California" smiled – behind Ramsey: such a different, surpassingly different Ramsey!

Near the *Enchantress's* bell these four and old Joy were gathered about Gideon Hayle, Watson, and Hugh Courteney – such an inspiringly different Hugh! Two or three showed a divided attention, letting an occasional glance stray down the waters ahead, where Old Town Bend swung from west to south.

At the same moment, in Horseshoe Cut-off, some twelve or fifteen miles below, another swift, handsome steamer, upward bound – the great river could hardly yet show more than one handsomer – swept into the north from an easterly course under Island Sixty-four and pointed up the middle of the stream to pass between Sixty-three and Sixty-two where, at the head of the reach, they parted the river into three channels and widened it to more than a league. She would have been an animating sight if only for the fact that every soul aboard who was not just then engaged in runningher was at the guards of one or another of her graceful decks. The forecastle was darkened by her crew standing in a half circle about the capstan, her larboard pantry guards were crowded with white-jackets, her roofs were gay with ladies and children. In elated oblivion of the charming picture presented by their own boat and themselves, all were awaiting a spectacle which their pilots and captain had said would surely be met within the next hour's run.

Although behind them was a tortuous fifty miles in which hardly more signs of human life had been seen or heard than if their way had been on the open Atlantic, the beauty of the wilderness alone, transfigured in the lights of the declining day, might well have satisfied the eye. A red sun was just touching the horizon. Its beams and the blue shadows that divided them lay level, miles long, athwart the glassy stream and its green and gray forests and tapered and vanished in a low eastern haze. The tints of autumn already prevailed along the shores, and the indolent waters mirrored the reversed images of the two islands in outlines clearer than their own and from bank to bank took on in enriched hues the many colors of the sky. At the far end of the reach, between and somewhat beyond the islands, stood well out of the shrunken flood a sand-bar, its middle crested green and gold with young poplars and willows, all its ill favor made picturesque and the whole mass glorified by the sunset. By this bar the waters of the central channel were again divided, north and south, and the steamer, withanother eastward turn, straightened up for the southern passage between the bar and Sixty-three.

"We'll pass her close," said one of the boat's family to those who hung on his words. "In this low water she's got to come round the bar and well over to the left bank, same as us."

On the boiler deck and on the roof passengers of the kind that see for themselves pointed out to the kind that see only what they are shown the smoke of another boat, across the forests on the Arkansas side, in Old Town Bend. There were ways for some to know even at that distance that she was a craft they had never yet seen, but every two minutes the distance grew less by a mile. Presently, as the nearer boat, giving the bar's eastern head a wide berth, swung once more into the north, the *Enchantress* glided into view on the larboard bow hardly two miles away. But before the *Enchantress* as well, looking south across the same interval, gleamed a picture worthy of her delight. For there came the *Votaress,* curling white ribbons from her cutwater, her people waving and cheering, a swivel barking from her prow, and the whistles high up between her chimneys roaring in long salute.

By no premeditation could the unpremeditated scene have been finer. The *Votaress,* as she took the wider circuit against the Mississippi shore, caught the whole power of the setting sun on all her nearer side while she swept close along an undivided curtain of autumn forest drenched in the same sunlight and quaking toher sudden breeze. North and west of her, where the sand-bar lay bare of trees, the *Enchantress,* larger, stronger, swifter, moved in her own shade but was set against the far splendor of a saffron, green, and crimson sky in which the fiery sun showed only its upper half sinking beneath the landscape. The lights of all her decks, just lit, gave no vivid ray but glinted like gems on a court lady. Her bridal whiteness was as pure hid from the sunbeams as her sister's bathed in them. From both the high black smoke streamed away through the evening calm and from their twinkling wheels the foam swept after them like trains of lace. We speak for our poet, who, lacking fit imagery of his own, recalled one of Jenny Lind's songs:

"I see afar thy robe of snow,
I see thy dark hair wildly flow,
I hear thy airy step so light,
Thou com'st to wish thy love good night
Good night, my love, good night."

Good night, *Votaress!* He could not know, nor Ramsey, nor any of those among whom they stood, that these bends were never again to see you in your beauty – though in tragedy, yes! yes ! They knew that in the shipyards of the Ohio you were to receive a beautiful rejuvenation; but knew not that then, as a dove may be caught by a lynx, you were to be caught by a great war, a war greater than the great river, and should return to these scenes a transport; a poor, scarred, bedraggled consort to gunboats; slow reptilian monsters of iron ugliness and bellowing ferocity. They knew not of days when you must swarm with blue soldiers – including Marburg – sometimes hot and merry for battle, sometimes shot-torn, fever-wasted, yellow-eyed, a human rubbish of camp and siege, lighter part of the deadly price of conquered strongholds and fallen cities – Forts Henry and Donelson, Columbus, Island Ten, Fort Pillow, Port Hudson, Vicksburg, Memphis; or that, after all, in recovered decency, honored poverty, you should wear out a gentle old age as a wharf-boat to your unspeakable inferiors. And neither could they, those voyagers on the new steamer, foresee the happier vision of their *Enchantress* living through the war charmedly unscathed, sharing the palmiest days of the Mississippi's navigation without ever being surpassed in speed or beauty, even by younger Courteney boats, and at last falling asleep peaceably at her moorings hard by the vast riverside railway warehouses on the outskirts of a greater New Orleans.

All this forces its way through the mind while we see the meeting boats cover half the run between them. On the *Enchantress* a deck-hand mounted the capstan.

"They're going to sing," hurriedly said Ramsey to Hugh. "I wish they'd sing "Lindy Lowe" that I've heard about!"

And whether by happy chance or on some signal dropped down from him or because the chantey was a new one and the crew were glad to show it off, it waschosen. The two steamers passed close with a happy commotion throughout both and the song swelled. Then the wooded crest of the bar hid each from each, and Hugh turned to Gideon: "Now, commodore, if Miss Hayle is willing I'd like to take you both below and show you over the boat – before supper."

When their descent brought them to the boiler deck the song was yet in full swing. When, passing on down, they reached the engine room the fact was amusingly clear to many on all decks, among them the Gilmores, the Californian, and Watson, that the singers had lit on a new bearing for their lines and were singing them now in compliment to a certain two whose story was by this time known to all on board. Whether, back between the sweeping cranks and shafts of the two great engines and wheels, behind the "doctor" and the "donkey" and with Hugh and Ramsey at his elbows, the alert Gideon heard the song at all was doubtful; so deep in debate were the two men, the quiet and the loud, on dimensions and powers: length, beam, hold, stroke, diameters of cylinders and of wheels, in such noted cases as the *Chevalier,* the *Eclipse,* the *I. M. White,* the *Natchez, Antelope, Paragon, Quakeress,* and *Autocrat.* The three were there yet when the song's last echo died, with Island Sixty- four eastward astern, Sixty-five southward ahead, the brief twilight failing and the supper bell ringadang- dinging.

At table a far-away whistle softly roared and the *Enchantress* sonorously responded.

"A Hayle boat," said Ramsey to Hugh; "the *Regent."*

"And we're singing 'Lindy' again!" said Mrs. Gil- more.

Gideon, busy talking a few seats away, talked straight on, but a cloud on his brow showed now that he had heard the song the earlier time. Every one tried hard to listen to him and the melody with the same ears. Under the table somebody's toe had no better manners than gently to beat time.

35

SECTION 35

Lviii
   'lindy Lowe
   COME, smil in' 'Lind-y Lowe dc pooti - *tts* gal I
   know,... On de fin-ess boat dat ev-di float, In de O - hi -
   -g j j-d1 'r c C – e-l – r=l-m
   o, De Mas - lis - tip - pi aw de O hi - o.
   Come, smilin' 'Lindy Lowe, teef whiteh dan de snow,
   On de finess boat dat eveh float,
   In de O – hi – o,
   De Mas – sis – sip – pi aw de O – hi – o.
   Come, smilin' 'Lindy Lowe, to de Lou'siana sho',
   (Chorus)
   Come, smilin' 'Lindy Lowe, by de Gu'f o' Mexico,
   (Chorus)
   Come, smilin' 'Lindy Lowe, to de bayous deep an' slow,
   (Chorus)
   Come, smilin' 'Lindy Lowe, whah de moss wave, to an' fro,
   (Chorus)

Come, smilin' 'Lindy Lowe, de bell done ring to go,
(Chorus)
Come, smilin' 'Lindy Lowe, whah de muscadimons grow,
(Chorus)
Come, smilin' 'Lindy Lowe, befo' de whistle blow',
(Chorus)
Come, smilin' 'Lindy Lowe, de pride o' Lake St. Jo',
(Chorus)
Come, smilin' 'Lindy Lowe, I love' you long ago,
(Chorus)
Come, smilin' 'Lindy Lowe, I'll love you mo' an' mo',
(Chorus)
Come, smilin' 'Lindy Lowe, how kin you treat me so?
(Chorus)
Come, smilin' 'Lindy Lowe, whah de sweet pussimmon grow',
(Chorus)
Come, smilin' 'Lindy Lowe, de steam-kyahs runs too slow, (Chorus)
Come, smilin' 'Lindy Lowe, whah de blue pon'-lily grow,
(Chorus)
Come, smilin' 'Lindy Lowe, O don't you tell me no!
(Chorus)
Come, smilin' 'Lindy Lowe, I's bound to be yo' beau,
(Chorus)
Come, smilin' 'Lindy Lowe, whah de wile white roses grow,
(Chorus)
Come, smilin' 'Lindy Lowe, de fust of all de row,
(Chorus)
Come, smilin' 'Lindy Lowe, eyes sweeteh dan de doe,
(Chorus)
Come, smilin' 'Lindy Lowe, whah de white magnonia blow',
(Chorus)
Come, smilin' 'Lindy Lowe, an' awake up, fiddle an' bow,
(Chorus)
Come, smilin' 'Lindy Lowe, we'll a-dance de heel an' toe,
(Chorus)
Come, smilin' 'Lindy Lowe, to de tchune o' Jump, Jim Crow,
(Chorus)
Come, smilin' 'Lindy Lowe, come, de pootiess gal I know,
On de finess boat dat eveh float'
In de O – hi – o,
De Mas – sis – sip – pi aw de O – hi – o.
LIX
"CONCLUSIVELY"

Alone in the wide light of a harvest-moon that wrapped all shores in deep shadow and turned the mid- channel to silver, Hugh and Ramsey stood at the low front rail of the texas roof.

There were but few to see them, but every eye in range was aware of her and of a refined simplicity of dress adorning a figure whose pliant grace was the finishing touch to her joyous erectness. Hugh's gaze was frankly on her, and his mind on the first night he had ever seen her, when, with her hair wind-tossed in loose curls, she had stood at this spot on the *Votaress* and in carelessness of a whole world had sung "The Lone Starry Hours."

Equally distant from them were the pilot-house behind and above and the bell down forward on the skylight. To right and left on a thwartship line just back of them towered the chimneys softly giving out their titanic respirations. Watson, though off watch, was up at the wheel beside his partner, pretending not to see the two beneath. In other words, he was still, after eight and a half years, "hi the game." The Gilmores were with him, both in body and spirit.

Out forward of the bell, below it on the main roof, one of the boat's builders, responsible for her till she should reach New Orleans, sat in the captain's chair.

"After eight years and a half," Hugh himself had gravely begun to say to Ramsey, when two men, "California" and a fellow smoker, sauntered across the skylight roof close below. Gilmore, up in the pilot-house, was annoyed.

"Our poet," he murmured to his wife, "will spill the fat into the fire yet, if we don't stop him."

But the Californian had purposely encumbered himself with this stranger to make it plain that, hover as he might, he waived all claim to her attention. What better could a man do? And now he forbore even to look her way. The abstention was as marked as any look could have been. As they passed, Hugh was silent, but Ramsey spoke, her speech a light blend of response and evasion.

"On the *Votaress,*" she said, "the front of the texas didn't stand out forward of the chimneys, like this."

"Doesn't this make a handsomer boat," the lover asked, "seen either aboard or from the shore?"

Ramsey said yes, she had noticed the improvement from the Memphis wharf-boat. "She was a splendid sight; yes, out in the stream, just before her wheels first stopped. At least she was to any one loving boats and the river."

"Then you haven't changed?" asked Hugh, not for information but in the tone that always meant so much beneath the speech.

Her answer was merely to meet his gaze with a gentle steadfastness, each knowing that the other's mind was overcircling all the years that had divided them. Through those years they had exchanged no spoken or written word. Yet according to Watson true love finds ways, large love large ways, pure love pure ways. Sometimes love's friends really help; help find ways, or keep ways found; even make chutes and cut-offs. Gilmore, Watson, and the Vicksburg merchant happened to be Odd Fellows, and the Gilmores, to whom letter-writing was, next to their profession, their main pleasure, had been a sort of clearing-house for Friendship, Love, and Truth – and especially for social news – to all the *Votaress's* old coterie; Hugh, the pairs of Milliken's Bend,

Vicksburg, and Carthage, the boat's family, Phyllis, Madame Hayle, even old Joy –
with madame for amanuensis – and Ramsey herself. She and Hugh had followed
every step in each other's course, upheld by a simplicity of faith in friendship, love,
and truth, which hardly needed to ask the one question abundantly answered by this
steadfastness of eye.

Now she looked away to the moon's path on the river, and the question of change
came back from her: "Have you?"

"Only to grow."

"You have grown," she said, "every way."

"And you," he replied, "every beautiful way. I have just said so to your father."

Her response came instantly: "How did that happen?"

"We made it happen."

She looked at him again. "We," of course, meant "I." Truly she had grown every
beautiful way, but it was yet as wonderful as ever to stand, saying what she had said,
hearing what she was hearing, eye to eye, open soul to open soul, with one who could
make words – words at any rate – happen between himself and Gideon Hayle. She
looked this time not alone into his eyes but on all his unhandsome countenance, and
in a surviving upflare of her younger days' extravagance thought whether, among
all time's heroes of the world's waters, there had ever been one too great for Hugh
Courteney's face. So looking she thrilled with the belief that there was nothing such
men had ever done which this one might not some day, the right day, equal or surpass.

Again she looked away and as she looked the hovering Californian murmured to
his new-found confidant:

" You can't see the glory of her in this light nohow, unless you'd seen her already
in the full blaze of the cabin, or of broad day, with the light in that red hair. If you had
you wouldn't need even the moonlight now. You'd only need to know she was there
and you'd see her without looking. I seen her in her first long dress, jest a-learning to
fly and some folks showing no more poetic vision than to call her 'almost plain.' I saw
the loveliness a-coming, like daybreak in the mountains. And *he* saw it. I saw he saw
it. And now? I tell you, sir, her brow is like the snowdrift, her throat is like the swan,
and her face it is the fairest – I neverseen Annie Laurie, but if she's better looking or
sweeter behaving – I'd rather not. Anyhow they're enough alike to be sisters. I've
writ a poem on this one. Like to show – hmm? Hold on. It don't quite suit me yet but
– what's your hurry? When it does, I Joel it'll be a ripsnorter. I've worked eight year
and a half on it and they say genius is jest a trick o' takin' in- finitessimal pains. . . .
No, I'm not sleepy. Reckon I'll go up to the pilot-house. So long. Pleasant dreams."

While he so spoke Ramsey had said: "Here comes another boat, down in the next
bend. Or is she in the chute?"

"The chute," replied Hugh. "That's the old *An- iekpe.*"

"Ah, up and running again! I know all about you and the *Votaress* saving her people
that awful night she sank."

"Who told you?"

"Oh, a dozen, at a dozen times; but the best was Phyllis, writing to us."

"Phyllis behaved heroically that night; made up for all the past – though really
she'd done that before."

"I'm glad you feel that way," murmured Ramsey and suddenly asked: "Why did you take my father to your room just now?"

"To show him the plans for another boat."

"Humph!" What crystalline honesty was in his answers, she pondered. They were as prompt as a mirror's.

"Rivals," she remarked, "don't ordinarily show plans."

"Your father and I are not ordinary rivals."

What did that mean? Her, and not mere boats' plans? She did not look at him this time. Like " California" she could see without looking. "Think I'll rejoin the Gilmores," she sighed, as certain couples came up to see the *Antelope* go by. She feared a recurrence of " 'Lindy Lowe." On the way to the pilothouse she leisurely inquired:

"Do you think you'll ever build a finer boat than this?"

"Yes, and larger, and faster."

"Not this season?"

"No, I should hope not for many. Yet "

"Boats' lives," she prompted, "are so uncertain."

"Yes, grandfather thinks "

"Oh, if only he were here!" She paused to let Hugh notice that she had "were" and "was" in hand at last. Then:

"How long will that boat be?"

"Three hundred and thirty feet. She'll have ten boilers. Her cylinders will be forty-three inches, her stroke eleven feet. She'll cany eighty-five hundred bales of cotton."

"Goodness! How wide will she be?"

"In the beam fifty. Over all, at the wheelhouses, ninety. Her wheels will be forty-five feet in diameter and their buckets nineteen feet span. You still like figures, boats' figures, I hope?"

She still liked, for second choice, to make him, to herself, ridiculous; liked it even now while inwardly laughing and weeping at him for not coming to personal matters infinitely more important. "Go on," she said, "I like cabin figures. How long, wide, and high will the cabin be?"

"Two hundred and sixty-three by nineteen by sixteen."

"What'll her name be? Another e-double-s, of course?"

" No, I've just been telling your father – here comes the *Antelope*. I was telling him that grandfather "

An overhead roar of reply to the signal of the approaching boat drowned all words, but Ramsey had learned on coming aboard that the grandfather was still sound though beyond four score, and her one vivid wish now was to know more not of him but of Hugh and her father. Yet she had to let Hugh hand her up the pilot-house stair, and without him rejoined the Gilmores while Watson spoke down to the man in the captain's chair as to the light-draught *Antelope* having come up through the chute of Island So-and-so. She was just in time to accept her share in the splendor and gayety of the two boats' meeting and passing. As the picture dissolved, Mrs. Gilmore slyly pinched Ramsey's finger while asking Watson:

"Why don't our men sing? 7 want some more Xindy!"

Had she not heard the signal for the lead? No, in the excitement she had not, though both Ramsey and"California" had, there being to them an unfailing poetry in the casting of the lead, whether by day or, as now, by the glare of a torch basket let down close to the water under the starboard freight guards. At one end of the breast-board the two ladies, at the other the actor and the Californian, looked out and down. The boat's builder had left his seat and stood with Hugh at the forward rail. From the freight guards, far below, the leadsman, unseen up here except to experienced "poetic vision," sent up a long-drawn chant telling the fathoms of depth shown on the sounding- line that flew forward from his skilled hand into the boat's moonlight shadow, plunged to the river's bed, vibrated past his feet in the glare of the pine torch, stretched aft while he chanted, and was recovered in dripping coils and hove again.

"Mark under wa-ater, twai-ai-ain."

As the notes resounded Hugh looked up to the pilots and in his quietest speaking voice repeated:

"Mark under water, twain."

But our concern here is mainly with those for whom the scene, the calls, veiled two private conversations. Three or four times the one melodious cry, following as many casts, rose from below, and each time, with all its swing and melody left out, Hugh passed it on up to the pilots. Between the strains Gilmore said softly to "California":

"My dear fellow, no. Every time we show ourselves their partisans we make heavier hauling for them. They'd tell us so, only that – don't you see? – they can't even do that. It would be *infra dig."* But in fact Ramsey was just then telling something much like that to his wife.

"Yes," admitted the Californian, full of a new scheme, yet always generous, "and that was a ten- strike, your wife, after supper, taking Miss Hayle away from Hugh and Gideon in such gay style. Did you see how't sort o' eased the old man's mind?"

The leadsman's cry changed and so came twice or thrice, Hugh as often repeating it to the pilots, while Ramsey and Mrs. Gilmore, though hearkening, whispered busily.

"Shoaling," commented Mrs. Gilmore to Ramsey.

"Not seriously," said the river-wise Ramsey. "Go on. What did you get out of him at last?" She had a merry sparkle.

Once more the far-below cry rose to them and was restated by Hugh without color or thrill. Ramsey well knew that so it was always sung and spoken, yet she remarked:

"Hear that absurd difference – in those two voices."

"That's the difference between him and other men, Ramsey; even between him and your father."

She liked that, though now she felt bitter toward him for not being more like ordinary mortals.

"Go on," she lightly repeated. "If he won't make words happen with me I must take him secondhand."

"You naughty girl ! He'll tell you all you'll let him."

"Oh, I'll let him, all he'll tell me. What did he say?"

"He said the very best was, that under all your mantle of new charms "

Ramsey's soft laugh interrupted. "He didn't. He never said that, my lady. He wouldn't know how. You said it."

"Well, he did say that under it all there's nothing lost of the Ramsey we began with."

"The slanderer!" They laughed together. The calls of the lead were passing unnoticed. " Mark above water, twain; mark, twain; quarter less, twain; half, twain; nine and a half; by the mark, nine; nine feet."

"The slanderer! Why, that's actionable! I'll have the law on him!" The speaker's mirth was overdone. As the leadsman sang another cry and Hugh sedately spoke it she tinkled as of old and said: "Don't get excited, captain. Keep cool."

Mrs. Gilmore sobered. "You may laugh, but I believe he's talked with your father conclusively and will to you to-night, if you'll allow it."

"Humph! you don't know that he'll come near me. Aboard his own boat, on her trial trip, he's got other fish to fry. But even if he should, don't you see how absolute the deadlock is? Oh, you must have seen it these eight years and more! – in spite of everybody's silence."

"We didn't. We don't see it even now, Gilmore and I. We don't believe Captain Hugh sees any deadlockwhatever. He merely knows you think you do. You think to accept him would condemn him to death? "

"Mrs. Gilmore, I know it would. My brothers – may have broken promises but they – keep – their – threats. You know that's the fashion of all this country, from Cairo down."

"Ma-a-ark, twai-ai-ain," chanted the leadsman for his final call, and not only Hugh but an echo from the land repeated it. To many an ear, poetic ear, that echo is there yet, in all that country, from Cairo down. But that is aside. Watson and his partner threw the wheel over and the *Enchantress* swept round for the chute.

In the bright moonlight Hugh and the boat's builder turned back toward the solitary chair, placidly conversing. Gilmore talked on with "California." His wife and Ramsey drew back into the corner behind them.

"Your brothers," murmured Mrs. Gilmore, "threatened Hugh's life just the same before you came into the issue at all."

"Yes," said Ramsey, "and they're watching their chance yet. Julian told me so this summer and Lucian berated him for 'showing his hand.' Oh, that isn't the deadlock, by itself. The deadlock is that as long as Hugh Courteney holds off the feud will keep, but when he doesn't I come in and it won't; everything's precipitated. And so, you see? . . .

"Hmm! Hugh Courteney won't put himself, or me, or mom-a, where, in a fight for his life, no matterwho's killed the killing would be in the family, and the killed would be ours, mom-a's – and – and mine. The twins see that. Jule says it, and, what's worse, Luce says nothing. That's why *they* are entirely satisfied with the deadlock. . . . Look."

The boat's contractor was leaving the deck. Hugh had started toward the pilot-house. But when Mrs. Gilmore looked she looked beyond him in meditation.

"I know what you're thinking," said Ramsey. "But it'll never happen. They've settled down to the ordinary term of a decent life, thank God! . . . Here becomes.

Think he'll talk to me? Yes, he will. He'll begin where he left off." She laughed. "He's going to tell me the name of his next boat, if he ever builds another. Anything 'conclusive' in that?"

Mrs. Gilmore was grave a moment longer and then brightly said: "There might be! There may be! I can see – I can see how he – " She could not finish. Hugh had entered.

His coming broke in upon another conversation, that of Gilmore and "California."

"Old boy, no. Suppose it should work out as you plan. You leave us at Natchez; that's easy. You live there a week, a month, free with your gold and making friends – of the sort gold makes. You get into a political quarrel with the twins – nothing easier – and in a clear case of your own self-defence the two are: –

" ' – Laid in one grave. Sing tooralye/ etc."

"Wouldn't that be poetic justice? and ain't I a poet?"

" Undoubtedly. Then by miracle you come off scot- free."

" Not essential. I take my chances."

"Still, you have that hope; freedom is sweet. Moreover, miracle of miracles, what you did it for is never guessed. But, my dear fellow, there are two who'd never need to guess. Like us they'd know and that knowledge would sunder them forever. They'd never willingly look into each other's faces again."

"Nnn-o. No, course they wouldn't. I seen that from the jump but I sort o' hoped you'd maybe know some way to get round that; it being the only real difficulty."

" Sorry, but I don't. Odd how narrow-minded one's friends can be, but when they are – what can we do?"

"Yes, that's so. ... Mr. Gilmore, you're not narrow-minded; I've got a poem "

It was there Hugh entered. But it was there, too, that Watson made a move in his modest part of the game.

With his eyes out ahead down the chute they were entering – "If any one," he drawled, "wants to see a scandalous fine moonlight picture of this river, one they'll never forget, the best place from whence to behold it is the texas roof, down here, out for'ard o' the chimneys."

"If Captain Hugh would go with us," pensivelysaid Mrs. Gilmore, "we'd all go." And soon the pilots were alone.

"Now," growled the younger, with his gaze down there on Ramsey, " don't that beat you? Her making California stay so's Cap'n Hugh can't pair off with her!"

"Be easy," said Watson; "that's according to Hoyle. Don't shoot till they settle. . . . There. Now I'll go down and take care of California. By cracky! run smooth or run rough, I believe it's going to go this time."

LX

ONCE MORE HUGH SINGS

Between that great eastward bend nearly opposite the mouth of the Arkansas, which in later years was cut off and is now, or was yesterday, Beulah Lake – between it and Ozark Island below – a white-jacket came up from the passenger deck far enough to show his head to the watchman above and warily asked a question.

"Six," was the reply. "Including me – seven."

The inquirer ran wildly down again, but the *Enchantress* sped on through the glorious moonlight as though he scarcely mattered. On the texas roof Mrs. Gilmore sat with "California," her husband with Watson, Hugh with Ramsey. But only the last two were out on its forward verge. Mrs. Gilmore had found it cool there and with the others had drawn back a few steps, into the pleasant warmth of the chimneys. For average passengers the evening was far gone, but not for players, pilots, Californians, or lovers – of the river.

A mile or so farther on, the white-jacket reappeared and, gliding by all others to reach his captain, said, with mincing feet and a semicircular bow, while presenting a tray of six, not seven, sherry cobblers:

"Sev'l gen'lemen's comp'ments, an' ax, will Mis' Gil' "

"What gentlemen? Who?"

"Sev'l gen'lemen, yassuh. Dey tell me dess say, sev'l gen'lemen. Sev'l gen'lemen ax will Mis' Gilmo' have de kin'ness fo' to sing some o' dem same songs she sing night afo' las' in de ladies' cabin an' las' night up hyuh. . . . Yass'm, whiles dey listens f'om de b'ileh deck."

"Has my father gone to bed?" asked Ramsey.

" No'm, he up yit. He done met up wid dese sev'l gen'lemen an' find dey old frien's – callin' deyse'v's in joke Gideon' Ban' – an' he talkin' steamboats wid 'em "

The speaker tittered as Ramsey inquiringly extended her arms out forward and crossed her wrists. " Yass'm," he said, "hin' feet on de front rail, yass'm."

It seemed but fair that Mrs. Gilmore, to meet the compliment generously, should sing at the very front of the hurricane roof, just over the forward guards of the boiler deck. But Ramsey and Hugh kept their place. Ramsey wanted to be near the sky, she explained, when songs were sung on the water by moonlight, and eagerly spoke for two or three which her friend had sung of old on the *Votaress* to spiritualize the "acrobatics" of the Brothers Ambrosia.

The singer's voice was rich, trained, and mature, and her repertory a survival of young days – nights – before curtains and between acts: Burns, Moore, Byron, and Mrs. Norton, alternating with "TheLavender Girl," "Rose of Lucerne," "Dandy Jim o' Caroline," and "O Poor Lucy Neal." And now she sang her best, in the belief that while she sang the pair up between her and the pilot-house were speaking conclusively. Let us see.

"Ramsey," said Hugh, and waited – ten seconds – twenty.

Well, why should he not? In eight years and a half there were ten million times twenty seconds and she had waited all of them. At length she responded and the moment she did so she thought she had spoken too promptly although all she said was, "Yes?"

"The hour's come at last," said Hugh.

"What hour? – hour to name that boat?"

"Yes, to name that boat. Only not that first. Ramsey, I've told your father all I ever wanted to tell you."

"Humph!" The response was so nearly in the manner of the earlier Ramsey, "the Ramsey he had begun with" and whom she remembered with horror, that she recognized the likeness. The further reply had been on her tongue's end, that to tell her father only that could not have taken long, or some such parrying nonsense; but now it would not come. She felt her whole nature tempted to make love's final approach steep and slippery, but again without looking she saw his face; his face of stone; his iron face with its large, quiet, formidable eyes that could burn with enterprise in great moments; a face set to all theworld's realities, and eyes that offered them odds, asking none. So seeing she knew that if she answered with one least note of banter she would make herself an object of his magnanimity, than which she would almost rather fall under his scorn – if he ever stooped to scorn. Suddenly she remembered the deadlock and was smitten with the conviction that these exchanges were love's last farewell. Now it was hard to speak at all.

"What was it you told him?"

"I told him how long I'd loved you, and why."

"We both love the river so," murmured Ramsey in a voice broken by the pounding of her heart.

"Yes. I told him that, for one thing. And I told him how gladly I would have asked for you long ago had I not seen myself, as you so often saw me on the *Votaress* "

"Condemned to inaction," she softly prompted; for if this was farewell a true maiden must speed the parting.

"Yes."

"By an absolute deadlock," she murmured on. "My father sees it. He knows it's one yet and must always be one."

"No, a lock but not a deadlock. It's a lock to which your brothers do not hold the key."

The pounding in her breast, which had grown better, grew worse again. "Who holds it?"

"Your father. I have just told him so. At no time would I have hesitated to ask for you if the key hadbeen with your brothers. I would have got a settlement from them, sink or swim, alive or dead. I believe in lover's rights, Ramsey, and I'll have a lover's rights at any risk or cost that falls only on me. Those old threats – yes, I know how fiercely they are still meant – and they have always had their weight; but they've never of themselves weighed enough to stop me. I've held off and endured, waiting not for a change of heart in your brothers, but for an hour counselled, Ramsey, by my father on his dying bed."

"What hour? Hour of strongest right? strongest reason? "

" Not at all. The hour I've waited for was the one which would best enable me to meet your father on equal terms as measured by his own standards."

"Oh, I see. I believe I see."

"Yes, the hour when I should be not owner merely, but captain too, of the finest boat "

"Dat eveh float' – " she tenderly put in.

"Yes, on this great river."

"Oh, Captain Courteney "

"Don't Courteney or captain me now, Ramsey, whether this is beginning or end."
There was a silence, and then –

"Hugh," she said, as softly as a female bird trying her mate's song, "you mustn't ask my father. You mustn't ask any one. I can't let you."

"Your father's already asked. If he consents I go ashore at Natchez, having telegraphed ahead from

Vicksburg "

" You shan't. You shan't go to my brothers. You shan't go armed and you shan't go unarmed."

"Yes, I shall. I'll go and settle with them in an hour without the least fear of violence on either side."

" Armed with nothing but words? You shan't. And armed with anything else you shan't."

" Ramsey, words are the mightiest weapon on earth. The world's one perfect man – we needn't be pious to say it – set about to conquer the human race by the sheer power of words and died rather than use any other weapon. Died victorious, as he counted victory. And the result – a poor, lame beginning of the result – is what we call Christendom."

"You shan't die victorious for me."

"No, I shall not. I talk much too vast."

"Humph! you always did." She smiled, but a moonbeam betrayed a tear on her folded hands.

"True," he admitted. "I talk too vast. I'm only claiming the power of words in small as well as large. I've no hope of martyrdom; I'm only confident of victory."

" No matter. You *won't* go ashore at Natchez."

"You mean your father won't consent?"

" I do. There's one thing, at the very bottom of his heart, that you've never thought of."

"I think I have."

"What is it?"

"That as the Hayle boats are all one day to be yours, and our union would unite the two fleetsunder the one name of Courteney, he will never allow it."

"He never will."

"Ramsey, he says he may. If we and the boats are so united the fleet will be, while grandfather lives, the Courteney fleet; but each new boat from now on will be named for a Hayle, beginning with you, or your father, or your mother, as you and they may choose. At Vicksburg, if he consents in tune, we can telegraph her – we must have her – to come aboard at Natchez for the rest of the trip. Grandfather, I suppose you've been told, is now waiting for us at Vicksburg. He came up on the *Antelope.*"

"The Antelope! How do you know?"

"By a despatch received at Memphis."

"Mmm! what a blessing is the telegraph! But, ah, Hugh" – the name was almost naturalized – "this is a mere castle in the air! My – my brothers "

"I'll take care of them."

"You can't! You can't! Oh, Hugh, they – keep – their – threats." She caught a breath and looked at him. If he went seeking them she would go at his side! He must have read her mind, for hi his ma- jestical way he smilingly shook his head.

Mrs. Gilmore had ceased to sing and with the others had risen and turned Ramsey's way, confident that up there the conclusive word had been spoken. Ramsey called down:

"Don't stop. Sing 'My Old Kentucky Home' or that thing in which 'the river keeps rolling along' aid'the future's but a dream.' We're song hungry up here."

"Then sing to each other," was the reply. "You can do it."

"Let Captain Hugh sing," said Watson. "He's off watch."

"He says," said Ramsey, "captains don't sing on the texas roof." She moved to join the group on its way to an after stair. Watson bent his steps for the pilot-house. At the stair the actor's wife let her husband and "California" go down before her and as Ramsey and Hugh came close said covertly:

"Sing, captain. Sing as softly as you please, just for us two while the world is in dreams and sleep, won't you?"

The lover's heart was big with happiness, his solicitor had just been singing pointedly in his interest, the seclusion here was all but absolute, the quoted line was from Ramsey's song of that first night on the *Votaress,* and to the bright surprise of both his hearers he laid a touch on Mrs. Gilmore's arm and in a restrained voice so confidential as to reach only to the pilot-house above and to the two men at the stair's foot below began to sing.

Before half a line was out the Californian had seized both of Gilmore's shoulders. "My poem!" he gasped. "I gave it to him last night to grammatize! He's fit it to a tchune. Partner, he's the only man that's listened "

"Sh-sh-sh! listen yourself," whispered the actor, and this is what they heard:

O come and grace my gar - den, From all the world a -
part. Thou on- ly may'st the won-der see Of birds and flow'rs that
in it be, For all of them are dreams of thee. My
gar - den is my heart, My gar - den is my heart.
" If heaven might make my garden
An empire wide and great,
Fidelity should close it in,
The joy of life bloom evergreen,
And love be law and thou be queen,
Might I but keep the gate.
"For where would be my garden,
Dear love, from thee apart?
Whose every bush and bower aod tree,
Its founts, perfumes, and minstrelsy
And all its flowers spring all from thee,
Thou sunlight of my heart."

"You say that's your poem?" murmured the actor. "Oh, he's doctored it," stealthily admitted the Cal- ifornian. "He's doctored it a lot."

LXI

WANTED, HAYLE'S TWINS

Early in the next forenoon another of the Cali- fornian's benevolent schemes threatened to miscarry.

At the settlement of Milliken's Bend there were people already at the landing, and people running to it from three directions. Yet not a hat, hand, or handkerchief did they wave until the *Enchantress,* in full view up toward the head of the bend, was too near to mistake their salutes for a sign to stop. Then there were wavings aplenty and cries of acclaim. By the "River News" daily telegraphed down to the New Orleans, Vicksburg, and other papers, from Louisville, Paducah, Cairo, and like points, and brought up in those papers by such boats as the *Antelope,* it had been known here and at every important landing below that this latest bride of the river was coming and the time of her appearance had been definitely calculated. And now behold her, a vision of delight, a winged victory, the finest apparition yet. Up in front of her bell could be seen Captain Hugh, and who was that beside him, twice his bulk, but Gideon Hayle!

"Well, well, what's going to happen next?"

No one offered an answer, though the question echoed round.

So early in the season the new wonder carried no cotton, but her lower deck showed "right smart o' freight," and wherever passengers were wont to stand stood a crowd looking so content that on the shore one lean and hungry native with his hands in his trousers to the elbows drawled sourly as his eye singled out the boiler-deck throng:

" Kin see thah breakfast inside 'em f'om hyuh."

Now they read her name in gold on the front of her pilot-house, now on its side and splendidly magnified on her wheel-house, and lastly again on the pilot-house, at its back, as she dwindled away eastward for Island One-hundred-and-three, called by Ramsey and Watson "My Wife's," and now known as Pawpaw Island.

"California" was a general disappointed of his reinforcements. The pair at Milliken's Bend having failed him, what better hope was there of the Carthaginians or even of the Vicksburg couple? Yet at Vicksburg, two hours later, he had joy. For down at the wharf-boat's very edge, liveliest of all wavers and applauders, with a "Howdy, Cap'm Hugh?" before the lines were out, and a "How you do, Miss Ramsey?" were the three pairs at once, foregathered here, they said, "to make the spree mo' spree-cious," and wild to be the first on the "sta-age plank." Close after them came Commodore Courteney, and Vicksburg faded into the north.

"Why, Mis' Gilmo'!" said the three pretty wives, sinking with a deft sweep of their flounced crinolineupon the blue-damask sofas and faintly teetering on their perfect springs, "why, my deah la-ady, yo' eight an' a hafe yeahs youngeh! – Ain't she? – She certain'y is! An' that deah Commodo' Co'teney! He's as sweet as eveh!

"But you, Miss Ramsey, oh, – well, – why, – you know, – time an' again we heard what a mahvel you'd grown to be, but – why, – lemme look at you again! Why, yo' just divi-i-ine! Law' ! I'd give a thousand dollahs just fo' yo' red-gole hair. Why, it's the golden locks o' Veronese, that Cap'm Hugh's fatheh showed you, – don't you remembeh? – on the *Vot'ress,* an' you showed us, – in the sky. They there yet!

"An'" – the five heads drew close together – "Cap'm Hugh, oh, he ain't such a su'pri-ise; we've seen him f'om time to time. But ain't he – mmm, hmm, hmmm! An' so a-a-able! Why, Miss Ramsey, – oh, you must 'a' heard it, – they say excep' fo' yo' pa he hasn't got his equal on the riveh an' could 'a' been a captain long ago had he 'a' thought best himself. He certain'y could. But ain't this boat the splen- didest thing in the wi-i-ide, wi-i-ide world? It certain'y is! It's a miracle! an' he her captain and deservin' to be!

"Mis' Gilmo', – Miss Ramsey," – the lovely heads came together, – "the's a hund'ed pretty girls – an' rich as pretty – that ah just cra-a-azy about him. But they might as well be crazy about a stah. They certain'y might, an' they – know – why!" (Laughter.) "They certain'y do – Law'! ain't Miss Ramsey gotthe sa-a-ame o-o-ole la-a-afe, on'y sweeteh'n eveh? Sweeteh an' mo' ketchin'! You certain'y have. No wondeh yo' call' the Belle o' the Bends. But, all the same, yo' cruel. Yo' fame' fo' yo' cruelty!" (Laughter.) "They say he's just telegrayphed yo' ma to come aboa'd at Natchez. That's just ow Southe'n hospitality. But won't that be fi-i-ine? It certain'y will!"

The three husbands came bringing the actor, the junior pilot, the Californian, and his confidant of the evening before. Incited by Ramsey the wives fell into queries on the coming election, rejoicing that even should Lincoln be made President, and that incredible thing, a war, come on, the great river and its cities – New Orleans, Natchez, Memphis, and especially Vicksburg – would be far from the storm. While they made merry Mrs. Gilmore got Ramsey aside.

"If Captain Hugh's telegraphed, why, then, your father "

"Oh! my father, he's roaming over the boat somewhere with Commodore Courteney! I'm going to change this hot dress for a cooler one. I'll be back before a great while."

"Let me go with you. Are you not well?"

Not well! The girl laughed gayly. But as she drew her friend out upon the guards and to her stateroom's rear door she talked with a soft earnestness all the way.

"I don't see how I could have been so blind! If *he* saw those things why couldn't I see them? I thoughtof them, over and over; but always the other things crowded them back into the dark – and there was plenty of dark. He's right, my father does hold the key, and if I'd seen things as I see them now I'd have made the twins give in, somehow, long ago. If you should see mammy Joy, or Phyllis, or both, please send them to me."

She shut herself in, dropped to the berth's side, and let the tears run wild. The nurse and the still handsome Phyllis appeared promptly, together. But they found her full of sparkle; so full that Phyllis saw under the mask; a mask she herself had worn so often in her youth under a like desperation.

"Mammy," said her mistress, "want to go somewhere with your baby, about sundown this evening?"

For explanation the old woman glanced at Phyllis, but Phyllis's eyes were on Ramsey with a light whose burning carried old Joy's memory back twenty years. "Sundown?" echoed the nurse to gain time, "yass'm, o' co'se, ef – but, missie – sundown – dat mean' Natchez. You cayn't be goin' asho' whah Cap'm Hugh dess tell Phyllis yo' ma comin' aboa'd?"

"Not ashore to stay," was the blithe reply as Phyllis aided the change of dress. "There'll be two or three of us."

"Well, o' co'se, ef you needs me. Wha' fo' you gwine?"

"To see the twins," sang Ramsey, "if we go at all."

Then Phyllis knew she was trusted, and while with a puzzled frown the nurse watched her manipulate hooks and eyes she blandly asked: "Miss Ramsey, if Cap'm Hugh give' me leave kin I go too?"

"Yes, you might ask him. Nobody's going unless he goes."

The light came to old Joy. " Law'! missie, now you a-talkin'! Now you a-talkin' wisdom! Dah's whah I's wid you, my baby. I's wid you right dah, pra-a-aise Gawd!"

All three, parting company, were happier for several hours. But the Californian's were not the only fond schemes, aboard the *Enchantress,* that could go to wreck.

Nor had "California" met his last disappointment even on this journey. As he and his reinforcements came out on the boiler deck with a hundred others from the midday feast the deck-hands below, for quicker unloading at Canal Street on the morrow, were shifting a lot of sacked corn from the hold to the forecastle-deck and were timing their work to a chantey. The song was innocently chosen in reference solely to the piece of river in which they chanced then to be, but all the more for its innocence it touched in that gentle knight a chord of sympathy.

"My own true love wuz lost an' found –
O hahd times! –
An' lost ag'in a-comin' round
Hahd Times Ben'.
Found an' lost, lost an' found,
An' lost ag'in a-comin' round
Hahd Times Ben'."

So it ran, while the *Enchantress* turned southeast with that Lake Saint Joe of which " 'Lindy " was " the pride" lying forest-hidden a few miles away on the starboard beam. The melody opened with a prolonged wail on its highest note and bore the tragic quality which so often marked the songs of slavery. Helped on by names of near-by landmarks – the Big Black River and the once perilous Grand Gulf – at the bottom of Hard Times Bend – it played on "California's" mind like summer lightning and seemed to call to his romantic spirit supernaturally. He could delay no longer to take his companions into his confidence.

By guess, he said, by inferences, and by modest inquiries he had discerned that Hugh was going ashoreat Natchez to – they understood. All right, he would go, too, and ordinarily he would be enough. But the present need was not a fair fight but peace. Hence the propriety of overwhelming numbers. Wouldn't they like to take a hand?

"But he'll see the twins privately," said the invited.

"Of course, but 'though lost to sight' they'll know we're too close for them to get away from, and that's a very convincing situation to 'most any man, even twins."

"Yes, but we can't turn a feud into a fox-hunt. You don't know these things as we do."

"Don't? Why, my friends, I'm a Kentucky high- lander. Might as well say I don't know the smell of whiskey because I keep sober, when, in my day, I've been so drunk I've laid on my back and felt up'ards for the ground."

However, he yielded sweetly. But it was plain to see that he would certainly, con- tentedly, go with Hugh alone. Indeed, only this would he have preferred – that Gideon Hayle might go instead. But one square look at the big, grim, baffled commander had told him earlier that Hugh's perilous isolation was wholly acceptable as a final test of his fitness to belong to Gideon's Band. He parted with his companions and stood at the front rail taking comfort in the thought that whoever might disappoint him the twins would not and looking down on the toiling singers in placid defiance of their lines:

"My true love's heart to mine 'uz boun' –
O hahd times! –
Dey broke dem bindin's comin' roun'
Hahd Times Ben'.
Boun' an' broke, broke an' boun',
An' broke ag'in a-comin" roun'
Hahd Times Ben'."

Watson's partner touched the listener's arm, who smiled and said:

"Only four hours more."

"That's all," replied the pilot. "But I've just thought of something. Suppose the twins shouldn't be in Natchez." LXII

EUTHANASIA

A Few steps aside from Hugh and his grandfather at the forward rail of the hurricane roof, in a glow of autumn twilight, the Gilmores and the three couples taken on at Vicksburg observed the *Enchantress,* under Watson's skill, lay her lower guards against the guards of the Natchez wharf-boat with a touch as light as a human hand.

Down on the wharf-boat, in its double door, as beautiful in her fuller years as in *Votaress* days, and more radiant, stood Madame Hayle. A man-servant at one elbow, a maid at the other, saw the group on the roof fondly bidding for her smiles, but except one sent earlier to the two Courteneys they were all for her husband and daughter, who, unseen from above, awaited her half-way down the main forward stairs. When the maid, however, leaned to her and spoke, her glance went aloft and her gestures were a joy even to the strangers who crowded the boat's side. Now while the stage was run out and her husband met her and gave her his arm, and white-jackets seized her effects, the man-servant answered a question softly called over to him by Ramsey, and the group overhead caught his words:

" De twins couldn' come. No, miss, 'caze dey ain't in town. No, miss, dey bofe went oveh to de Lou'si- ana place 'istiddy. . . . Yass, miss, on a bah hunt in Bayou Crocodile swamp."

Mrs. Gilmore stole a glance at Hugh, but the only sign that he had heard was a light nod to the mate below, and a like one up to Watson.

"Take in that stage," called the mate to his men. The engine bells jingled, the *Enchantress* backed a moment on one wheel, then went forward on both, fluttered her skirts of leaping foam, made a wide, upstream turn, headed down the river, and swept away for Natchez Island just below and for New Orleans distant a full night's run. She had hardly put the island on her larboard bow when merrily up and down the cabin and out on the boiler deck and thence down the passsenger guards rang the supper bell.

" Bayou Crocodile," said a Carthaginian descending the wheel-house stair, "that's where one of the sons- in-law has his plantation, isn't it?"

"On the Black River, yes," said he of Milliken's Bend.

"Near where it comes into Red River," added Vicksburg.

Once more Hugh and Ramsey sat alone side by side under a glorious night sky, at that view-point so rarely chosen by others but so favored by her – the front of the texas roof. Down forward at the captain's station sat the two commodores and up in the pilot-house were the two pilots, the Gilmores, "California," Madame Hayle, and they of Vicksburg and the Bends.

In the moral atmosphere of this uppermost group there was a new and happy clearness easily attributable to a single potent cause – Madame Hayle. Her advent and the moon's rising had come in the same hour and with very similar effect. Every one was aware for himself, though nobody could say when any one else had been told, that while Gideon's decision was still withheld, madame, in her own sweet, absolute way, had said it would be forthcoming before the boat touched the Canal Street wharf, and that in the interval, whether Hugh and Ramsey were never to sit side by side again, or were to go side by side the rest of their days, they should have this hour this way and were free to lengthen it out till night was gone, if they wished.

It was not late in any modern sense, yet on the passenger deck no one was up but the barkeeper, two or three quartets at cards, the second clerk at work on his freight list, a white-jacket or two on watch, and Joy and Phyllis. Thus assured of seclusion the lovers communed without haste. There had been hurried questions but Hugh had answered them and Ramsey was now passive, partly in the bliss of being at his side as she had never been before and partly in a despair growing out of his confessed purpose to leave the *Enchantress* at Red River Landing. The grandfather had already assumed Hugh's place and cares aboard, and it was Hugh's design to make his way, by boat or horse, up to and along Black River in search of the twins.

To allay this distress Hugh's soft deep voice said:

"Suppose you were a soldier's wife. This is little to that. This is but once for all."

"Yes," murmured Ramsey, "but I'd have one advantage."

"That you'd be his wife?"

"Yes," whispered Ramsey, who could not venture the name itself, for the pure rapture of it.

"Why, you're going to be mine. As the song says: 'I will come again, my love, though a' the seas gang dry.' "

"Hugh, didn't you once say I didn't know what fear was?"

"I certainly thought it."

"Well, now I do know."

He made no reply and she sat thinking of his errand. If he should find her brothers he would meet them in the deepest wilderness. Only slaves, who could not testify against masters, would be with them, their loaded guns would be in their hands, and their blood would be heated with – She resorted again to questions in her odd cross-examining way.

"You say you think there's going to be a war?"

"I fear so."

"Humph! fear. If there should be will you fight?"

"Certainly."

"Humph! certainly. I should think – you'd hate to fight."

"I'd fight all the more furiously on that account."

"Humph! ... On which side?"

"Ramsey, I don't know. I *don't know* till the time comes."

"Then how do you know you won't fight my brothers – now?"

"I shan't be armed."

"But if in an outburst you should snatch up some weapon?"

"I don't burst out. I don't snatch up."

"Humph! Wish I didn't."

They were rounding Point Breeze. The long reach from Fort Adams down to Red River Landing lay before them. "Hugh, did you ever have a presentiment? Of course not. I never did before. I got it a-comin' round Hard Times Bend."

"Then I can cure it – with a new verse, one our poet has made and given me. It shall be our parting word. Shall I?"

"Oh, yes, but not for parting! I don't want any parting!"

He spoke it softly:

"I dreamp I heard a joyful soun' –
O hahd times! –
Love once mo' foun' de last turn roun'
Hahd Times Ben'.
Los' an' foun', broke an' boun',
Love foun' an' boun' de last turn roun'
Hahd Times Ben'."

Ramsey barely waited for its end. "What's that light waving far away down yonder? It began as you did."

"It didn't know it. It's only some one on the Red River wharf-boat, wanting us to land," said Hugh, and before his last word came the *Enchantress* roared her assent to the signal. But Ramsey had spoken again:

"What's this, right here?" She sprang up and gazed out on the water a scant mile ahead. There, directly in the steamer's course and just out of the moon's track, another faint light waved, so close to the water as to be reflected in it. The moment the whistle broke out it ceased to swing and when the whistle ceased the engines had stopped.

"What is it?" she asked again as Hugh stood by her looking out ahead with eyes better trained to night use than hers.

"A skiff," he replied, "with some message."

She could see only that Watson had put the light on their starboard bow. It seemed to drift toward them but she knew that the movement was the steamer's, and now the light was so close as to show the negro who held it. He stood poised to throw aboard a billet of wood with a note attached. And now he cast it. The lower guards were out of Ramsey's line of sight but a cry of disappointment told her the stick had fallen short and would be lost under the great wheel, which at that moment, with its fellow, "went ahead." But as the *Enchantress* passed the skiff its occupant called out a hurried statement to the mate, on the forecastle, and as the skiff and its light swept astern the mate repeated the word to the commodores.

"Man at Red River Landing accidentally shot. Must be got to the city quick or he can't live."

The commodores, and then the lovers, resumed their seats.

"Poor man," murmured Ramsey, "poor man! he's got *his* trouble without going in chase of it."

"If he'd gone in chase of it," rejoined Hugh, "he might never have met it."

The *Enchantress* swung more directly toward the dim lights of the wharf-boat and at top speed ruffled through a freshening air with the goal but a few miles away. Yet the lovers sat silent. Once parted they would think of many a word they should have spoken while they could, but now none seemed large enough to break such silence with. To be silent and best content with silence was one of the most special and blissful of lovers' rights.

Presently a glow rose from the forecastle, reddening the white jack-staff up to its black night-hawk. The torch baskets were being lighted. Hugh stirred to go but Ramsey laid her touch on his wrist and he stayed.

She spoke. "Mustn't you wait near your grandfather till you see who it is that's coming aboard?"

"lean. I may as well."

The *Enchantress,* in mid-river, began to "round to" in order to land bow up-stream. When she cameround, the half dozen men on the wharf-boat were close at hand in the glare of her torches, eye to eye with those on the forecastle, but prevented by the light itself from seeing those on the upper decks.

Ramsey sprang to her feet with lips apart to cry out to her mother up behind her, to Gideon down before, to Hugh at her side, but all these saw and knew. A face in the centre of the torchlight and of the wharf- boat group was Julian's bearing the mute intelligence that the writhing man on a rude stretcher borne by two negroes was his brother. The lovers parted without a word, but in a moment were near each other again as Hugh joined the commodores while Ramsey and her mother crouched at the roof's forward rail to see the wounded man brought across the stage.

"In my room!" pleaded madame to both Courte- neys at once, and the elder assented as Hugh hurried below with the three Hayles following.

It was heart-rending work getting the sufferer into the berth while he poured out meanings of agony mingled with frantic accusations of his bearers, railings against God and all his laws, and unspoken recognitions of mother and sister. Ramsey, seeing his eye fall on Phyllis and remain there staring, and knowing from old Joy that he had grown enough like his uncle Dan to have been his twin, suffered for her as well as him.

"Who are *you?"* he cried, still staring. "Where am I?"

The maid did not reply, but her unfaltering gaze met his as if it neither could nor would do otherwise. Ramsey intuitively followed the play of her mind. To look again on Gideon Hayle had already recalled emotions she had striven for half a lifetime to put away, and now they kept her eyes set on this tortured yet unrelenting advocate of all the wrongs from which those emotions sprang.

He looked to his mother. "Great God! mother, is this the new Courteney boat? Well, if this isn't hell's finishing touch! Jule! Where's Jule? Go, get meJule!"

Phyllis turned to go but – "No," he cried with a light of sudden purpose in his face, "you stay. Everybody else go! And send me Jule. Don't send a doctor, I'm the doctor myself. Get out, all of you, go! This isn't my death-bed. God! I wish it was, for I'm a cripple for life and will never walk again – leave! go! and send me Jule!"

Guided by a cabin-boy to Hugh's room, Ramsey found Julian confronting his father, "California," and the Gilmores. Hugh had led them there for privacy and stood close at one side. Julian seemed to be suffering a shock scarcely less than his brother's though it made a wholly different outward show. His face wore an appalled look, his voice was below its accustomed pitch, and his words, words which could not have been premeditated, seemed studiously fit and precise.

"Fortunately," he had been saying before Ramsey appeared, "he never" – meaning his brother – "goesinto the country without his drugs and instruments – we have them with us yet – and he could tell me what to do and I did it, or he would have died right there in the swamp."

"But you don't say how the accursed thing happened," said Gideon as Ramsey entered hardly aware that she was pausing at Hugh's side. The brother turned and stared on the two.

"Come," said Gideon, "never mind that. How did it happen?"

"It happened, sir, through my own incredible carelessness and by my own hand. *Don't say a word!* I would to God I had been the victim and had fallen dead in my tracks. If I had killed him I would have put the other load into my brain."

"Oh, if!" solemnly sneered the incredulous father. While he did so Julian, the profoundness of whose mental torture his father poorly saw, received from Ramsey his brother's summons and with her was turning away. He stopped and flashed back a look of agonized resentment, but Gideon met it with a beetling frown and neither gaze fell until Ramsey stepped between, facing the giant, and she and the brother backed away and were gone.

They sought the passenger deck. Between anguish for Lucian's calamity and anguish for his father's contumely there poured from Julian's lips in hectoring questions to Ramsey a further anguish of chagrin for the seeming triumph of Hugh's love. Two or three challenges she parried and while in a single utterancehe launched out as many more they encountered at a wheel-house stair their mother and old Joy. He cut short all inquiries with a proffer to return to them and Ramsey post-haste and give a full account of the disaster.

Meantime down in the sick-room Lucian said to Phyllis, when they had been a few minutes alone:

"And now give me my medicine."

"Yes, sir; where is it?"

"Oh, damnation! in my saddle-bags on the wash- stand. What are you trying to talk white folks' English for?" He hardly spoke three words without a moan or an oath. "Do you find a measuring-glass?"

She found it.

"See a small bottle – dark liquid – about twice the size – of the glass?"

"Yass, suh, but it's full, suh."

"Hell! what of that? Fill the glass and give it to me!"

She filled it but paused. "It – it looks like la'da- num."

"Oh, damn you, so did your great-grandmother. It's not laudanum. Did you ever smell vinegar in laudanum, or nutmeg? Give it here! God A'mighty, if I could reach you with my fist – Give me that glass!"

"Misteh Lucian, if this is la'danum "

"You hell-fired idiot, it isn't! And if it was, such an overdose would only vomit me. Don't you know that?"

"Yass, suh, I know it would." But still she held back.

"Then give it here!"

Julian came in with alarm added to his other distresses.

"Oh, Luce! do you want to start that bleeding again?"

" I'd just as lief as not! Make that wench give me that glass or mash her head! She knows if it was laudanum it would merely puke me. Damn it, it's a simple euthanasia." The crafty sufferer felt assured his brother would neither know nor ask the smooth word's meaning.

Julian turned savagely upon the maid. Heated with drink, enraged at himself, his father, Hugh Courte- ney, his sister, and his mother, he was in no mood to humor the contumacy of any freed slave and least of all this one. "Give it to him this instant," he cried. "Do you want to kill him?"

"No, Misteh Julian, that's exactly "

He drew and levelled his revolver and then motioned with it a repetition of his command.

With a woe of protest in her eyes, Phyllis obeyed. Lucian swallowed the draught and sank to his pillow. Julian watched Phyllis slowly set down the glass and bottle.

"What did you say that stuff is?" he asked his brother, with an assumed lightness.

"Oh, a palliative for these infernal pains. Have you told the family what happened? Go do it." Thespeaker's tone grew lofty. "I want them to know it was all my fault! This girl can stay with me till you come back, and you can take your time. I shan't need you for an hour. Go, Jule, my brother. Ob don't harry me with idle questions."

As Julian presently shut himself out Phyllis, her fears for the patient disarmed by his transient excitement where she had looked for heaviness, laid her hand on a, chair; but he stopped her. "You white nigger! would you presume to sit down in my presence? If you can't stand go outside – and shut the door. Oh, go anyhow! Life's more tolerable with you out of sight. If I want you I'll call."

The room was close abaft the wheel, where a widening of the guards made an inviting space, and out there Phyllis drew a chair up beside the door. A white- jacket came from the cabin in behalf of passengers in neighboring staterooms to ask what the commotion meant, and as she began to explain it away Ramsey and old Joy came down a near-by stair to watch with her or in her stead and to them she ampli6ed her explanation. Ramsey listened at the door. The patient seemed to be asleep, so audible was his breathing.

She had a sudden thought: a doctor's saddle-bags always contain laudanum. Had Phyllis seen any – in another bottle, untouched? That would confirm the patient's denial. She beckoned and asked. Yes, Phyllis had seen it, labelled.

"And besides," Ramsey thought on, "neither twinhas ever spoken falsely to the other." Why, then, sleep was good!

Even in outer sights and sounds there was solace and reassurance: in river and shore forever passing majestically up-stream through floods of moonlight; in the rhythmic flutter and rush of wheels and foam, and in the keen quiver of the *Enchantress* flying to New Orleans on the swiftest wings steam could give. Ramsey sent Phyllis up to bid Julian be at ease, and the maid, returning, announced that both the Com- modores had gone to rest but that madame was anxious to come back to the invalid the moment he would permit. She added, unasked, that Captain Hugh was in the captain's chair.

The hour passed and Julian reappeared. The partial relief of mind which had come to all the others had in degree reached him. It enabled him, as he came down the wheel-house stair, to reflect, though with a shudder, upon that furious treatment which alone, he had somewhere heard, would counteract an opium poisoning, and upon Lucian's utter inability to endure any part of such a treatment. He found Ramsey hearkening at the door again, newly disquieted. The two servants were out at the rail of the wide guards.

"Ought his breathing," she said, "to sound like that?"

Julian thought not, but even a sister's solicitude offended his lifelong sentiment of paramount owner?- ship in his brother. "Stand away, I'll let you know," he replied, passed in, and closed the door.

Then all at once, as so often has happened to so many of us, he saw his heedlessness where he had fancied himself vigilant. The light was dim. He knelt close to the sleeper. One long stare into the pale yet livid face was enough. Lucian was dying. Julian leaped to his feet to seek aid but saw its futility and fell again to his knees. Lucian was dying of the "black-drop" which his brother, in haughty ignorance, by the hand of Phyllis, had given him.

Presently Julian found voice, yet, mindful still of the listening Ramsey, let himself only softly murmur: "Oh, Lucian, my brother! Oh, Lucian, my twin brother! I've killed you, killed you twice over, my twin brother! God! but you're right not to live a cripple. And it was I who crippled you! Oh, Lucian, I'm the cripple now!"

Ramsey tapped. He sprang to the door and without opening it answered: "Yes, in a minute. He – he's all right."

At the wash-stand he lifted the phial of black-drop still half full. As quietly as if the dose were a dram at the bar he filled the measuring-glass and drank its last drop. Then he turned to the door and barely opened it.

"He's all right, Ramsey. . . . Yes. . . . Yes. He's done just the right thing. So have I. Now, go away, please, wherever you like, only don't – stay – here just to bother us. I'll merely lie down beside him without – What? . . . No, go away! You'll find us all right in the morning."

LXIII

THE CAPTAIN'S CHAIR

On the next afternoon but one, while hundreds went down to the steamboat landing to view the new *Enchantress,* there was a double funeral in the old French cemetery, Saint Louis Street, New Orleans.

Returning from it together, Watson and his forme..' "cub" spoke of Gideon Hayle.

"He takes the loss of them boys harder'n what I'd 'a' thought he would," said the younger pilot.

And Watson replied: "Yes, but he don't take it as hard as what, years ago, he tuck their fust refus'n' to go with him on the river."

They said no more all the way up Rampart Street to Canal, out Canal to the steamboat landing, and across the levee to the *Enchantress.* An hour later they stood in her wheel-house, looking down on the same Saturday afternoon five o'clock scene that Watson and Ned had thus contemplated from the *Votaress* a hundred months before.

Here were the same vast piles of harvest wealth, the same crowds and little flags, the same shouting and tumult only grown greater, the same open sky – though of October – the same many-pillared cloud of black smoke, the same smartly painted bumboatsselling oranges, bananas, pineapples, corals, and sea- shells – many of the latter treated with puritanic art, having, that is, the Lord's Prayer bitten into them with muriatic acid. Here lay the same yellow harbor with many more fussy little tugs in it, its water low yet still mast-deep, its yard-long catfish and fathom- long gars leaping and wallowing after their prey, its white gulls flashing about the steamers' pantry windows. Here was the same black forest of ships in the up-stream and down-stream distance and here, finally, the same public hope and pride grown wider and loftier in their last affluence before entering that purgatory of civil war which now seems but a bad dream outlived.

Steam was up on the *Enchantress,* and every now and then her mighty wheels tugged on her hawsers. In the crowd gathered on the wharf to see her go were the Gilmores and the half dozen from Vicksburg and the Bends. Up on the hurricane-deck were two or three small knots of passengers, chiefly ladies, unknown to the Gilmore group; but beside a derrick post, where we first saw Hugh on the *Votaress,* stood the three Hayles, old Joy, and "California" – bound once more for the gold-diggings. Near the Hayles, yet nearer the bell, was Hugh, in command.

"You don't reckon," said a voice in the throng, "that that's her captain, do you?"

"No," said another, "I should think not."

"Yes," said the very human Gilmore, "that's the captain."

Vicksburg and the Bends sent up smiles and faint wavings to Ramsey and her mother and only did not call to them because they were in a great city. It made them very proud and happy to see Hugh the master of this, to them, matchless wonder of utility and beauty, and they could not help saying things to each other with voice enough to let strangers around them know he was their personal friend. While they did so who should alight from a cab and glance up to Hugh but his grandfather. Hugh answered with a gesture toward the Gilmores, to whom the old gentleman promptly turned. There had arisen among the boats a good-natured custom of giving friends a free trip eight miles up the river, to the suburb of Carroll- ton. So a word from the commodore was enough; the players and their group hurried aboard with him and as they touched the lower deck the last bell sounded and the lines were cast off.

When they reached the hurricane-deck they were in the middle of the stream. They did not join the senior Hayles at once; Ramsey met them and with her they stood on the skylight roof watching the shores to see when they should stop drifting and gain headway. Over on the "Algiers" side of the harbor lay the *Paragon,* repairing a smashing she had got at the wharf through the bad handling of another boat, else the Hayles would hardly have been going home on the *Enchantress.*

The crew of the *Enchantress* stood about her capstan and their chantey-man, ready to sing when theswivel should peal and her burgee run down; but the Gilmore group were too far aft to see them. The player's wife, speaking gravely with Ramsey in low tones, remarked with sudden gayety:

"I see why we're here behind the bell. You're afraid they'll sing "

Ramsey made a pleading gesture.

"Why, what can you expect," asked her friend; "not 'Bounding Billow'?"

Ramsey, laughing, could only repeat the gesture. The swivel pealed, down sank the burgee, a wind began to ruffle their brows, and up rolled the song:

"Come, smilin' 'Lindy Lowe, whah de sea ships come an' go, On de finess boat dat eveh float," etc.

It was still coming up when a young man not of the Gilmore group surprised the actor a moment aside.

"Mr. Gilmore, is that Commodore Hayle over there? ... I thought it must be. I suppose he's going up home to settle his two sons' affairs. Mr. Gilmore, they wan't bad, they were only wild. Sad, their having to be buried in the city. But in this climate, you know – hmm! – yes."

The song and his observations crossed back and forth.

"Come, smilin' 'Lindy Lowe, you'd ought to come befo' " –

(Chorus.)

"You don't remember me, Mr. Gilmore, but I was on the *Votaress* with you and your lady and MadameHayle and those twins and all. I married the young lady I was keeping company with then. There she is. Don't you re-collect my lending you my field- glass at the Devil's Elbow?"

"Dear me! was that you at the devil's elbow! I – I hope I returned them."

"Oh, you did! You remember the first clerk of the *Votaress!* He's her captain now. And Ned – you remember Ned, the pilot, don't you? Well, he's on her yet. I see you're lost in admiration of this most unusual sunset. We almost always have these unusual sunsets. This is a wonderful country."

"Come, smilin' 'Lindy Lowe, whah de sweet cane honey flow'.

(Chorus.)

"Come, smilin' 'Lindy Lowe, love a-knockin' at de do'."

(Chorus.)

Now the boat was in the pilot's hands. Hugh joined Madame Hayle and the' two commodores at the derrick post. The same shrewd texas tender who had once abstracted the weapons of the twins from their stateroom set a second chair beside the captain's. Hugh offered the two seats to the commodores, but both declined. They of Vicksburg and the Bends watched the gorgeous October sunset beyond the low, flat orangeries on their right. "California" was with them and told them of the sunsets on the great plains. Gilmore generously kept the one-time lender of the field-glass and the lender's mouse of a wife beguiled with anecdotes while Mrs. Gilmoretalked on with Ramsey, making fond and welcome in. cursions into her confidence.

"Isn't it ridiculous," murmured Ramsey, "that he seems condemned to do everything in the tamest possible way? Not that he cares; he seems almost to like it so. It's so right now. He can't proclaim anything. And – you see why, don't you? – neither can I."

"Ramsey, you needn't. Only do one thing for us, Gilmore and me, and we'll know. When we've landed and the boat starts away again and he – " She finished in a voice too small for type.

At Six Mile Point the actor escaped his bonds and for a moment got Hugh into his sole possession.

"Certainly, under these conditions," he assented, "you can't *assert* anything – of that particular sort. But see here: You can tell me, just for us two Gil- mores exclusively, what your next boat will be named. Can't you?"

"Yes," said Hugh, "she'll be the – " He let Gil- more speak the name interrogatively and merely nodded, smiling.

The *Enchantress* was within five minutes' run of Carrollton when Watson dropped a quiet word to the roof, where both the Courteneys and Gideon were looking up-stream at a downward-bound steamer which had rounded to and landed under Nine-Mile Point.

"What is she?" asked Gilmore of Watson for hia group.

"A Hayle boat, the *Troubadour,*" said the pilot; "probably putting off some sugar-house machinery."

The *Enchantress* neared the huge Carrollton levee. "Good-by." "Good-by." "Good-by." "Good-by." Down they hurried, the old commodore, the players, the extraneous pair, and the six from Vicksburg and the Bends, followed to the stage plank by "California," and waved to from the after guards by Joy and Phyllis.

"Good-by." "Good-by!" The beautiful craft backed away and turned for Nine-Mile Point. And here came the *Troubadour,* with whistles trumpeting a troubadour's salute to the new queen of the river. The Hayle boat's people had espied their own commodore and the black mass on their forecastle were singing "Gideon's Band."

With whistles above and song below the *Enchantress* replied. The whistles ceased; the song was " 'Lindy":

"Come, smilin' 'Lindy Lowe, to meet to paht no mo',
On de finess boat dat eveh float'
In de O – hi – o,
De Mas-sis-sip-pi aw de O – hi – o."

Back at Carrollton on the crown of the levee, standing apart from their companions, the players gazed after the *Enchantress*. The three Hayles had returned to their stand by the derrick post. Hugh was near the two chairs. The actor softly spoke:

"Shall I tell you what Hugh told me?"

"Yes," said the wife.

"Then tell me what Ramsey told you."

"Nothing. She's going to tell it now. Watch!"

They watched together. Ramsey crossed to Hugh, and seemed to speak a word or two, not more. He sat dowri in the captain's chair and she took the one beside him.

Even Vicksburg and the Bends understood that. "He told me," murmured the actor, "that the next

Courteney boat will be the *Ramsey Hayle.*"

Lightning Source UK Ltd.
Milton Keynes UK
UKOW051917141111

182047UK00002B/102/P